MARIE
BONAPARTE

MARIE BONAPARTE

A LIFE ❦❦ BY CELIA BERTIN

❦ ❦❦❦A HELEN AND KURT WOLFF BOOK
HARCOURT BRACE JOVANOVICH, PUBLISHERS
SAN DIEGO   NEW YORK   LONDON ❦❦❦ ❦

Requests for permission to make copies of any part of the work
should be mailed to: Permissions, Harcourt Brace Jovanovich,
Publishers, 757 Third Avenue, New York, N.Y. 10017

Library of Congress Cataloging in Publication Data

Bertin, Celia, 1921–
Marie Bonaparte, a life.

"A Helen and Kurt Wolff book"
Bibliography: p.
Includes index.
1. Bonaparte, Marie, Princess, 1882–1962.
2. Psychoanalysts—France—Biography. 3. Psychoanalysis—
History 4. Bonaparte family. I. Title
RC339.52.B65B47   1982   150.19′5′0924 [B]   84-47679
ISBN 0-15-157252-6   AACR2

Printed in the United States of America

First edition

B C D E

to Helen Wolff

CONTENTS

ILLUSTRATIONS

Between pages 142 and 143

Princess Marie-Félix Bonaparte, née Blanc

Prince Roland Bonaparte

Marie Bonaparte, age seven. Photo Roland Bonaparte

Princess Pierre Bonaparte

Christian de Villeneuve

Jeanne de Villeneuve

Marie Bonaparte with her family of dolls.
Photo Roland Bonaparte

Marie Bonaparte, dressed for her first reception, at seventeen

Marie Bonaparte, age sixteen

Marie Bonaparte at the Villa Giramonte, Nice-Cimiez

Marie Bonaparte, age twenty-three

Princess Pierre Bonaparte with her Villeneuve grandchildren
and Marie

Prince George of Greece with his uncle Prince Waldemar
of Denmark

Princess Pierre Bonaparte, Prince Roland and Marie in the
"grand salon," Avenue d'Iéna, Paris

Marie Bonaparte with her fiancé, Prince George of Greece

Prince and Princess George of Greece at their wedding,
Athens, December 12, 1907

ACKNOWLEDGMENTS

My thanks and gratitude go first to H.R.H. Princess Eugénie of Greece, who not only provided the abundance of documents and copies of manuscripts without which this work would not have been possible, but also graciously authorized the use of them and guided my research. From the adventure of devoting five years to those personal notes and diaries, I have come to know an exceptional woman—Marie Bonaparte—who never faltered in her unblinking search for the truth in herself and her life.

I specially thank my husband, Jerome Reich, for his patience and unfailing encouragement. I would like to acknowledge my gratitude and indebtedness to Professor Serge Lebovici, who aided my project from the beginning, and to Dr. Frank R. Hartman, who gave generously of his time to help me with my manuscript; to M. Michel Richard for his friendly assistance and to Mrs. Natalia Danesi Murray and Mme Danielle Hunebelle, whose confidence sustained me. Among the many others who have helped me by giving generously of their time, recollections or support and to whom I would like to record my gratitude are: Mme Eliette de Beaurepaire, Dr. Richard Berczeller, the late Dr. Grete Bibring, M. Edmond Bordier, Mme Jacqueline Chevalier, Dr. Carolyn Cohen, Mrs. Jane Cohen, the late Helene Deutsch, Mrs. Anna Ducharne, M. Philippe Erlanger, Mme Robert van Eyck, Miss Anna Freud, Dr. Sandford Gifford, M. Thomas Gunther, Dr. Henri Hoesli, the late Dr. Marianne Kris, Mr. Raymond A. Mann, Mr. Joseph Murumbi, Miss Camille Naish, M. Jacques Nobécourt, Mme Blandine Ollivier de Prévaux, Mme Janice de Saussure, M. Jacques Sédat, Mr. John Shepley, Dr. Bluma Swerdloff, Mme

Geneviève Tabouis, Mme Annette Troisier de Diaz, Professor Robert Vivian, Mme Françoise Wagener and Mme Louise Weiss.

Grateful acknowledgment is made to Sigmund Freud Copyrights Ltd for permission to print the letters of Sigmund Freud to Dr. René Laforgue and also the Freud letters to Marie Bonaparte. I also wish to express my indebtedness to Mme Délia Laforgue, who made available to me the letters from Marie Bonaparte to her husband; and to thank J.-B. Pontalis, Director of *Nouvelle Revue de Psychanalyse*, who granted me his kind permission to use the correspondence between Freud and Laforgue and the introduction by Professor Bourguignon from volume 15 of his publication.

"Biographers and psychologists will reply that a biography that is as real and human as possible will not detract from the reputation of the dead. Through the medium of the written word they will at least live on in the reflection upon paper of the thoughts in their minds and of the feelings in their once beating hearts. They will be far more vividly represented than in the pages of some frigid and false idealization. Biography indeed has another and higher function than the mere satisfaction of an idle or unhealthy curiosity. For those who understand—and they are the only people who count—biography reaching out beyond the uncomprehending thousands, becomes a means of communing with a wider humanity. . . .

"In order that these portraits should be faithful likenesses it is however essential that the subjects' most loveable characteristics, although they may be considered by some as the least desirable, should not be removed for what is supposed to be respect but is in reality sacrilege. And these are the very characteristics that are usually preserved in intimate papers such as letters or diaries, which are so often threatened by the devoted persons who inherit them."

MARIE BONAPARTE, "DEFENSE OF BIOGRAPHY,"
INTERNATIONAL JOURNAL OF PSYCHOANALYSIS,

VOL. XX (1939), p. 239

MARIE
BONAPARTE

THE LAST BONAPARTE

*"If ever anyone writes the story of my life, it
should be called* The Last Bonaparte, *for I am the
last. My cousins of the imperial line are only
Napoléons."*

MARIE BONAPARTE,
Chronologie biographique en 8 cahiers,
notebook 8, unpublished

"I LIKED MURDERERS; I THOUGHT THEM INTERESTING. HAD
not my grandfather been one when he killed Victor Noir,
the journalist? And my great-granduncle Napoleon, what a
monumental murderer *he* was!"[1]

Marie, the last Bonaparte, made this observation in 1952; she
was referring to her childhood. At the time, she was seventy and,
as a psychoanalyst, accustomed to looking back, into the past.
Marie probed into her own with the impassioned, patient insistence she had inherited from her father—a geographer, anthropologist and botanist. But the liberality of her way of life and
mode of thinking contrasts sharply with the manner of Prince
Roland Bonaparte, a withdrawn man who devoted his time to
work in his library and scientific study in the field, but secretly
craved success in society.

Marie Bonaparte owed her moral courage and her clarity of
mind to no one but herself. The same is true of her career achievement, which her social circle preferred to ignore because it was
too difficult in those days to accept the fact that a princess, married to a king's son, could become first a disciple and intimate
friend of Sigmund Freud and later one of the most famous analysts
of Europe. This she achieved in spite of the obstacles that were
put in her way by her immediate family, her royal in-laws and
society. Her Royal Highness Princess Marie of Greece and of
Denmark therefore had every reason to assert her place among the
Bonapartes; for in her fashion she was self-made, as they were.

The Bonaparte family claimed to have origins in tenth-century
Tuscany and to have been established on the island of Corsica

since the sixteenth century. As she herself knew, Marie was a true Corsican in many character traits, among them chiefly stubbornness and loyalty. As a child, she heard much of the island, and images of it filled her dreams. There were many Corsicans in the household of her father, Prince Roland, and of her grandmother, Princess Pierre Bonaparte. Eager for knowledge, Marie had in her very early years followed attentively the singular accounts of her ancestors' lives, carefully sifting over all that presented itself to her inquiring mind. No clue escaped her: she examined causes and effects with a remarkable sense of fairness and disregard for public opinion. Quickly she learned how inventive life was.

Letizia Ramolino, mother of the Emperor and of Marie's great-grandfather, Lucien Bonaparte, was only fourteen when, on June 2, 1764, she married Carlo Buonaparte, aged eighteen. Like her husband, she was descended from a patrician Corsican family. Fleuriot de Langle, the historian, describes her as a beautiful brunette—ignorant, like other girls of her class, but "as realistic as her husband was given to daydreams, as thrifty as he was prodigal and fond of luxury, as tight as he was extravagant."[2] Carlo Buonaparte's attachment to his native island led him to ally himself with the cause of General Pasquale Paoli, who managed briefly to unite Corsica as the long dominion of the Genoese republic was drawing to an end and as France was negotiating to purchase the island. Paoli ordered Carlo to join him at Corte, which he had declared his capital. In 1767, Carlo became his secretary and settled in Corte with Letizia. Subsequently, while pregnant with Napoleon, she followed her husband throughout Paoli's anti-French campaign. But in the aftermath of Paoli's defeat in 1769, she prevailed upon Carlo not to join those who followed their hero into exile in England.

For Letizia, nineteen years old at the time, life had not been easy. She had lost two children and given birth to a son, Joseph, the previous year. After Napoleon's birth in 1769, she was to lose two more daughters before having Lucien, who was born in 1775; five more children, three daughters and two sons, were to follow. Letizia was forced to assume the major responsibility for her large family; after Paoli's departure for England, her husband, who was ready to collaborate with the French, was more eager to seek honors than to obtain a comfortable position which would have improved his family's income. Somehow, though, Letizia managed and their three eldest sons were sent to school on the mainland with royal scholarships.

Napoleon and Lucien entered the military school of Brienne. From the start, Lucien had the feeling that Napoleon resented him as a rival. The competition continued after their father's death in 1785, when Napoleon became *il capo di famiglia*, the family's head, even though he was not the eldest son.

Lucien was ambitious, intelligent and restless, and he became involved in the turbulent politics of the French Revolution at the age of sixteen. His Jacobin sentiments eventually landed him in prison. Fortunately for him, Napoleon, who had risen to general and commander-in-chief of the "Army of the Interior," was able to obtain his release, and on October 28, 1795, he named Lucien Commissioner for War of the Army of the North. Subsequently, Lucien was elected a member of the lower house of the legislature, the Council of Five Hundred. As its president, Lucien used his position to serve his brother's interests.

In the coup of 18th Brumaire (November 9, 1799), Napoleon overthrew the ruling Directory and established the Consulate, with himself as First Consul. (He later stated: "For all who ask from when the House of Bonaparte dates, the answer is simple: it dates from the 18th of Brumaire."[3]) Napoleon and his followers sought the approval of the Council of Five Hundred. When, at first rebuffed and hooted from the assembly hall, Napoleon faltered, Lucien stepped in, ordered troops to clear out the opponents and called for a new vote. To quote J. P. Garnier: "There is no doubt . . . that by this decisive, clearheaded action he saved a situation clumsily compromised by the blunders and lack of sangfroid of the future master of Europe."[4] But in everyday matters, Lucien was less dazzling.

As minister of the interior, a post he occupied from December 24, 1799, on (it was a sort of Christmas present from his brother by way of thanks for the crucial aid he had given him a month before), Lucien looked after his own affairs rather than those of the nation; he stayed with the ministry barely a year. The waste and corruption he countenanced in his department and his liaisons with actresses, among them the famous Mlle George, were the talk of Paris.

What might have impressed the young Marie about this forebear of hers was that he was a writer, for she was a precocious writer. A pamphlet by Lucien entitled *A comparison between Caesar, Cromwell, Monck and Bonaparte: A fragment translated from the English* appeared anonymously, but the authorship posed no riddle, since it had been printed at the ministry itself. Napoleon felt himself unmasked by his brother, and a tremendous scene ensued. Lucien was dismissed from his ministry and dispatched as ambassador to Madrid.

During his ambassadorship, Lucien added to his wealth, accepting gifts from the court and from the Portuguese government. Upon his return, he cleverly ingratiated himself with Pope Pius VII by supporting the Concordat drawn up between Napoleon and the Pope to reestablish papal authority in France after the disruptions of the revolution.

The time was late November 1801: Lucien had asked Napoleon to place him in charge of the Cisalpine Republic established in northern Italy after Napoleon's victories. But a woman was to enter Lucien's life who would radically alter his destiny.

By birth, Alexandrine de Bleschamp belonged to the "petite noblesse." In 1797, her father, impoverished by the revolution, married her off to a merchant, Jouberthon, who four years later was to die of cholera. Alexandrine moved in a circle of young Parisiennes of daring elegance in that period of sexual liberation and became one of the most alluring and publicized ladies of the Directory. She was twenty-four when she and Lucien Bonaparte became lovers in 1802.

Lucien, then twenty-seven, was a senator and rich. He lived in outrageous luxury, played the market and granted, in return for bribes, scandalous monopolies. He took a lively interest in arts and letters. At his country estate of Plessis-Chamant, he presented excellent drama in his private theater to an audience of artists and scholars. Alexandrine appeared on his stage in Voltaire's *Alzire*. Lucien could not fail to notice the young, red-headed tragédienne with her fine white skin and big, deep-blue eyes. Lucien and Alexandrine became inseparable. Her house in Paris was connected by an underground passage to his residence, the Hôtel de Brienne, rue Saint-Dominique (now the War Office). On May 24, 1803, she gave birth to Charles-Lucien, the first of nine children.

On May 25, the baby was baptized by a priest who delivered a second document: a marriage certificate given to the "couple who have sworn to me that they will not be able to celebrate their nuptials before the civil authorities because of compelling political necessity."[5] The political necessity was Napoleon. In his opinion, it was through princely marriages that the Bonapartes could establish themselves. Nonetheless, a civil ceremony did take place at Plessis on October 26, 1803, and Lucien wrote his brother at Malmaison to inform him. (It was the second marriage for both. In 1801, Lucien's first wife, the illiterate sister of an innkeeper, had died, leaving him two young daughters.)

The only supporters of Alexandrine and Lucien were Letizia, Lucien's mother, and Joseph Bonaparte's sister-in-law and her husband, Jean-Baptiste Bernadotte, later to become king of Sweden. At the time the couple was married, everyone else—brothers, sisters, in-laws—bowed to Napoleon's orders. So Lucien knew that exile was inevitable.

Napoleon was attached to Lucien, the only one of his brothers of a stature comparable to his own. But after a tempestuous quarrel between the two brothers in 1803, Napoleon told his wife, Joséphine: "It's all over. I have broken with Lucien. It is difficult to meet with such resistance to such great opportunities. I will have to shut myself off and count on no one but myself."[6]

On May 18, 1804, the Senate elevated Napoleon, already head of the government for life, to "Emperor of the French." The imperial succession was soon established, from which Lucien was barred. Yet, the very next year the Emperor offered his favorite brother the Italian crown—with the proviso that his wife and children would be without a title. Alexandrine never doubted that Lucien would refuse. Their marriage had changed him. At no time did he betray even the slightest wavering in his loyalty to Alexandrine.

Lucien settled in Rome, where he acquired numerous palaces in town, in the surrounding countryside and in Tuscany. These properties were princely residences and sound investments as well. He surrounded himself with lordly splendor and played host to such dignitaries as the papal aristocracy. He presented concerts and tragedies; he undertook archaeological digs for Roman ruins on his lands, and he wrote.

Alexandrine seems to have found satisfaction in these literary endeavors. Throughout her life with Lucien, she shared his interests and adopted his points of view. She refused to give in to any of the compromises suggested by Napoleon, toward whom Lucien had his old feeling of rivalry. All Europe echoed with his brother's exploits, making his own marginal position humiliatingly felt. Lucien and Alexandrine decided to risk running the British blockade of the continent to flee to America on an American ship, the *Hercules*, provided by his brother-in-law, Marshal Murat, now king of Naples. The ship was intercepted by the British. After three months of detention on Malta, the couple was dispatched to Worcestershire, where late in 1810 Lucien rented Thorngrove Castle; there, the couple reestablished their pattern of entertaining the local aristocracy and artists.

Alexandrine was a courageous woman and lent her support to the political meddling her husband could not refrain from, though his republican ambitions were unrealistic. Lucien had a crackpot side to him, as she must have realized. After Napoleon was forced to abdicate at Fontainebleau, in April 1814, the couple was allowed to return to Rome. The Pope then offered officially to create Lucien a Roman prince. The title of Prince and Princess of Canino consoled them both for many missed opportunities.

When the couple first settled in Italy, Lucien's fortune was sizable, comprising, besides cash, an important collection of paintings and objets d'art acquired as "gifts" or appropriated. "If it is true that the Corsicans only love money because they like to spread it around, Lucien's efforts to amass wealth were equaled only by his prodigality and therefore should be thought of as an innate predisposition," François Piétri remarked.[7] In this matter, too, Alexandrine seems to have been a loyal consort. Their life might be described as one of bohemian luxury. They were preoccupied with themselves, with their worldly pleasures, and with the unjust fate of which they fancied themselves the victims.

The education of their sons and daughters was of little concern to Lucien and Alexandrine. The children lived as lords—omnipotent, unbridled, pleasing their own whims, reveling in stories of vendetta and bloodshed. Still, later on, most of them displayed interests that show some link to their parents' intellectual and artistic concerns. The eldest, Charles-Lucien, married his first cousin Zénaïde, the daughter of Joseph Bonaparte, a man of great wealth who chose to settle in New Jersey. Charles led a carefree life on a princely scale and devoted his time to science. In 1825, he published in Philadelphia an important ornithological work entitled *American Ornithology, or History of Birds Inhabiting the United States not given by Wilson*. Later he went to Paris, becoming a member of the French Constituent Assembly in 1848 and President of that body in 1849. (He was also a gambler and in 1852 broke the bank at the Homburg casino.)

Paul, Alexandrine and Lucien's second son, was the hero of the family. Following Lord Byron's example, he rushed to the aid of the Greeks rebelling against the sultan of Turkey. But he killed himself accidentally in 1824, at the age of nineteen, while loading his pistols just before the battle of Navarino. Through Paul, Greece plays a part in Marie Bonaparte's family history.

The third son, Louis-Lucien, who spent most of his time studying philology and science, served as deputy in the Constituent Assembly in 1848 and as senator during the Second Empire. The second-to-last daughter and eighth child, Alexandrine-Marie, published poems and novels in Italian. The youngest, Constance, took the veil.

These lives, which all tended toward some sort of fulfillment or achievement, seem paradigms of order by comparison with that of Pierre, Marie Bonaparte's grandfather.

Prince Pierre Napoleon Bonaparte was born in Rome on October 11, 1815, the sixth child of Alexandrine and Lucien. Talented, sensitive, passionate, he suffered the most from his parents' neglect. In a letter to his half-sister, Christine Bonaparte, one of his father's daughters by his first marriage, Pierre wrote: "My family does not love me and I have no future. . . . The best I can do is to take my revenge by risking my life."[8]

The lack of love he complained of, and perhaps the hero worship following Paul's senseless death, early on impelled him to dramatic deeds. He was thirteen when he risked his life for the first time, drawing a knife in a fight with an innkeeper. At fifteen, when Charles X was forced to abdicate the French throne and the supposedly more liberal Louis-Philippe became king, a struggle between liberalism and conservatism spread throughout Europe; Pierre took part in the revolutionary movement in Tuscany, fighting on the side of the liberals. Here he found the commitment he had been looking for: combat with honor at stake. But his father, fearing for the boy's life, requested that the authorities arrest him. From May 10, 1831, to early November of the same year, Pierre served his first term in prison. He came to a decision: henceforth he would scorn the role of a young prince who sets a good example. But no one had any notion of asking him to play it, and therein lies his tragedy. His violent revolt grew out of his fantasies. Fighting was the affirmation of his freedom and his manhood.

One day he decided to join his uncle Joseph in America, but the luxury and easy life he found in rural New Jersey were not what he was looking for. He traveled to New Granada, the country known today as Colombia, in search of adventure. Disappointed and ill with tropical fever, he returned to Europe by way of New York in June 1833.

Home in Italy, he and his brother Louis engaged in violent activities that ultimately led to imprisonment for both. The young princes of Canino behaved rather like leaders of street gangs in American cities more than a century later.

Pierre became more and more brutal. He risked his own life and endangered others. Complaint of his outlawry reached Rome, but no action was taken. When rumors of conspiracy against papal authority arose, however, the Vatican ordered his arrest.

Pierre was seized on Piazza Canino by a detachment of Pontifical Guards, but only after he had stabbed to death its lieutenant, Giacomo Cagiano di Azevedo. The twenty-year-old black sheep of the Bonapartes was imprisoned, tried, convicted and sentenced to death. The sentence was upheld on appeal. During this ordeal, Pierre received no word from either parent, both of whom were exasperated with him. The family did, however, manage to have his death sentence commuted to life imprisonment and then to exile in the United States. He joined his cousin Louis-Napoleon in New York City, where the latter had taken refuge after attempting to foment a revolt against King Louis-Philippe. Their temperaments, however, were too opposed for them to get along. Pierre returned to Europe and for a time settled in Corfu.

In 1838, Pierre moved on to Mohimont, in the Belgian Ardennes. Belgium, independent since 1830, was willing to give a home to a Bonaparte as long as he behaved himself—and Pierre from then on did, restricting his violence to hunting. He lived with Rose Hesnard, a Frenchwoman he had met in England, who remained his faithful companion for fourteen years.

Lucien's death in 1840, which followed three years of illness, seems not to have affected Pierre at all; he remained a romantic desperado. Women were eager to console him. He was handsome, a lord, a hunter, a horseman, and he needed to be loved, but beneath his dashing exterior he was so consumed with self-doubt that he never tried his luck except with women of humble origin.

The names of some of his mistresses are known only because the liaisons were of long duration or because they bore him children.

After the fall of Louis-Philippe in the revolution of 1848, Pierre returned to Paris and became a member of the Constituent Assembly. Restless as always, he set out for southern Algeria in 1849 to fight with the French Army of Occupation against Arab rebels at Zaatcha, which he did with thrilling panache. But when the battle bogged down, he returned to France once more, suddenly and without permission, to involve himself in politics.

At this time, after three legitimate kings and two revolutions, the Bonapartes were again in the ascendancy. Napoleon's nephew Louis-Napoleon, who was next in line of succession after the death of Napoleon's son in 1832 (Lucien could have been in this position were it not for his quarrels with Napoleon), staged a coup d'état in 1851 and appointed himself prince-president. One year later, he became "hereditary emperor of the French," by a plebiscite staged to give his reign an appearance of legitimacy. But he had already dismissed the parliament and put his enemies under arrest. He lacked his uncle's drive and genius, and his reign was swayed more by circumstance than by his actions.

Pierre's mistress, Rose Hesnard, whose love amounted to endless self-denial, died in 1852. Now that his cousin was emperor, Pierre was legally obliged to marry only with imperial consent. This meant that he should have sought the hand of an aristocrat. But he met Justine-Eléonore Ruflin in Paris and took her with him to Corsica.

Pierre called her Nina. She was the daughter of Julian Ruflin, a worker in a copper foundry. Her mother, née Justine Lucard, daughter of a schoolteacher at Metz, was a Bonapartist and had instilled similar feelings in Nina and her younger daughter Elisa.

To make Nina happy and to ease their situation in Corsica, Pierre secretly married the nineteen-year-old girl. The quasi-religious ceremony was arranged with the complicity of Abbé Casanova, who had been tutor to Pierre and his brothers. But in a letter dated May 13, 1867, Pierre asserted that no religious ceremony had taken place. Had he forgotten? Or did he still fear the Emperor's wrath?

Pierre now would remain out of favor with the Bonapartes in power.

The Princess of Canino disapproved of her son's match, not on political grounds but for reasons of social propriety, which she might have called simple common sense: one did not marry a workman's daughter. Though she must long have given up hope that Pierre would ever mend his ways, she could hardly have thought he would go so far as this. As for seeing her own marriage as a parallel to her son's, this would never have entered her mind: she was of a social class different from that of Nina Ruflin's.

After the death of her husband, Alexandrine had, with governmental approval, settled in Paris, where she again mingled with men of letters; Lamartine, Victor Hugo and Alphonse Karr were among her friends. Her great-granddaughter, Marie Bonaparte, was to share similar interests. From her early years Marie, too, sought the society of writers, artists and scholars; for her, true aristocracy was the aristocracy of the mind. Marie arrived at this view in spite of the influence of her uneducated, small-minded grandmother, Nina Ruflin.

Alexandrine had no confidence that Pierre's marriage would bring him any good. She did not live long enough to see how right she was—she died in 1855.

Like his father, Lucien, Pierre lacked moderation though not resolve. But his marriage, unlike his father's, did not change his life at all. His womanizing continued; he seduced young peasant girls or servants of the house. No woman, not even Nina, whom he seems to have loved very much, could give him a sense of security or fulfill his sexual needs.

To please him, the Parisienne of working-class origin learned to ride and to shoot and followed him tirelessly wherever he led her. Her life in Corsica was by no means romantic. When he was not with other women, she had to share him with men. He gathered a large group of peasants who were at once friends, servants and hunting companions. He would ride off with them when the whim struck him or sit with them telling tales by the hour. She had not envisioned such a disordered life when she had let Pierre seduce her—and whenever she thought she was about to become used to it, Pierre would head back to Paris. His ties with the capital and family power were important to him.

Near Calenzana in Corsica, Pierre bought a large piece of land and built his home, Lutzobeo, on a peak near an old Genoese tower. The house was a virtual eagle's nest, perched above the surrounding countryside, which opens majestically to the sea. It offered good hunting—and fertile ground for fantasies of grandeur.

There, on May 19, 1859, just after the passing of Donati's comet (this was a detail it greatly pleased her to recall), Nina gave birth to a son, whom she christened Roland—the same name she had given to a boy born four years earlier who had died. Originally, this energetic woman had had little use for superstition, but now she drew great hopes from the coincidence of the comet and the birth of her second Roland. She had lost three children in a row and blamed this on the unwholesome climate of the island.

It may have been to please her on this point that Pierre, who so loved Corsica, decided to leave. He again settled in the hunting and forest country of the Belgian Ardennes, which was to become his true home. In September 1861, the couple had another child, Jeanne, who, like her brother Roland, prospered in the healthy environment.

Nina at twenty-eight was still as much a lover as a mother, and eager to share her man's activities. Pierre had taught her to shoot, and she spent hours on the lookout for boar in the copses of the Ardennes. She took a liking to the hunt, and it appealed to her romantic streak to live in the old abbey of Orval. There she and her prince led a rough and simple feudal existence, surrounded by freely roving animals. Like all true hunters, Pierre loved animals, which Nina never did. He raised litters of boar (having killed their mothers). One day he bought a lioness, which followed him like a dog.

The incident with the lioness took place in Paris, where Pierre and Nina spent part of the year in a house with a large garden on rue d'Auteuil, living with both their legitimate issue and Pierre's bastards. Among them was Pascal, born in Corsica twelve years before Roland. He was to play an important role in the life of Prince Roland and is one of the key figures in Marie Bonaparte's history.

Although the civil marriage of Nina and Pierre took place at Les Epioux, in Belgium, on October 2, 1867, the Emperor refused to recognize it. The marriage did not count; it did not legitimize the couple's children. Nina was aware that Pierre suffered from being ostracized on her account. Without her, Pierre's entire past as a hothead might have been forgotten. Their relationship was not nearly as strong as that of Lucien and Alexandrine, but it was nonetheless out of the question that Nina would set her prince free. She had developed a habit of patience, and her ambition sustained her.

When they were in Paris at the house on rue d'Auteuil, Pierre would slip out for a reason Nina could tolerate even less than his other escapades. He, the rebel, persisted in his wish to appear at court, and the Emperor and the Empress would not receive her. He did not inherit his father's Jacobin, republican spirit or fight his cousin Napoleon III as his father had fought Napoleon I.

By the end of 1869, the Second Empire was in political trouble. The republicans forced a liberalization of the regime under Emile Ollivier. Pierre then wrote an inflammatory and provocative article insulting the republicans. On January 19, 1870, when Victor Noir, a republican journalist, came by appointment to rue d'Auteuil to challenge him to a duel, Pierre shot and killed him.

The uproar this murder set off in Paris threatened to trigger a revolution. Pierre gave himself up and was jailed at the Conciergerie, then arraigned before the High Court sitting at Tours. Nina faithfully followed with their two children, aged eleven and nine, to be present at the trial. Pierre pleaded self-defense and was acquitted. He refused the government's request that he go into voluntary exile in Belgium. But soon after, the Emperor was at war with the Prussians and Pierre did flee with his family to Rochefort, Belgium. By September 1, 1870, from their home, Pierre and his children heard the cannon of Sedan, where defeat sealed the Second Empire's fate.

After their cousin's fall, Nina and Pierre celebrated their marriage for the third time; the ceremony, the only valid one of the three, took place on November 14, 1871, in Brussels. Only then, thanks to the advent of the Third Republic, did their children Roland and Jeanne receive the right to bear the name of Bonaparte and their mother the right to become a princess.

Nina attached great importance to her title; in her eyes it must have made up for the sacrifices Pierre's conduct had demanded of her, which had taken their toll, aging her before her time. It was still plain to see what a beauty the new princess had been. With her dark eyes, her luxuriant hair and commanding height, she seemed a huntress, even an Amazon. In the present situation, she had to muster her every resource and her undiminished forcefulness: new challenges lay ahead.

Nina and Pierre were ruined. The house on rue d'Auteuil had been plundered and burned during the Commune, the period of civil and social strife that ravaged Paris from March to May 1871. Les Epioux, their country estate, had been sold to meet debts. Nina prided herself on always having been loyal to her husband, but was now heard to say that she cared only for the future of her children. The new princess knew that she would have to secure it alone.

Pierre had vainly tried to mold his son Roland after his own image. He saw the need for the boy to learn to ride and hunt, but what good would it do him to learn to read? He apparently forgot that he himself had published a volume of poetry, *Loisirs.* Writing counted in the Bonaparte family, even for those among them who said it did not.

Pierre had chosen a gamekeeper as his son's tutor, but Roland was more interested in plants, rocks and stars than in firearms, snares and decoys. At the age of ten, he began to read on his own, encouraged by his mother, who had pricked his curiosity by reading to him from a popular book she thought would arouse his interest: *The Mysteries of Science.*

Things had changed for Nina. For years she had hoped for position and power through her husband. Now she had a title and Pierre could give her nothing more. Her ambition shifted to their children. Her future and theirs depended on what she could help them to obtain intellectually and socially. She left home and took the children with her.

Pierre objected but could not stop her. He remained in Belgium until the last months of his life. He died in Versailles on April 8, 1881, in the company of a servant-mistress.

When Nina resolved to leave her prince, she chose London as the most promising destination. Many fugitives of the Second Empire were there already, sharing the exile of the Emperor and the Empress Eugénie. They did not accord her family status, but that is a point she may not have considered.

To make a living, she opened a millinery shop in New Bond Street. Her discretion was hardly equal to her determination; hoping to attract customers, she emblazoned the shop window with her name—Princesse Pierre Bonaparte—in oversize letters, unleashing a storm of indignation. She was believed to be playing a game of blackmail, setting herself up as a milliner to extort an allowance from the ex-sovereigns. Besides, what could she have known of fashion? She had spent most of her life among hunters. Her venture was a fiasco.

Marie Bonaparte later wrote: "My father always remembered the evening when, at sunset, in Trafalgar Square, at the foot of the statue of Nelson, conqueror of his great-uncle, he suffered hunger pangs, not having eaten all day."[9] Her projects defeated, Nina determined that it would be simplest to go back to Paris. There, at least, though she remained isolated from Parisian society, some friends of more modest means might be willing to help her; one of them was Pierre's natural son, Pascal, who had earned some money working in the imperial stables. Nina was resourceful, and she managed to have her daughter Jeanne tutored and to send Roland first to the Institut Hortus, then to the Lycée Saint-Louis, where, because he was an exceptional pupil, he skipped grades. He dreamed of entering the Ecole Navale, but his weak vision made this ambition impossible. His mother was set on his becoming an officer, the sole acceptable profession for a prince.

It was not easy to come up with the funds for completing his costly education. Boldly, Nina turned to Prince Pierre's cousins, who had never acknowledged her, and convinced them of their duty. Thus it was that the children of Napoleon's brother Jérôme —Princess Mathilde and her brother Prince Napoleon (after 1883 pretender to the throne)—paid for the final stages of Roland's studies and for his uniform for the Saint-Cyr military academy.

Marie Bonaparte rightly describes her grandmother as a "truly phallic woman." Princess Pierre exercised her power over her son for the rest of her life. Having instilled in him a passion for work and study and pushed him into a military career—Roland graduated from Saint-Cyr as one of the top of his class—she also arranged his marriage (which took place on November 17, 1880) to Mlle Marie-Félix Blanc, one of the most moneyed heiresses of Europe. Princess Pierre, an uneducated workman's daughter, held the Blancs in contempt, but Mlle Blanc represented a dowry of 8,400,000 francs in various assets, plus 6,082,566.81 francs in trust, with the life interest to her mother.

François Blanc, the young woman's father, was born in 1806 in the Vaucluse, north of Avignon, the posthumous son of a registry clerk who had earlier worked as a silk spinner. With his twin, Louis—the two were inseparable—François started working immediately after having finished elementary school. The brothers washed dishes and waited on tables at restaurants and took odd jobs at banking houses, first in Avignon and later in Lyons. They even ventured as far as Paris. Both were gamblers and had a way with cards; they began to frequent gaming clubs and to invest their profits in the stock market.

They invested their money with flair, and by the age of twenty-eight were in a position to start their own business. In 1834 they opened a small stockbrokerage house in Bordeaux. At that time, Chappe's telegraphy had already been in service between Bordeaux and Paris for eleven years. The Blanc brothers had the idea of using this system, in which signals were passed with the aid of a semaphore and telescopes from mountaintop to mountaintop, for their own profit. They developed a code of their own and bribed a telegraph official to inform them of the highs and lows on the Paris exchange. In two years, their business was flourishing, but their contact fell ill and, stricken with conscience, confessed his sin before he died. In March 1837, the Blanc brothers stood trial at Tours and pleaded guilty; in their defense they pointed out the use of carrier pigeons and other means of communication employed by businessmen richer than they—the Rothschilds, for example. Although they had bribed an official, they were sentenced only to defraying the costs of the trial.

But it was time to change their type of business. They persuaded the Landgrave of Hesse-Homburg to let them open a casino in the spa of Homburg, the capital of his principality. The casino, a reflection of nineteenth-century opulence, opened on August 16, 1843, and Homburg (today Bad Homburg, in West Germany) immediately became the most fashionable resort in Europe.

A small man of calm appearance, mustachioed, bespectacled, with piercing eyes, François Blanc was not easily rattled, but on one occasion he did appear to be worried. Between September 26 and 29, 1852, Prince Charles-Lucien Bonaparte, Pierre's brother, played the Homburg casino and won, walking off with 180,000 francs. Until then, no one had broken the bank.

After a two-day rest, the prince returned to the casino and won again—this time 560,000 francs! The casino was in danger. That evening, October 2, François Blanc recognized the advantage he might derive from the disastrous event by giving it all the publicity he could. The news of such enormous winnings drew a flood of new gamblers eager to equal or surpass them. They left tremendous sums behind on the green felt.

By then, François Blanc was alone. His twin brother and his

wife, the two people most dear to him, had died. An elderly house-keeper ran his unpretentious home and looked after his two little boys, Camille, aged six, and Charles, aged four. One day she introduced to him a young girl who spoke French, Marie Hensel.

Marie was born in 1833; her father, a cobbler of French descent, had twelve children besides Marie. She was a stunning girl, with black hair, a straight nose and big, brown eyes. François immediately thought of marrying her, but she was sixteen years old, wild and uneducated. Willing to take a risk, he went to the cobbler with the following proposition: at his own expense, he would send Marie to a good convent school in Paris for four years; if, at the end of this time, she would accept a husband twenty-seven years her senior, they would marry. The cobbler could not refuse, and François sent his instructions for her education to the school. It was necessary that Marie improve her knowledge of the French language and speak without an accent and that she learn history, etiquette and how to dress. The *Almanach de Gotha*, with its detailed information on the royal and titled families of Europe, was to be her bedside reading—for though he did not tell Marie, he foresaw the kind of life they would lead together. His fortune was already considerable and he was determined to go further still.

From time to time, he went to visit the young girl at her school to assure himself of her progress and to confer with her teachers. The results exceeded his hopes. Marie became a most beautiful and elegant young lady. She had an inquisitive mind, took a keen, intelligent interest in business and developed a remarkable passion for precious stones and jewelry, in which she became an expert. François and Marie were married in 1854, and she soon proved an indispensable advisor to him.

During the first three years of the marriage, she bore him a son, Edmond, and a daughter, Louise. Marie-Félix was born on December 22, 1859.

In 1863, Blanc bought ninety-seven percent of the casino in Monte Carlo and made it the most famous in the world. He also became the principal real-estate developer of the tiny principality of Monaco. His holdings there included the Société des Bains de Mer and the Cercle des Etrangers. Marie Blanc played an important role in the expansion of her husband's business in Monaco. It was she who pushed for the construction of the renowned Hôtel de Paris.

As business in Monaco prospered, the casino in Homburg continued to flourish, but it was also threatened by its new territorial owner, Prussia, with a prohibition against gambling. François's luck held, though, and he did not have to close the Homburg casino until 1872.

Blanc also kept a close eye on the French political situation. He hired, as secretary, Count Bertora, who had been a postal official and held a position at court during the Second Empire. Bertora, who subsequently became Marie Blanc's principal collaborator, and perhaps her lover, kept Blanc informed of events in Paris and during the Franco-Prussian War of 1870–1871 sent him daily dispatches. To insure friendly relations with the Third Republic (which replaced the Second Empire), Blanc lent it the money to finish the Paris Opéra. Everything he touched turned to gold: he received six percent interest on the sum he had lent the government and managed to double the number of trains between Paris and Monaco. The French economy actually improved and Blanc's business success in Monaco was more spectacular than ever.

Charles Garnier, the architect, was so grateful to François Blanc for facilitating the completion of the Paris Opéra, which he considered his masterpiece, that he consented to work in Monte Carlo. In 1879, he added a theater to the casino.

At the time she asked the architect to build this hall, Marie Blanc was making decisions on her own. Her husband had died in 1877; he was seventy-one then and she forty-three. He left the business in her hands. She was used to the responsibility, since during his last years asthma attacks had kept François Blanc out of the office with increasing frequency. She also inherited most of the cash of his fortune, estimated at 88 million francs. François Blanc's remaining heirs received shares in the business. Generous provisions were made for charities: 1 million francs was left to the church of Saint-Roch, in Paris, 400,000 for infirm priests, and so on. The obituary in *Le Gaulois*, dated July 31, 1877, read: "One may say that M. Blanc was king twice in his life! King of Homburg and King of Monaco."

When Princess Pierre told her son of the marriage she had arranged for him with François Blanc's daughter, Roland acceded out of filial obligation—and it is likely that he fell into line with his mother's wishes easily enough. His poverty and his mother's ambition had taught him to love money.

On Wednesday, November 17, 1880, the day of the wedding, it

rained. The religious ceremony took place at noon in great splendor at Saint-Roch, the Blanc family's parish church. A reception followed at Mme Blanc's at 194 rue de Rivoli, after which the young couple was to proceed to Château d'Ermenonville, one of the Blanc properties. They were expected to dine with numerous guests, and an apartment had been prepared for them. But, under cover of the confusion produced by a traffic jam of carriages carefully engineered by Roland's half brother, Pascal, the couple disappeared. Several days before, Pascal had been entrusted with the secret leasing in the prince's name of a house on the hill of Saint-Cloud. The couple was driven there at full speed.

Marie-Félix realized at once that the carriage was headed in the wrong direction. "Where are you taking me?" she demanded in fright. "To my house," Roland replied calmly, adding nothing to reassure her. His cryptic demeanor must have thrown the girl, trusting till then, into utter disarray.

As Mme Blanc awaited her daughter with mounting anxiety amid the festive lights and decorations at her château, there began at Saint-Cloud a life no less strange for Roland than for his wife.

A LONESOME CHILD

> *"Nature has no concern for our prudery. She goes her way without giving it a thought, and that is why, as early as childhood, the little human being finds himself prepared by her for the great tasks he will later have to perform. Now the most sacred task devolving on the species is that of perpetuating itself. And it has taken all of mankind's age-old repression to make it close its eyes so stubbornly to the fact that childhood is not asexual."*
>
> MARIE BONAPARTE,
> *Psychanalyse et biologie*, p. 54

MARIE-FÉLIX, THE YOUNGEST OF THE BLANC CHILDREN, HAD been both pampered and protected by her aged father, her mother and her godfather, Count Bertora. Marie Bonaparte carefully noted the rumors about the count and her grandmother Blanc: "It is whispered by certain people [that he was] more than her [Marie-Félix's] godfather."[1]

Marie-Félix's brother Edmond was still unmarried. Her sister Louise had made what was considered a splendid marriage, three years before, to Prince Constantin Radziwill. François Blanc had made careful inquiries about the Polish prince, who was poor, before consenting to the match. But he had died before Prince Roland was introduced to Marie-Félix. The slender, pale young woman with long chestnut-colored hair fell in love with the young prince in military uniform bearing the famous name Bonaparte.

Her mother was less enthusiastic about the match. She distrusted the vulgar, foul-mouthed old princess, who was still shunned by society, but she accepted the marriage, to please her daughter. Whether or not Marie-Félix was at the time aware that she was stricken with tuberculosis must remain speculation.

Certainly Mimi, as she had been known since childhood, was not the most mature of twenty-one-year-old brides. She was still terrified of thunder and lightning and preferred to take refuge in the cellar during storms. She did not possess the strength of character to keep her on an equal footing with her husband and mother-in-law.

The Bonapartes, mother and son, saw in Roland's bride only a spoiled, high-strung child, devoid of both judgment and will-power, with ridiculous fears and deplorable hygienic habits, de-rived from German governesses (how on earth could she enjoy taking ice-cold tub baths?). Her superstitions and piety also pro-voked their sarcasm; what was more, she loved cats and ducks! Even worse, she was charitable and generous with her money. Pascal, the head groom, saw a certain sentimentality in her, a sweet and docile nature forced to live in constant anxiety, like a prisoner in a golden cage that she herself had supplied.

The house at Saint-Cloud, called a "château" in newspaper arti-cles[2] and a "little villa" by Marie Bonaparte,[3] was situated on avenue du Calvaire (which has since become rue du Mont-Valérien), on the hillside overlooking the Paris–Versailles railway line. It was demolished in 1975 to make way for several apartment houses built around its vast grounds, which had been planted with splendid trees. For days on end Marie-Félix was alone in this house, with no visitors.

When Roland discovered that her favorite pastimes were music and reading French and German poetry—sins in his eyes and ears, and in those of Princess Pierre—he scolded her no less severely than he did for her piety. Like all Bonapartes, he prided himself on his hatred of music. He could not stand Schubert or the sonatas of Beethoven. On the other hand, he rather liked the "Beautiful Blue Danube," so Marie-Félix played this waltz to please him. But as soon as he returned from the barracks, he shut himself up in his study to work, away from the wife who had been waiting for him to come home. She was completely defenseless, lost in an un-familiar world. Prince Roland's retreat into his study and his pre-occupation with his books was to become a lifelong pattern.

Soon Marie-Félix was impatient to have a child. Each time her menstrual period came she was thrown into turmoil. New doctors, novenas, various treatments—she was ready to try anything to become pregnant. She was surprised to see that her mother-in-law and Roland discouraged none of these proceedings. They wanted a baby as much as she did, but for different reasons.

Did Princess Pierre and Roland surmise that Marie-Félix was ill? Most likely they did and took care not to broach the subject to Mme Blanc. After the young couple had settled at Saint-Cloud, their first concern had been to take out an insurance policy on the life of the bride. As she often spat blood, they said she had "granulations in her throat" and blamed it on the cold baths. With the doctors, they were discreet, pretended to suspect nothing and asked no questions. Mme Blanc was to die without ever finding out how much they knew. Her death, which occurred unexpectedly on July 25, 1881, brought about great changes.

The stance now taken by the son-in-law was as unforeseen by the two daughters and the son of Mme Blanc as their mother's demise at the age of forty-seven: Roland insisted that Marie-Félix renounce her portion of the estate. This caused a permanent break in relations with the Radziwills and a temporary one with Edmond Blanc. In taking this step, Roland dropped his mask, but for the moment it mattered little. He showed that he was perspicacious, or well informed, for it was soon discovered that apart from her fabulous jewel collection, Mme François Blanc, *née* Marie Hensel, had left nothing but debts—the responsibility, under French law, of her heirs. She had squandered an enormous fortune in a few years. To be sure, much of it had gone in lavish spending, but she had also made generous gifts to each of her remaining siblings, other poor family members, and friends.

The rupture with the Blancs favored the schemes of Princess Pierre, who was able to take immediate advantage of it. So far she had been doing her best, without being entirely successful, to keep her daughter-in-law's relatives away from her, and here at one stroke she was rid of them! She swiftly drew up a skillful strategy which eventually enabled her to secure the fortune that she had been dreaming of for her son.

If her daughter-in-law were to die without issue and intestate, her estate, according to the law, would revert to her natural heirs, her brother and sister. To pass so close to the fortune without being able to gain control of it would have been a disaster that she refused to contemplate. But how to maneuver so that the distraught girl would not take fright and alert her whole family? Obviously she could not approach her directly about the need to make a will in her husband's favor. Roland too must keep quiet. And time was pressing, with death visibly close. As Marie Bonaparte wrote, with her customary lucidity: "Professor Pinard, who attended her confinement, assured me later that my mother was consumptive and that the whole of one lung was affected. He told me that in the course of her pregnancy she actually had several hemoptyses. But her consumption was something to be denied; they wanted to be able to count on her death without seeming to do so."[4]

Since there was no baseness in her character, Princess Roland was unaware of the rapacity of her husband and her mother-in-law and her early death spared her the painful revelation. She never knew that she was, as her daughter wrote, the "scapegoat" for the "Monte Carlo crime," the crime of accursed money, which was to weigh so heavily on Marie, the crime in which Princess Pierre participated by her determination to appropriate this wealth.

Princess Pierre relied on the loyalty of women in her entourage to bring pressure to bear on her daughter-in-law. Two among them were assigned to enter into relations of seeming friendship with the shy and dreamy princess. Their husbands were both in Prince Roland's employ. Mme Escard, a placid wife and mother, and a friend of long standing, was married to the prince's librarian. Her father had once been subprefect in Corsica, and she had assisted Princess Pierre financially in the education of her children.[5] The other, Mme Bonnaud, the wife of Roland's secretary-steward, was much more intelligent; she was given the task of persuading Marie-Félix to make a will in favor of her husband. A practiced but amiable schemer, she spared no pains in her assiduous attendance on the young woman.

When Marie-Félix discovered that she was pregnant, her mood changed entirely. Though the early stages of her pregnancy were uncomfortable, she was so elated that God had finally granted her the child for whom she unceasingly prayed, that all her warm impulses toward others, temporarily curbed by seclusion, illness and disappointed love, were reactivated. This made Mme Bonnaud's task easier. She worked on her victim at every propitious moment, that is, whenever the princess was not incapacitated by her illness, which happened too frequently not to be alarming. She returned so often to the attack that the young princess lamented to Pascal: "Am I really all that ill? . . . Am I going to die soon?" She had by now arrived at the mid term of her pregnancy; Pascal thought she looked much better and did his best to reassure her. He even tried to dissuade her from drawing up a will. Mme Bonnaud nevertheless prevailed. On March 27, 1882, Princess Marie Bonaparte, née Blanc, wrote: "Wishing to give my husband, Prince Roland Bonaparte, a proof of my attachment, I leave to him in entirety: The whole of my fortune . . ." listed in succinct fashion in a short document that ended, "If I leave issue of our marriage, I leave to my husband all that the law permits me to dispose in his favor."[6]

In the note in which Marie Bonaparte copies "the text of my mother's will," she adds: "The amount which my mother could dispose of in favor of her husband if there were a child consisted of one quarter in capital and one quarter in life interest. In the absence of a will, I should have inherited the whole of my mother's fortune, my father, as my legal guardian, only having the right to enjoy my income until I reached the age of eighteen."

These unusual provisions, made at the instigation of her grandmother, were to have painful repercussions for Marie. For a long time, she believed that it was only her coming into the world that had made it possible for her father to appropriate her mother's fortune, as though the will in favor of Prince Roland would have had no validity if she had not existed.

On July 2, 1882, Professor Pinard, who had not left the bedside of Princess Roland Bonaparte, in labor for three days, decided to use forceps for the delivery. The patient was weak and her state of health had worried him throughout her pregnancy. Now at the end of her strength, she would never succeed in giving birth normally. Her labor pains were becoming dangerously less frequent.

When the little girl came into the world, she was inert and already turning blue. She was rushed into an adjoining room, where the celebrated obstetrician applied mouth-to-mouth resuscitation to combat asphyxia. His efforts lasted three quarters of an hour, an infinity for the exhausted young mother, waiting in anguish for someone to bring her the long-desired child.

In the days that followed, Marie-Félix seemed to be making a slow recovery from the fatigue of pregnancy and childbirth. She rested quietly in her bedroom, which was separated from that of the prince only by a small shared sitting room. Visits were, as always, rather infrequent. Princess Pierre hardly ever appeared at Saint-Cloud. A newborn baby held no attractions for her and she had nothing to talk about with her daughter-in-law.

As for Prince Roland, he too was constantly absent. The baby's birth had in no way changed his habits. Still he could hardly forget it, for he must have heard a great bustling about on the floor above him. The cradle had been installed in the wet-nurse's room, situated just over his own. Since it was impossible for the young mother to nurse her child, this task had been entrusted to Rose Boulet, a good-looking, healthy peasant girl from the Nièvre.

On August 1, Princess Roland seemed well enough to get up, in the opinion of Professor Pinard, who had continued to attend her. Her brother Edmond was invited to dine at Saint-Cloud to celebrate the event. He took his leave around nine o'clock, and Marie-Félix went back to her room. But suddenly, as she was helped into bed, she felt so sharp a pain in her leg that she let out a cry. Immediately she asked for a doctor and a priest. She was gasping for air and said that she was going to die. Her maids tried to reassure her. They called the prince, who had gone to show his brother-in-law out. "My poor Roro, I'll never see you again," she told him when he appeared, and then her head fell back on the pillow. The prince thought that she was sleeping. She was dead, of an embolism.

Bonnaud was dispatched to Paris to carry the news to Princess Pierre. Pascal, the head groom, was summoned from Bouviers. He later told Marie that when he arrived on horseback in the middle of the night, he was greeted by Princess Pierre, who cried out on seeing him: "What luck for Roland! Now he gets the whole fortune!"[7]

Princess Marie-Félix Bonaparte was buried at the Versailles cemetery. The mourning imposed on the household must have been of the briefest and most perfunctory sort. Whether true or apocryphal, the comment reported by Pascal was a perfect expression of Princess Pierre's state of mind in response to her daughter-in-law's death. However, according to French law, if the child were to die, her share would revert to the Blancs.

Princess Pierre soon gave up her apartment at 17 rue de Grenelle to live with her son at Saint-Cloud, in order to help him raise the little Princess Mimi.

Once under Princess Pierre's control, the house was to change its atmosphere. It became filled with noise and shouting. The service changed its pace—the reins were tightened. The staff reacted to her strong presence and kept an interested eye on newcomers. Princess Pierre had brought with her her chambermaid, Marguerite, and her reader, Mme Proveux. This shrewish companion of hers, whom Mimi was to nickname Gragra (literally "Fat-Fat") because of her bulk, had once been on the same terms with her employer as Mme Escard, the wife of the librarian; she had a bitter grudge against her former debtor, on whom she now depended for her livelihood. The reversed roles fueled her envy. Nevertheless, the two old friends shared the same points of view in politics, and their reading was confined to the newspapers. They also spent a good deal of time criticizing the actions and behavior of the servants, in a tone of petulant complaint.

Nurse and baby were not among their concerns. Indeed, for the first three years of little Mimi's life, no one, neither the grandmother nor the father, seems to have supervised the relations between Rose Boulet and the child. Nounou, as Mimi called Rose, became the child's psychological mother. She nursed, changed, bathed, weaned and trained Mimi. Small wonder that she played such a decisive role in the formation of Mimi's personality. As is usually the case, much of the relationship with Nounou was lost to Mimi's conscious memory, but this unconscious part of the relationship became a crucial factor in her life. Still, there were times when Princess Pierre had to intervene, just as she had to settle the rivalries and jealous disputes of the staff in which the child was used as a pretext. She was most displeased when her personal maid, Marguerite, accused the nurse of secretly having pap sent upstairs for the baby. Rose, the handsome nurse with the pink ribbons, protested. Good food and red wine had not spoiled her milk, as Marguerite claimed. She demanded, and obtained, the departure of her slanderer. They probably chose this way out because it was easier to replace a chambermaid than a wet-nurse.

The family continued to live in the house in Saint-Cloud; its purchase with the infant Mimi's money and in her name was arranged by her father before she was a year old. Beginning with the second year, and for most of Mimi's childhood, Princess Pierre took the household to Dieppe for the summer. This Norman port, from which Giovanni da Verrazano sailed for America, was then the most fashionable seaside resort, since Paris was only four hours away by rail. Princess Pierre hated the place but Prince Roland had inherited a house there from Marie-Félix. He himself spent the summers traveling; in 1884, to Norway, Sweden and Finland.

On February 2, 1885, the family moved to 22 Cours la Reine, Paris, a large, three-story mansion, built in sixteenth-century Italian style.

It is from the beginning of the move to Cours la Reine that Mimi's earliest three memories date. The first has to do with her nurse: "I am sitting very low down, on a little chair or a box, in Cours la Reine, in my wet-nurse's room. She is standing before the mirror on the chimney piece, where the fire is burning; I am looking at her attentively. She is putting cream on her parted black hair. The pomade, in a little white jar, is on the marble mantelpiece: It is black. I feel disgusted. My nurse has a long yellowish face and looks like a horse."[8]

This vivid early memory is a distortion of reality, for Rose Boulet certainly did not look like a horse. However, this strange detail as well as others in the memory proved to be unconsciously determined.

The second memory relates to her father: "He and I are in the long hall opening on his bedroom to one side and his study to the other, the large hall with dark walls all covered with arrows and lances from distant, hot, and savage countries, where men, they say, are black and naked. Papa, very tall, very handsome, with his mustache and his black eyes, stands there in the uniform of a French officer, in red trousers; I, very small, am next to him. With my two little arms, I embrace one of his red legs, I squeeze it very, very hard, I love and admire my Papa so much!"

This memory was to arouse a certain anxiety in Marie Bonaparte. Her love for her father was an essential part of the princess's life. She wanted to do what he was doing. She wanted to study, she wanted to write, and she did at a very early age. She wanted to be like him, in order to get his attention, but, of course, it did not work.

The third memory is the strangest. She sees herself all alone on July 2, her birthday, in the annex her father had built behind the house to hold his library. She is waiting for an old valet of her grandfather François Blanc, whom everyone calls "Baron Phylloxera" because he claimed to have discovered a remedy against these plant lice, which were destroying most of the vineyards in France. " 'Baron Phylloxera,' a big, heavy, flabby man wearing gold earrings in his ears, to improve his eyes, he says, comes every year, accompanied by his pale daughter, to greet me on my birthday and bring me a bouquet of white flowers, wrapped tightly in lace paper, flowers that are a perfumed enchantment, something that is not found the rest of the year. In the summer heat of the library, the expected fragrance of the enchanting bouquet overwhelms me. Yet I am thinking: I'm four years old! How old that is!

And the poignant feeling of the passage of time which was never again to leave me, oppresses my young heart for the first time."[9]

By the actual time of this third memory, Mimi had been without Rose Boulet for some months. Nounou was abruptly dismissed in the autumn of 1885 for being impertinent to Princess Pierre. Needless to say, the princess did not consider the grief that the child might feel. By this time Mimi had begun to try to understand the fact of her mother's death. She had studied the watercolor of her mother on her deathbed, in the gloomiest corner of the small salon, and asked about it. Nounou's departure was different. She would not come back, but she was not dead. Lucie, her replacement, "was sweet, with her pretty smiling young face framed by small black curls." She was cheerful, she was young, she was pleasant to be with. Mimi had the feeling they would never be parted, or, rather, that there was no reason for such a thing to happen. She got along beautifully with Lucie, who was the witness and sometimes the instigator of discoveries that Mimi never forgot: a hill covered with violets above San Remo, the sound of the sea when a shell is held against the ear. Lucie was also a devoted nurse at Mimi's bedside when the little girl was ill.

Shortly after Lucie's arrival, before Mimi was four, her father decided that she should learn languages. The study of English and German was indispensable for her education. The young woman whom he engaged as a tutor was Irish; her husband was Prussian and a tutor in a Parisian family. Mme Reichenbach was for a long time to be the little girl's link with the outside world. She occupied a special position, like Gragra, since she too did not live in the house. She arrived in the morning and left each evening to go back to her husband and children.

On April 10, 1886, Mimi's first cousin, Pierre de Villeneuve, was born. His mother, Princess Jeanne Bonaparte, had married Comte Christian de Villeneuve–Esclapon, Marquis de Vence, an aristocrat of old stock, in 1882. Marie-Félix's fortune had facilitated this marriage as well. Uncle Christian and Aunt Jeanne were to play important parts in Marie's life.

Shortly after Pierre's birth she was taken to see the newborn cousin at his mother's bedside. She was fascinated with his tiny hands and wished to know where he had come from. She also wanted to know why Aunt Jeanne was in bed. Gragra explained to her: Aunt Jeanne was exhausted from walking to the marketplace where children were bought; boys were found in cabbages and girls in roses. Mimi asked Mme Reichenbach the same questions and was told that the stork had brought the baby.

Mimi's first memory of music dates from Dieppe, when she was four and observed a merry-go-round with a barrel organ grinding out Rossini's *William Tell* overture. "So the earth contains such marvelous things! The children on the little horses go round and round, I don't envy them, I don't even see them any more, I'm so carried away by the enchantment of the music, this marvelous fairyland that has just been revealed to me! But, alas, Grandmother, who can't stand the spell of the music, gives me a tug and drags me away because the wind is blowing too strongly from the sea."

Mimi was no less isolated in Dieppe than she had been in Saint-Cloud and Paris, for proper society still did not accept Princess Pierre, and this bitter old woman did not think of providing playmates for her grandchild. But Mimi enjoyed Dieppe, even though she was forbidden to go into the water. She liked the view of the sea, the sound of the waves, their smell, and the pebbles on the beach. She even liked the house, which, as she later recognized, was frightful, narrow and four stories high.

It was cold in Dieppe in September 1886, which made Princess Pierre decide to return to Paris. Marie cried on the train. She thought that she had cried in order to have the window down so that she could feel the strong wind blowing on her, reminding her of the sea. This fragment of memory was connected to a second which was much clearer: three days later, in the Jardin d'Acclimatation with her grandmother, she watched in fascination the dance of big gray birds which, facing each other in pairs, spread their wings, leaped and pirouetted. Cranes? storks?—she was not quite sure. The following night, "on waking up in my little bed, I saw, standing upright on my stomach, one of the birds, but how much more beautiful! Luminous, diaphanous, it gave off all the colors of the rainbow, standing on one leg like a stork; its head and beak cocked to one side, it looked at me. It was terrible and marvelous at the same time; never have I seen anything so beautiful. . . . I cried out, Lucie came running, but in the meantime the vision, which seemed made of light and mist, vanished in the air. Then I remember nothing more, except that I learned the strange name of

this unreal vision—hallucination—and that day I stayed in bed."
Mimi did not feel feverish but she knew that something extraordinary was happening to her and that Dr. Josias, whom she knew well, had come. She was not left alone for a second.

Two days later, she had improved, but meanwhile her papa rushed back from his summer-long Balkan trip to see her. In the whispering, she overheard, "It is just like her poor mother"; but what had happened to her, "like her poor mother"? Useless for her to ask the question. Only years later did she learn of the report by Dr. Hardy, consulted by his pupil Dr. Josias on October 7, 1886. According to this document, she had, the previous month, a "tubercular lesion at the base of the right lung, with the complication of a brief but fairly copious hemoptysis [the colors of the bird represent the bleeding]. The illness had followed a regular course and, after about ten days, a complete cure had taken place."

This illness, mild tuberculosis, common at the time, and the reaction of those around her to it, were to have considerable repercussions. Her fortune and the consequences should she die before reaching her majority could not be overlooked. Henceforth Mimi was treated as an invalid and thus overprotected and further isolated. For her part, the idea that she was like her mother and therefore likely to die young took root. These factors were to have a strong influence on her later behavior.

The doctors recommended that she be taken to the south for the winter. The departure was delayed because Princess Pierre, Bonne-Maman as Marie called her, had to have an operation. The vision in her right eye had become obscured by a growth. The princess had delayed the surgery as long as possible but now gave in. For days afterward she remained bandaged in a darkened room awaiting the results. The operation failed. The princess's hunter's eye, which had served her so often in taking aim, had lost its vision.

In November 1886, the women of the Bonaparte household—Princess Pierre, Gragra, Mimi, Lucie, Mme Reichenbach—accompanied by Bonnaud and Pascal, left for San Remo by night train-sleeping car. It was Mimi's first such trip and she was wildly excited.

The princess had rented a villa overlooking the Mediterranean. Each morning, watched over by Lucie, Mimi played in the shade of the orange trees, wondering at their fruit. Each afternoon she was taken for a drive with her grandmother. The adults tried to point out Corsica ("the family island," they called it) but Mimi never made it out on the horizon. Once on an excursion the rock of Monaco could be seen in the distance. Bonne-Maman made certain that the experience was not repeated for she did not want to be reminded of anything to do with the Blanc family. In fact, she had banned card games from the household and forbidden use of the word "blanc," which means "white."

Mimi recovered from her illness and forgot all about being sick. Then early one morning, in February 1887, she was awakened with the household in an uproar. There was a major earthquake in San Remo. Before it was over, two hundred people were killed in the collapse of the church. This delighted her atheistic grandmother. Mimi was pleased to have seen Pascal in his night shirt. The Bonapartes hastily returned to Paris.

Back home on Cours la Reine, Mimi had the feeling of being in exile. Once more she was an invalid. With the weather being too cold, too damp or too foggy, she was forbidden to go out. Sadly she remained for hours at the window to watch the lucky children rolling their hoops along the Cours.

In a melancholy mood she waited for the leaves of the chestnut trees on the Cours to sprout. When the trees were in bloom and the weather was fine, her grandmother took her to the Bois de Boulogne. The rest of her time was spent in the study room.

Marie Bonaparte could not recall when and how she learned to read and write, but she never forgot the revelation that the English word "moon" was for her when her governess used it to designate the celestial body she was gazing at one spring evening. She remarks that she was less impressed later on by the story of the Tower of Babel. Mme Reichenbach, whom Mimi was quick to nickname "Mrs. Plom-Pudding" was "sweet and languorous" and her teaching entirely fanciful. As reading material she used storybooks and collections of songs, and since she played the piano well she preferred to sit down at it herself rather than torture Mimi by making her do exercises and scales.

Princess Pierre took no more interest in the study room than she had in the nursery.

For Mimi, the Villeneuves represented her family. Aunt Jeanne came to visit regularly. Over the years Mimi observed her aunt in the role of mother to her cousins and concluded that she had missed something by not being raised by her own mother. She yearned to rival her cousins in Aunt Jeanne's affection.

Meanwhile Aunt Jeanne's perfumes, lovely dresses and even her beauty were criticized by her mother, Princess Pierre, who wanted everyone to lead an austere existence, if possible as unhappy as her own had been. She lived withdrawn into her past and in the plans she was ceaselessly making for Roland and now for Mimi, whom she saw as a means of furthering her son's ambition.

Mme Reichenbach and Aunt Jeanne were both visibly pregnant in the spring of 1887. On May 21 Aunt Jeanne gave birth to a girl, named Jeanne, who was to become Mimi's childhood rival. A few days later, Mrs. Plom-Pudding also had a girl and took two months off to care for the child.

That summer, as usual, they went to Dieppe. This time, Prince Roland went first to Switzerland, then made a trip to Corsica in September and October. What went on in Dieppe did not interest him. But that year events took place there that would be of the greatest importance for Mimi. Lucie was discovered slipping out of the house to spend the nights with Pascal in his room across the street. Mimi overheard her grandmother's outraged comments. Lucie was as light as her curls and "had thrown her bonnet over the windmills." What could that mean? How could Lucie be so strong? But when Bonne-Maman threw her out, Mimi understood.

Mimi loved her, Pascal made love to her, and Lucie was sent away. This gave the child a feeling of insecurity and taught her the meaning of injustice. In sexual matters, why should Pascal, the man, be absolved and Lucie, the woman, be punished? Mimi was six years old. What she understood of the behavior of grown-ups upset her greatly. She wanted to keep near her those whom she knew, make them love her, get used to loving them so as never to be parted from them again. Who would take care of her, feed her, wash her, play with her? For a time Bonne-Maman's maid, Anna, grudgingly filled in.

Gragra, Mme Proveux, suggested a replacement for Lucie, and for Anna, who had protested that she did not have the patience to care for a child. As a result, a new woman entered Mimi's life.

Marie-Claire Bernardini, widow Druet, was a simple Corsican woman, daughter of a poor carpenter from San Pietro di Venaco, near Corte. She had been adopted at a very young age by an aunt in Algeria, who with her husband ran the Hôtel de France in Blida. Tortured and beaten by her sadistic aunt, she escaped at the age of fifteen by marrying a thirty-two-year-old merchant, a client at the hotel. It was a good marriage and they got along well. They had two children, both of whom died; when she was forty, she lost her husband. Together they had been fairly well-off, but as a widow, she found herself impecunious and isolated, and had to seek employment. Death and unhappiness were the principal themes in the recital of her ordeals, and Mimi never tired of hearing her stories.

Claire, as she was called for short, had been more deeply marked by her experiences than her physical appearance suggested. There were disturbances in her psyche that long remained invisible to a little girl, and to those who did not care to see. She was certainly reassuring at first, just the opposite of what one might imagine after so many tragedies. Marie Bonaparte has described her as she appeared to her one summer day in the year 1887: ". . . small, plump, well planted on her short legs; her blue eyes framed by her black hair reflect the light and smile at me, as do her pretty white teeth in her wide, pink mouth . . . The newcomer keeps smiling and, in a musical voice that begins to charm the musician's ears I inherited from Petite-Maman, she calls me sweetly, 'Come, my little princess, my child. . . .' " Mimi responded with tears—she did not want a newcomer to replace Lucie, to whom she was still attached. But Claire was able to "tame her" by offering her a caramel. "Claire the Corsican, primitive and passionate, must have suffered a great hunger for love. She lacked a child just as I lacked a mother. A kind of fate brought us together."

Marie Bonaparte also tells how mimosa blossoms suggested the nickname she gave her: "The name Claire seemed cold to me, like the overly clear brightness of a fine northern day. So all of a sudden, at the sight of some flowers of the South in her beloved hands, I had the idea of calling her by the warm name of the flowers. Mimau, I said, Mimau . . . keeping the two M's of Mama, the name I had never been able to say to anyone, and lovingly prolonging the second syllable."

Mimau was to be her confidante, her consoler, her source of joy and knowledge, her refuge during her childhood. Later their relationship was to be less simple, but their hearts remained united.

They lived together in intimate isolation, in adjoining rooms. In the evening Mimau stayed near Mimi. She sang and told her stories. On the sky-blue prie-Dieu that had belonged to her Petite-Maman, in the house of the atheist prince who had forbidden it, she had her say a prayer, in a low voice so as not to be caught by Grandmother. After putting her to bed, she told her other stories, while stroking her arms with the tips of her fingers, a caress that the little girl called "playing the charming mouse" and which she asked for.

In the morning, Mimau got ready first, in their shared dressing room. When the child opened her eyes, there she was, ready to kiss her. She had lighted or relighted the wood fire in the fireplace; the central heating was not enough, because of Mimi's fragility. She washed the child's face, hands and body with lukewarm water, and dressed her before the fire. In another room the child was served her breakfast: hot milk with a roll or a croissant. Then Mimi began playing, or watched the passersby from the window, and around ten o'clock Mme Reichenbach arrived.

At lunchtime, Bonne-Maman ate in the dining room with her son, Bonnaud, the secretary-steward, and Escard, the librarian. According to custom Mimi ate with her governess and Mme Proveux. Mimau, "who had only the rank of nursery maid, ate with the servants, though she came from the same middle-class background as Gragra." She resented this bitterly and let it be known.

But usually she and Gragra were united in their malicious opinions of others: Mme Reichenbach was filthy in her personal habits and Anna, Bonne-Maman's maid, a whore. Anna's liaisons with footmen and other servants kept the tongues of these two busy, but Mimau's imagination was the more fanciful; she alleged that Anna got her footman-lover to ejaculate into the soup intended for the main table.

In this enclosed little world where masters and servants spied on each other, where self-esteem was often wounded, where snubs were common currency, backstairs gossip by aging women, spiteful and full of hatred toward their employers, verged on calumny. Murder stories are truly exciting, even if one does not completely believe what one is hearing. Mimi did believe. Not all this talk made sense to her, of course, but she caught the drift of it.

Grandmother and Papa had done away with Petite-Maman in order to get hold of her money; that was what came through to her.

There are people who are said to be capable of anything. Princess Pierre was one of them. Behind her back, people whispered that in order to get rid of all traces of poison in the intestines, she had hastened to have the corpse embalmed, but that it was already black when the embalmers had taken it away. It was bruited about that Jean de Bonnefon, a writer and journalist, had published a pamphlet accusing the greedy mother-in-law. But Marie Bonaparte discovered later that her mother's body had not been embalmed, and the bibliography of the alleged accuser does not mention anything written about the "crime" of the Bonapartes. Furthermore, no libel suit was brought by the family. All the same, these assurances came too late. The harm had already been done.

Mimi's curiosity about her mother reached a new pitch. Mimau urged her to pray for her Petite-Maman. Bonne-Maman, when she spoke of her daughter-in-law at all, was critical. Now it was said that the young princess had been killed for her money. From all the talk around her the little girl concluded that she was like her "dreamy and poetic mother with her musical soul."[10] Certainly she was learning that she was like her mother in being rich, for the household talked as much of her money as it did of her mother's death.

The daughter of the victim in these tales was also the daughter of the criminal: "And the conflict between my ardent love for my adored father, and the dazzling horror that these imaginary crimes inspired in me, already lacerated the depths of my young heart," Marie Bonaparte wrote. This conflict, which was to mark her profoundly, would find its resolution only much later.

Then and throughout her life, Marie Bonaparte was fascinated with murderers and executions. We will see her again, as an old woman, fighting to save Caryl Chessman. As a child, she was excited by the crimes of anarchists, which the press related at length. Ravachol, Henry, Vaillant threw bombs into a restaurant, into the Chamber of Deputies, on the sidewalks, all over Paris. They were her heroes. She was also carried away by the exploits of Jack the Ripper, the mysterious killer of prostitutes in the Whitechapel quarter of London who has since passed into legend. For her he was the true superman, "a supermurderer and a super-anarchist."

Her childish imagination had another hero closer at hand, Jules Ferry, neighbor and former prime minister. She watched for him and followed him with eyes of admiration as he walked along the Cours, for she counted him among the murderers. Grandmother and Gragra blamed him for the massacres of French soldiers and sailors in Tonkin and Tunisia. He had just resigned because of the failure of his colonial policy.

Mimi had been baptized by the abbé Viallet. He still came to Sunday dinner from time to time and Mimi was intrigued by his story: He had killed his best friend in a duel over a woman and become a priest to expiate his guilt. Marie Bonaparte called him an "assassin monk" and wrote: "It did not displease me that the holy water should have been poured on my head by hands that had killed."

Although Mimi's daily life was restricted to the women's quarters, she was keenly aware that the household revolved around her father. He reigned downstairs where he shut himself up to work, and evenings he went out to dinner.

Princess Pierre protected him as much as possible from any disturbance from the house. Beyond that she continued to dote on him as if he were still a school boy. At the first sign that he had caught cold, she nursed him, usually giving liberal doses of *sirop de Flon*, which contained opium.

Prince Roland was a frustrated, unhappy man. He had hoped by his marriage and his academic success to find a place in society. However, the Blanc money did not help as he had expected, so Prince Roland remained as before his marriage—united with his mother in dreaming of the future and withdrawn into his books and his travels. In 1884 he published an anthropological work, *Les Habitants de Suriname*, which he dedicated to his mother ("la Princesse Pierre-Napoléon Bonaparte"). The book was put together from notes he had taken at the colonial exposition at Amsterdam the year before. He went on to produce several other monographs, of secondary character. He also published an album of a hundred photographs he had taken on a journey to Lapland in 1884, and the Société de Géographie soon invited him to give a talk on Lapland and Corsica. After June 1886, his time was his own, since a new law forbade all princes of families which had reigned in France from serving in the army.

Prince Roland saw little of his daughter, which is not surprising. Not only was he a busy man, but in the world to which he belonged by virtue of his name and wealth, children led a life quite separate from their parents. Mimi suffered because she did not have a mother to give her at least a minimum of love and attention. Mimau supplied what she could spontaneously, but she could not prevent the little girl from feeling rejected by the parental couple formed, in Mimi's eyes, by her father and grandmother. It was a matter of feelings and not of the way of life, which in itself was nothing out of the ordinary.

When the time came for it, Mimi was allowed to join the mother-son team for Sunday dinner. Usually it was just the three of them. The menu was always the same (Mimi found it monotonous): *pot au feu* and *riz à l'impératrice*; champagne was served, and to her glass, water was added. Next came what she had been waiting for all week: the moment when she entered her father's study. Her grandmother was seated to one side with her crochet work, "her everlasting shawls and petticoats of piss-yellow wool," and Mimi installed herself on her father's knees at the desk that was lit by a large oil lamp. For her this desk was covered with wonders that she never tired of contemplating.

Some evenings, the prince had her draw. He taught her to hold her pen correctly, or else he drew for her. Mountains most often, because she expressed a particular curiosity about Switzerland, where in her opinion he spent too much time traveling. He also showed her engravings illustrating the works of the Swiss natural-ist Friedrich von Tschudi. More astonishing still than the glaciers, lakes and waterfalls, was a receptacle containing mercury, with which he entrusted her for a few moments. She also held a magnet in her hands. Another evening, with a stick of sealing wax rubbed on the sleeve of his coat and a few bits of paper, he demonstrated for her the phenomenon of static electricity. He seems to have been a good teacher, and she was the ideal pupil.

Some Sundays, more wonderful still, he took her into his bed-room, where Grandmother did not follow, and let her look through the telescope placed before the open window, to see the stars, moon and planets. Throughout her life she was to enjoy observing the sky.

From such a father a daughter would inherit more than tall stature and dark eyes. Marie did all she could in a vain attempt to please him. She was quickly taught to respect her father's work. Under no circumstances was she to set foot in the library or the office where he pursued his scholarly studies; those rooms were a sanctuary and by general acknowledgment inviolable. Marie was proud of her father's excellence and dazzled by his knowledge. She loved him with all the passion she was already able to feel.

Nevertheless, he made her daily life miserable. He never tried to understand her aspirations, her joys or her fears, and (though she was following his own example) he discouraged her fondness for study so as to assure the success of rather different plans he and Princess Pierre had for the girl's future.

Frequently he left her with a "broken heart," as she tells in connection with a memorable sleigh ride. It was not often that one could use a sleigh in Paris, and Mimi wanted desperately to accompany her father. Permission was denied (it was too cold), and as he departed, he did not even think to raise his eyes toward the child who was watching him from behind her window. "Was it because of the mourning into which his departures and absences plunged me that I was often so sad, and that across all the years gone by such melancholy confronts me in my portraits from that time?" she asked herself when she had become an old lady.

These photographs, remarkable for their quality and upsetting since the little girl's expression reflects all the misery of the world, had been taken by him. This might suggest that he had some realization of his daughter's condition, but nothing is less certain. He seems to have delighted in the arrangement of the setting, and to have directed his model in what were then considered to be becoming poses, and the look on the face may not have struck him.

Marie never forgave him for his lack of any spontaneous affection and understanding of a child's needs and tastes. She was present at the inauguration of the Eiffel Tower and of the International Exposition of 1889; at the time, a reception was given in her father's house for Edison and his marvelous talking machine. The affair was a child's delight. American Indians in war bonnets would also be there because Monsieur Edison was American. Timidly Mimi asked her father if she might not pay a brief visit downstairs at the reception. He refused. Her answer, written later, was: "O Papa, cruel Papa! I am not an ordinary woman like Mimau and Gragra. I am the true daughter of your brain. I am interested in science as you are."

She was, for a long time, unaware of the full extent of his abandonment. On June 2, 1948, while supervising the removal of the library from her Paris mansion, she discovered some letters of hers that he had never opened. Mimi had written them during Prince Roland's second trip to America, and he had received them in Chicago on May 10, 1893. Meticulous as he was, he had taken the trouble to jot this fact down on the envelopes. In those unopened letters his little daughter had told him all about her days and spoken from the heart to her darling Papa. Even after fifty-five years, it was painful for her that they had remained unread.

In one way or another little Princess Marie felt estranged from life around her. Visits from her Villeneuve cousins added to this feeling. She was only seven years old when Pierre and Jeanne stayed for a month or two with their grandmother, while their parents were moving from avenue Marceau into their mansion on rue de Prony. Though they were under the same roof, Mimi's life was different from her cousins'. The only child was overprotected. The grandmother had two reasons for treating her this way: illness and money. She spoke constantly of the return of the tuberculosis she dreaded, and of the fabulous fortune that would open up possibilities to the daughter of her beloved son which her other grandchildren would never know. It was necessary to prepare Mimi for this exalted destiny by leaving her isolated as much as possible, which, according to the grandmother, was the prerogative of aristocrats and wealthy people. She thought that a gregarious instinct was the portion of the lower orders—a relict from her own early experiences.

Mimi turned more and more to her nursery maid for love. Mimau loved her little princess, but she was fast becoming a frustrated old woman. Too old to be seduced by Pascal, she saw some aspect of sexuality to be censured everywhere. "Nounou" had let Mimi straddle her foot and then bounced her up and down, thus stimulating the first remembered sexual pleasure, which the child later repeated by rubbing herself against a little armchair. Mimau said all that was needed to fill the child with a sense of guilt and fear. Mimi gave up the pleasurable activity, but developed a phobia of buttons which lasted for a long time.

She had already developed a morbid fear of illness, much like a phobia, because of the way she had been raised. Now she became fearful of being poisoned, like her mother, and developed a horror of medicines, especially *sirop de Flon*.

At night, she had fears, as many children do, but hers persisted far beyond youth. First she was terrified that she would awaken with Anubis, the Egyptian jackal-headed god of the dead, howling at the foot of her bed, in which she lay like a mummy; she had seen Anubis in her beginner's history book.

More frightening for the child was a nightmare that recurred for many years. She called it the Serquintué. She could hear the Serquintué knock three times to announce its arrival. Then she was sure that she would not succeed in hiding herself completely. If the tip of her foot or a bit of her nightgown stuck out, she was going to die because the monster would catch sight of her. The Serquintué was "a railroad, but animated, alive, a fantastic and terrible animal of iron, coal, and steam, which entered houses . . ." Here she drew on Mimau's stories of the coffins of those who perished on the ships and were thrown to the sharks in the China seas. Mimau recognized this nightmare, which each time made Mimi moan. When the Serquintué made its appearance she took Mimi into her own bed to comfort her; as Mimi grew older, she lay down beside her terrorized little girl.

During the day, Mimi took refuge in her favorite game of "playing houses": "Drawing chairs and tables together, she would cover them with shawls, thus making a dark, little, airless enclosure into which she would creep and remain for hours, ecstatically contented."[11]

Between the ages of seven and a half and ten Marie Bonaparte engaged in an activity unusual in a child of that age: she filled five small books with stories. As she later wrote: ". . . as early as in my eighth year there was established in me the psychological attitude which was to be mine for the rest of my life. Whenever my instinctual impulses, of whatever kind, broke against the wall of reality, it was by climbing the starry tree, i.e., by taking refuge in intellectual sublimation that I found peace and happiness."[12]

The little copybooks were found by Marie among her father's papers after his death in 1924. "I read them with strange feelings, for although I myself had filled them, I had lost all memory of their contents," she remarks in her introduction to the first volume, adding: ". . . the riddle of these little books was one among the reasons which prompted me, after my father's death, to seek an analysis with Freud."[13]

These five copybooks each bear the title *Bêtises* (Trifles). She wrote the first four in English and the last in German. Marie was later unaware of their meaning. Their content—"fantastic, absurd, grotesque"—provoked her curiosity. These school copybooks, with their dreary, black glossy covers, contain evidence not only of the conflicts that were tormenting her but also of her knowledge, her activities and all the things her memory had hidden. It is rare to possess such testimony concerning one's own early history. Few children at that age write so much. Thanks to her persistence, Mimi found in writing a way of shielding herself.

Marie Bonaparte published the *Five Copy-Books* in French and in English with Freud's and her own commentaries on the stories between 1939 and 1952. The texts themselves bring to life Mimi and her preoccupations:

My "I Would Try to Cry" [sic!]

> D. Sad, find you not, cry, sad, cry sad,
> Why, If I say it they will say it is not
> to work! music, I will play, I will,
> oh! they will say it is not to work.
> ("*Yes*") I would cry. Cry, cry, No, not the battle
> of flowers, if I am as so sad.
> I am sad, It is because I am sad, Poor me?
> No, so sad, never I was!
> I will cry, I want Mimau, it is she that
> will ("console") me. Dont play that it make
> me sad. Mme Proveux also will console me, oh!
> It is in this book I put all the thinks that
> can soulage me!!!!!!!!!
> Wery sad am I! oh! Papa console me I will
> work I will! sad never so sad was I! oh! I want
> to sleep, Don't speak to me or I will burst
> in "larmes" (Eclater en sanglonts!)*
> I am sure it is they will say if I say it,
> they will say it is not to work.
> Oh! my leg! it hearts me very much! No
> I will surmonte myself oh! sad am I!
> I want it say it . . . . [14]

Here is Mimi's daily life, and it is sad indeed. As we see, her very tears earned her a scolding. She was accused of using them so as not to have to practice the piano. It is interesting that Mimi, then only nine years old, realizes that her copybook is an outlet. Her mistakes in English are revealing. Thus in "It is in this book I put all the things that can soulage [relieve] me" (a sentence followed by nine exclamation points, it should be noted), she writes the word "thinks" for "things" or "thoughts." This is much less an error than a slip of the pen. When her English fails her, she uses

---

* In French, but misspelled in the English text.

French: "*console*," "*larmes*," "*éclater en sanglonts*" [sic] (console, tears, to burst into sobs), or French spelling, *surmonte* for "surmount."

La Photographie

—In a wood a little girl saw
a man making a Photographie
but at the same minut a "*meikäfer*"
came and Mme - - - - - - - - - - - - - - - -
Kreichenbachen (Mrs. Plompudding. Nom surnoming)
gave him a knock and he fell as—a dead
man—but he was not a man! He was
a "*Hanneton*." But Mme Kreichenbachen took
him and put him in her mought. Then he
became large, large, that she was obliged
to open her mough as great as a house,
and by the same occasion she swalowd
up a house! But her stomac bursted inside
because there was *Dy* and she didjested
by the lungs. Then the maikaifer became
more large more large then five houses
and it finished he was so great
as the wold and then more then
the sky and all the Planets that
existe and they made   the
Photographie   of   this formidable "*Hanneton*"
Then Mrs. Kreichenbach swallowed
him up, and she burst out.
But all was a dream Fortchenly for her.[15]

Here the symbols become clear. "Meikäfer," for example, is German (*Maikäfer*) for *cockchafer*, an insect which had a phallic meaning for the little girl (*hanneton* in French). We find in the copybooks numerous stories inspired by reminiscences of the primal scene. The actors may vary but in each story there is the same ambivalence of attraction and fear in relation to the penis, which is moreover sometimes openly coveted. The solitary little girl, deprived of games appropriate to her age, shows perhaps more than the usual interest in sexual matters.

The rest of Mimi's school work was poor owing to the laziness of her tutor. Mme Reichenbach probably never realized how exceptional her pupil was. She taught her popular songs, and read with her Perrault's fairy tales and the fables of La Fontaine.

Mimi probably never knew just how mediocre Mrs. Plom-Pudding really was, but she had begun to see herself as different from the other women in the house. She thought she had found a kindred spirit in Mme Bonnaud. She had heard Mimau and Gragra telling how the wife of Prince Roland's secretary-steward had extracted from her Petite-Maman the famous will that so outrageously favored her father at her own expense. This wicked action, denounced by the two women, crowned Mme Bonnaud's brow with a halo of glory and placed her just below murderers in Mimi's secret pantheon.

Mme Bonnaud was old, she had no children, and she too had lost her mother as a child. The little girl had learned this from her lips and quickly became passionately fond of her friend. In addition to their similar family situations, she tried to find other resemblances. She decided they were both intellectuals. An intellectual Mme Bonnaud most certainly was, compared to the other women in the house. She became for a time the secluded child's favorite companion.

Mme Bonnaud taught her ancient mythology. Mimi loved to hear "the melodious voice" reciting to her the adventures of the gods and goddesses, of whom she went on thinking long afterwards. But her old friend, with her gray hair and long yellow teeth, began to lose weight and to stop eating. Then she stopped going out, even to come and see her. She was too weak. Her death, in October 1891, was a new experience, and one that Mimi was unable to come to terms with. She had known mourning, she was told ceaselessly about the deaths that had already taken place around her, but the void caused by the disappearance of a beloved person—this she was feeling for the first time. A familiar presence was no more. Never again would she tell Mimi her own story, or those of the gods and heroes of Greece and Rome. "Never more," Mimi repeated, using these words for the first time.

Occasionally Mimi was given a companion for her studies. Rolande Escard, two years her junior and the prince's godchild, was the first daughter of the Escards, who previously had had three boys. Jean, the third, was Mimi's contemporary. They got on well, but it was to Pierre Escard, the second son, handsome and "naughty," that she was attracted. One day, Mimau scolded her because they had been rolling on the ground together, and, Marie Bonaparte recalled, "I was crushed by a huge feeling of shame, proof of the pleasure that I must have taken in it."

With Rolande—up until the time when they shook bottles of beer so that the foam expelled the cork and splashed over the table and even on Mme Proveux's bodice or that of the tutor—the games were more innocent. While practicing this one, Mimi recognized that it gave her a strange feeling; her laughter, as well as her little companion's, was the result of the embarrassment and uneasiness they experienced. The adults who scolded them for the damage caused and for their bad manners did not appear to see what the shaken bottles represented for them.

Against grownups, the little girls stood united, but Rolande was never to play a large role in Mimi's life. Having an affectionate family, a mother and father who loved her, Rolande had no inkling of the motherless girl's problems.

Mimi's relationship with her Villeneuve cousins was more complicated. Over the years their number grew to six and their Sunday visits were an institution. Cousin Jeanne, five years her junior, became Mimi's principal rival. Mimi was certain that she could never be roguish and sparkling like Jeanne, and that she would never be liked. People only liked charming superficiality. These were the pessimistic conclusions she drew from her observations.

Jeanne was a beautiful little girl with black eyes set far apart, a delicate nose and a full mouth. She had two major trump cards: the self-assurance of those who are loved, and wit. When she made fun of her brother Pierre or of Mimi, she made everyone laugh, even Uncle Roland. As if these natural attributes were not enough, she was dressed in the English fashion with bare calves and wore pretty dresses and nice petticoats when Mimi was still bundled up in woolens, shawls and long woolen stockings that scratched her legs.

Unfortunately there were many opportunities to compare herself with Jeanne, since Aunt Jeanne and her children spent their summer holidays with Princess Pierre and Mimi.

One happy memory of these summers persisted, though it started inauspiciously. In 1890, Marie and her grandmother watched the regattas from the pier in Dieppe. Mimi flinched at each cannon shot. Bonne-Maman was furious. "How dare you? A Bonaparte mustn't be afraid of cannon!" She forced the frightened child to remain on the pier and afterward Mimi had "a small attack of nerves" nursed by Mimau. Her grandmother then tried to overcome her fear of gunfire by bursting paper bags filled with air near her.

During the summer of 1893, spent with the Villeneuves in Malabry, near Paris, Monsieur Bonnaud came to shoot rabbits. He bought Aunt Jeanne a small hunting rifle and urged Mimi to fire it. Mimi was ecstatic; when she felt the recoil of the gun against her shoulder she went wild. She and her younger cousins bought cap pistols. They shut themselves in the dark in order to enjoy the spark, noise and smell. Mimi was drunk with pleasure. "A reversal from the passive to the active [had taken place] since the aggression inherent in my explosion complex had changed direction . . . and was released,"[16] she recognized later.

Returning to Paris for the long winter was always a saddening experience. Marie wanted pets and had in the past been given a red squirrel and two marmosets. The squirrel soon died and the marmosets disappeared the night of their arrival. Aunt Jeanne had two pet female dogs and that summer she gave Mimi a female puppy with pearl-gray fur, soft, thick and silky. She was the mongrel offspring of Aunt Jeanne's collie bitch and a fine Great Dane. Mimi was delighted and named her Diablette. The dog disappeared the day of their return to Paris.

To console her, Pascal, the head groom, brought her another dog, a tiny one that would not get any bigger. This one was all black, except for the red tips of its paws and red circles around the eyes. Mimi named him Zéphyr and loved him at first sight. To everyone's surprise, Prince Roland also became attached to the little animal. It was doubtless due to his protection that Zéphyr was tolerated by his mother. Later Zéphyr had a companion, a puppy of Blanchette, Pascal's fox terrier bitch. Mimi first chose from the litter an all-white puppy, but since her grandmother refused to let her call him Blanc-Blanc or even Blanchet, for obvious reasons, Mimi chose another one and called him Satellite, in homage to Jules Verne, whom she was reading with enthusiasm.

"Little Louis," the seventeen-year-old groom who accompanied Mimi and her grandmother when they went out in the landau, was also a fervent reader of Jules Verne. Mimi liked Little Louis and they exchanged brief opinions about their reading. He became one of the many distant acquaintances in the large household whom she considered "friends" as she grew up.

The outings by carriage were usually to the Bois de Boulogne or to Saint-Cloud, to her own private park. Mimi was proud of owning the house and its beautiful gardens.

The trip to Saint-Cloud was pleasant and lasted about an hour. Mimi observed each detail of the journey. The minute they opened the entrance gate, she was happily back among the tall chestnut trees, the large pine, the paulownia, and the mixed odors of boxwood, elder, spindle tree and syringa. The lawn extended south of the garden, beyond the transverse walk bordered by lindens trimmed to a round shape. There a goat browsed, tied to a stake. When the carriage stopped before the stone steps of the villa, Mimi jumped out and ran on the grass.[17]

When she was little she ran to Eugène, the gardener, for a basket of snails to throw to the chickens. By telling Mimi it was cruel, Mimau stopped this game, as she had put an end to other pleasurable activities.

Mimi was eleven now and growing up. Even so she still delighted in the domestic animals at Saint-Cloud, in the goat's milk and fresh jellies and preserves made by the gardener's wife. These pastoral interludes were cherished events, and remained pleasant memories in the solitary child's life.

The year 1893 was the last time she felt herself "still truly a child."

· 3 ·

ADOLESCENCE AND BLACKMAIL

"I prefer truth to love."

MARIE BONAPARTE,
unpublished notes, 1927

OVER THE YEARS, AS MIMI HAD MATURED, SHE HAD REALIZED that the "mothers" who cared for her—Rose, Lucie, Mimau—were less important than Princess Pierre. Her grandmother became the dominant female figure of her adolescence. Marie's distrust of her began early, but she was nevertheless dazzled by Princess Pierre's tales of the Bonapartes. At some point, with Mimau's help, she realized that her source for most of what she knew about the Bonaparte relatives was despised and rejected by them. As she listened, she also learned to recognize one of the most common of human obsessions: fascination with what one cannot overcome. It was not an obsession she shared.

Early in 1893, her grandmother informed her: "You know, Mimi, don't be frightened: every month women bleed down below. And one day that will happen to you. So don't be scared!" Shortly thereafter, when Aunt Jeanne gave birth to her fifth child, in April 1893, Princess Pierre added: "I'll tell you something, Mimi. Women have children by going to bed with their husbands." This information was insufficient and Mimi did not know whom to ask to make it more complete.

Birth remained a mystery. She wanted to be informed, and she could not find the explanation by herself. One day she decided to ask Mme Escard, who, like Aunt Jeanne, had five children. Averting her gaze, the librarian's wife replied that she didn't know; that earned the resentment of a furious Mimi.

Mimi began menstruating at the age of eleven and a half. What a pleasure it was to understand all of a sudden what Mimau and

Gragra whispered about on certain days, the requirements of hygiene that they hid from her but which she had glimpsed. Another piece of the mysterious puzzle fell into place.

The pride of becoming a woman was relegated to the background by her first communion. Her father and grandmother told her that she must receive her first communion because it would be ridiculous to have to worry about religious instruction at the time of her marriage. (They spoke more often now of the fabulous marriage to be arranged for her.) The Abbé Paoli, a Corsican friend of the family, would prepare her and Rolande Escard, her playmate and study companion, for first communion.

The priest, "round, bald, graying, his face ruddy and jovial," lived on rue Raynouard, not far from the site of Prince Pierre's old house that had been destroyed during the Commune. He kept doves, two of them in a cage, in a corner of the room where he received his young visitors. Because of the birds, the young girl liked him immediately. She was ashamed of crossing herself incorrectly and of making mistakes in the recital of the Lord's Prayer and the Hail Mary, which her grandmother had hastily taught her the week before. Mimi would soon look forward impatiently to these Tuesday catechism lessons.

Inspired by the abbé's faith, she became an excellent catechumen. She outshone Rolande and dreamed in secret of converting her grandmother and her father. On Sundays she went to mass; since she was preparing for her first communion, they could hardly prevent her. Mimau alone rejoiced, imagining that her dear little girl would be a fervent Christian for the rest of her life.

With the enthusiasm that she put into everything, Mimi received the Sacraments for the first time in exaltation, sobbing with happiness. "I no longer knew where I was, whether my grandmother was there with Mimau, whether my father had refused to accompany me, I didn't even know what in a moment I knew very well—that I was hungry."

At home, there was no party to celebrate the occasion. Lunch was like any other, no guest had been invited. Mimi spent the day alone, seated on the sofa in the study room in her white communion dress, which she had refused to change. Her father's secretary took a photograph. By dusk she had fallen asleep from fatigue and sadness.

Marie kept her religious feelings to herself but began composing devout poems in secret. Soon her writings were discovered and immediately forbidden by Princess Pierre. Mimi was resentful, but she was still trying to make herself loved by her formidable grandmother. When she discovered that the half-blind princess played billiards and was willing to teach her this game, she was overjoyed. During her walks, she had occasionally glimpsed through the half-open door of a café groups of men around a billiard table, and had noticed that no women were among them.

Her pride in this initiation was matched by fear because her grandmother warned her that if she tore the green cloth it would be a disaster: the whole covering would have to be replaced. Yet, on the days when the two of them dined by themselves, without Gragra to finish reading the newspaper to the princess, Mimi waited impatiently for the moment to go upstairs to the study. They moved aside the desk which during the day was placed against the billiard table, lighted the two hanging gas lamps, and the lesson began. This was the only form of play that Mimi ever shared with her grandmother.

By now Mimi had begun to think seriously of what she would do "when she grew up"—a magical formula for all children. Certain aspects of her grandmother's personality fascinated her. For her, the masculine woman represented life. She already knew that she herself would not be "like one of the others, feminine, weak, ailing, lethargic," accepting their "sad fate." Grandmother, the huntress, horsewoman and politician, had gone so far as to be able "to piss standing up, like a man, in the very midst of a crowd, merely by spreading her legs and skirts." This was Mimi's ambition also.

The billiard table was not a permanent part of their lives; it belonged to a house where the family was only temporarily installed while awaiting the construction of a new dwelling. Prince Roland had bought a lot, on avenue d'Iéna, that overlooked the Seine and the Champ de Mars, and there had built a true palace of gray stone in the Neoclassical style, in which the prince was to live until his death.

The following summer, 1894, again taking the Villeneuves with them, the Bonapartes rented a château in Villereau, near Orléans, where the marquise was taught to ride a bicycle by her husband's secretary. Mimi was not allowed to join them. Bicycling was forbidden to her, like everything else that gave joy to others. Pretty Aunt Jeanne was adored by the tall young man who bore the name of the only king of Corsica, Théodore. Mimi was as intrigued by this couple as she was by the symptoms of Mimau's menopause which had begun.

That autumn, Prince Roland at last took an active interest in his daughter's education. He decided to replace Mme Reichenbach. His mother vehemently opposed him, and finally it was agreed that Mimi should be examined by a school inspector to test her knowledge of elementary skills. The results were disastrous; it was obvious that Mme Plom-Pudding had to go. Unfortunately, at this point the prince again withdrew and left the choice of her replacement to his mother.

The princess's choice, a Mme Jéhenne, was a small-featured woman, shriveled, with gleaming false teeth and gray eyes behind a pince-nez. The new teacher shared with Princess Pierre a certain rigidity and limitation of mind. Her relations with her pupil remained strained, and Mimi never became attached to her.

By that time Mimi had already written a good deal ("the movement of the pen dipped in ink over the pure, smooth paper was a physical pleasure for me, as it has remained ever since"). Mme Jéhenne pronounced her handwriting defective, not noticing that Mimi had deliberately developed a script modeled on her father's. She had no wish to amend her handwriting. Mme Jéhenne did not back down so easily, and though Marie was twelve years old, she humiliated her by obliging her to practice her strokes and individual letters in copybooks designed for beginners. She tried to give her pupil a feeling of intellectual inferiority. Grudging with compliments, she found fault with everything.

Nevertheless, she fought for the Latin that Mimi was so anxious to learn, while the prince feared that a knowledge of this language would lead his daughter to religion. He had the narrow-mindedness and intransigence of the freethinkers of his time. When Mimi was finally allowed to begin her lessons, the light green cover of Lhomond's Latin grammar, brought one morning by Mme Jéhenne, seemed to her a thing of surpassing beauty.

Mme Jéhenne also intended her pupil to learn to play the piano correctly. Though Marie wanted to play with the skill of her mother, she balked at the discipline of scales and correct fingering. Finally, however, Mme George-Hainl, a first-rate music teacher, was engaged for her, whose hands, "plump and muscular, master the keys of the piano with a velvety sweetness," and who cost thirty francs a week for a one-hour lesson. The princess had taken her time in agreeing to this step.

Mimi looked forward to her first summer break from Mme Jéhenne's teaching. Her vacation was spent, with the Villeneuves, in Javersy, a château situated among the wheatfields of La Beauce. Princess Pierre did not stop complaining about the heat, while Mimi was scrutinizing her two new teachers, Fräulein Frieda and Miss Kathleen.

Fräulein Frieda was a pastor's daughter from a village near Karlsruhe, twenty years old, short of stature but long of face, with straight flaxen hair, a wide mouth, and small gray, very lively myopic eyes behind a pince-nez.

Miss Kathleen was a twenty-eight-year-old Irishwoman with reddish chestnut hair. Marie was enchanted. "I loved her hair, her beauty, the gentleness of her gestures, including a certain morbid refinement of her frail limbs and high pink cheekbones."

Immediately Miss Kathleen "dared" to initiate her into the plays of Shakespeare. She began with *Julius Caesar* but got no further, for she did not return to Paris in the fall. Grandmother first announced that she was on a month's vacation, later she said that the Irishwoman was not in good health, and according to Dr. Josias, who supposedly had been consulted, she might have been able to infect Mimi. Once more the girl felt caught in the trap of her grandmother's lies. Miss Kathleen had vanished, like the dog Diablette, like the animals Mimi had wanted to adopt. Why?

The lies had become so troubling for her that she had difficulty spotting them and even then she still believed them a little. Did Grandmother have an unerring talent for separating her from those she loved, or was Miss Kathleen really consumptive and was she going to waste away in some distant place and end by dying like Petite-Maman? Mimi did not succeed in establishing the truth. Everyone in this house seemed to indulge in lies, at least by omission. To make matters worse her study of Latin was banned that fall. Mimi comforted herself with books, and Mimau scolded her for reading too much.

There was some consolation. Fräulein Frieda had "a broad and powerful brain, a man's mind. And it was this mind that day by day won me over, all the more so since it was also warmed by the emanations of a heart as ardent as mine in its aspirations toward life, beauty, art and love." Soon Fräulein Frieda became Frifri and a great friend.

Mimi had not forgotten that her Petite-Maman had had German governesses and a perfect knowledge of the language of the country where her other grandmother, Mme Blanc, had been born. She listened enthusiastically to the descriptions of the Black Forest, of the walks Frieda had taken there, of the animals that inhabited it. Frieda and her pupil also discussed literature. They talked about life and love. To Frifri alone, Mimi dared to speak of what was bothering her. It was Frifri who revealed to her the mystery of the intimate relations between men and women. Mimi, who had been trying to puzzle this out for herself over a long time, had thought she had solved the riddle while watching a performance of Molière's *Tartuffe*.

The scenes between Tartuffe and Elmire fascinated her. Especially the second, in which Elmire, who was trying to unmask Tartuffe, had hidden her husband, Orgon, under the table. Elmire, pressed against the table by the hypocrite whose physical touch she wanted to avoid, leaned back more and more. "All of a sudden, I think I understand. Their position indicates that the man, in his relations with the woman, makes peepee on her!" Mimi was proud of her discovery. At the same time, she had the impression that "that's not quite right . . ." Finally she asked Frifri, who told her: "*Etwas geht hinein . . .*" Whereupon she was seized with terror at the thought that such a thing would happen to her when she married. No wonder Petite-Maman died. . . . Her inner turmoil that evening dulled the brightness of the lamps and, in the days that followed, the brightness of the sun. Then, she could not say how, little by little calm was restored. "I had accepted the law of nature to which I would have to submit."

Mimi did not confide in Mimau, whom she still loved but from whom she did not want to have to put up with evasions or lies. Nor did she say anything to her Aunt Jeanne, who on other occasions had shown kindness to her, for here the affection lacked depth. She also felt that perhaps her aunt might pity this too rich niece and find her awkward and clumsy. Mimi herself recognized that she was awkward and clumsy compared to her cousin Jeanne.

She was then fourteen years old and almost as tall as her grandmother, whose height was five feet seven inches. At night, after undressing for bed, she liked to look at her naked body, which was changing and seemed to her both attractive and strange.

Except for the Villeneuve and Escard children, the young princess saw no one her own age. She had no friends. So what a joy it was to be invited by Mme Émile Ollivier, the wife of Napoleon III's last prime minister, to meet her daughter Geneviève.

In her own home, Mimi had first met Daniel, Émile Ollivier's son by his first marriage, to Blandine, eldest daughter of Liszt and Mme d'Agoult and sister of Cosima Wagner. Geneviève was Daniel's half sister, twenty years his junior and four months younger than Mimi.

The Ollivier house stood in the center of a garden filled with lilacs and birds' song. Mimi was impressed by M. Ollivier, then an old gentleman of seventy-one, who took the trouble to welcome her with much good grace, "seeming to bend his noble mind, like his fine face, toward the adolescent that I was."

At the Olliviers', Marie found tenderness between parents and children, sharing of interests between the generations, and a stimulating intellectual and artistic atmosphere that were new to her. Her relations to her father suffered greatly by comparison, and Uncle Christian de Villeneuve, about whom there were rumors she did not yet understand, was not an impressive father either. The girls discussed music and literature. Mimi had recently become a follower of Rousseau. Geneviève was a Voltairian; she had become familiar with Voltaire's correspondence through her father, who read it aloud during the winters they spent at La Moutte, their estate on the Mediterranean.

Geneviève talked about this house, the tall palm trees, the pines, the nightingales and the sea, and Mimi recalled the hill with violets, the orange trees, the jasmine, all the intoxicating scents of San Remo from which the earthquake had driven them away. She had always wanted to return to the South.

Though the two girls argued constantly over their literary tastes, Mimi felt enormous relief at being able to express herself at last. Geneviève remained her friend throughout her life, occupying an exceptional place since Marie was to have few women friends.

Raised without a mother, by women who lacked the empathy to respond intelligently to the girl she was, Marie was long on the defensive as regards her own sex. She was conscious very early on of the disadvantage of being a woman. She knew they would never dare to treat her the way they did, had she been a boy. Her intelligence was of no account; it was her sex that determined the behavior of her grandmother and father. Later she would write, in a volume of recollections: "In the culture created by men, women do not have the position, the freedom, the happiness that they ought to; I feel myself to be one of the oppressed.

"But, from certain points of view, it serves women right. Basically I do not like women, who are either simple-minded, like Mimau and Gragra, or stupidly virtuous, like my austere Grandmother, who was deceived and made a fool of by Grandfather but could only go on repeating in her old age, 'At least, I've been a decent woman . . .' Or else women are flirts, who sport with love and men, and make fun of everything and everybody, like little Jeanne, or Molière's Célimène."

This text dates from 1958. The feminists had not yet thought to accuse her of not being one of them, as they would do later on. During her whole career, however, Marie Bonaparte had been acutely conscious of the particular problems of women, never forgetting the difficulties of her own early years.

The first months of 1896 were a time of anticipation and preparation for the household as the palace on avenue d'Iéna was nearing completion; Marie paid little attention—she was taken up with discoveries of her own. Mme Jéhenne, the daughter of an actress, had the love and knowledge of the theater in her blood and urged Princess Pierre to take Mimi to see plays. For this girl living in isolation the theater was a great school. Mimi discovered by turns the musical stage, the classics and the emotions of love.

In July 1918, Marie Bonaparte added another memoir to her many unpublished manuscripts, this one entitled *Les Hommes que j'ai aimés* (The Men I Have Loved). It reveals that her first love was "a light opera singer who sang the role of Ganymede." She was thirteen years old, and Victor Massé's *Galatée* was the first operetta she had seen. "Her" singer was nineteen years old, as Gragra, to whom she could not help talking, informed her. "Youth attracts youth," was the comment of the princess's reader, who was clearly an unsatisfactory confidante. Some time later, still burning with the same flame and unable to turn her thoughts elsewhere, Mimi asked her aunt Jeanne for an explanation. "You'll be married when you're seventeen," declared the latter, kissing her. Mimi was perplexed. The prediction indicated that the feeling that engulfed her had something to do with marriage, but she still did not know that it was a matter of love.

The very first time that she went to the Opéra, the young Ganymede was supplanted by the second love, a young Spanish tenor named Alvarez who sang the monk in *La Favorita*. Fortunately this time Frifri shared her enthusiasm. "And it was good not to be alone in undergoing these languorous and painful ecstasies, and to be able to talk about them, albeit in German!" Not only did she talk about them, but at night she couldn't sleep. She would have liked to stroke the Spaniard's hair and his attractive little beard. Frantically she hugged her pillow until finally she dropped off to sleep.

April, the month of the move to avenue d'Iéna, was for Mimi principally the time of her discovery of Mounet-Sully. The great tragedian performed Sophocles' *Oedipus Rex* at the Comédie Française. Mimi was puzzled that she found it so difficult to grasp the meaning of the play, not realizing that the play was as much the thing for her as the actor. She had no way of knowing that, in this very same year, the word "psychoanalysis" appeared in print for the first time in an article by Freud,[1] first in French on March 30, 1896, then in German on May 15.[2] Freud's discovery of the Oedipus complex was still to come. Mimi noted the reactions of her companions: Bonne-Maman objected to the cries that set her teeth on edge, Mme Jéhenne remained impassive, and Gragra pointed out that Mounet-Sully squinted. She herself was transported. She had never seen anything so sublime, and it struck her dumb. Though she had had her period two weeks before, waking up the next day, she was bathed in blood. This was to her the proof of the depth of her feelings. Everything in her had changed. What she loved the night before, she loved no longer. She no longer loved Mimau, who brought her breakfast as usual. She no longer loved her dog, sweet little Zéphyr. She was in Thebes, not in Paris about to move to avenue d'Iéna.

During the move, the little dog was lost. Mimi felt no grief, even when Mimau suggested that it might have been strangled by one of Anna's lovers. She was indifferent to what went on around her. She resented her grandmother since she failed to understand the beauty of Oedipus' cries; she resented Gragra; she did not succeed in making Frifri feel what it was that obsessed her. She could not speak to anyone, and certainly not to Aunt Jeanne, who, about to be delivered of her sixth child, walked around with a big belly, asking Mimi to feel the baby's movements.

The spell was to last. With her grandmother's permission, Mimi bought two photographs of Mounet-Sully in the role of Oedipus. But soon her grandmother had the photographs removed from her bedside, at Prince Roland's command. The prince despised actors; he called them "mummers" (*cabotins*) and rated them no higher than actresses, whom he called "whores." But never mind! Mimi was allowed to see *Oedipus* several times.

Hamlet, another of the celebrated tragedian's triumphs, transported her just as much. She may have seen herself as a female Hamlet. The performance of Shakespeare's tragedy, which, like *Oedipus*, she insisted on seeing again whenever the opportunity arose, overwhelmed her. Nor did she fail to notice that her grandmother, who oddly enough did not refuse to accompany her, was strangely ill at ease.

That summer, spent in her house in Saint-Cloud with the Villeneuves, Mimi herself had a chance to act. With Mme Jéhenne's help she staged Racine's tragedy *Athalie*, with herself in the title role and Gragra and her cousins playing the supporting parts. In a queen's costume made of veils embroidered with gold and silver, she declaimed the famous dream quite well and the audience applauded her, just as if she were Mounet-Sully. Her teacher found a way to spoil part of her pleasure by pointing out that her breasts shook. Trying to overlook this unpleasant fact, Mimi awaited impatiently the return to Paris and the new theater season.

The fall brought a resumption of her studies. Aside from her method of instructing through the theater, Mme Jéhenne was a wretched pedagogue. Princess Pierre was suspicious of new people, but she had at last found a replacement for Miss Kathleen. Mimi took an instant dislike to her new English teacher. Nevertheless, Miss Hetty[3] was to remain with her from 1896 to 1903. She came from the shires of central England. Marie Bonaparte describes her as having "the small mouth of a mocking rodent. She made fun of all enthusiasms, ceaselessly upholding self-control and matter-of-factness. This horrified me."

It is likely that Princess Pierre was aware of Miss Hetty's lack of affinity with Mimi. She distrusted friendships that Mimi's spontaneity might elicit and over which she would have no control. It was becoming obvious that Mimi was gifted, although she had been kept from serious studies. However little or badly taught, she showed an insatiable desire for literary activity.

She created a "monthly magazine" which she called *Le Sphinx*; its two issues appeared in May and June 1897. Her contributors were given pseudonyms borrowed from Greek history and mythology. Prince Orlando was the editor-in-chief, and she herself a member of the administrative council, signing herself Rhadamante.

Le Sphinx's articles were inspired by current events—a local fire, the coming of the telephone, the Diamond Jubilee of Queen Victoria. The second issue contained an anti-Greek and pro-Cretan article: *Eastern Courier: The Greeks Want to Dominate Crete.*

The summer of 1897 brought Marie a new experience; Prince Roland had long before become an expert alpinist and his love for mountains led him to the study of glaciers. His work in this field is still authoritative.*

For the first time the entire household, as well as the Ville-neuves, were allowed to accompany him. To accommodate this large group, it was necessary for the prince to rent two "extra postes" (private stage coaches). The group traveled from canton to canton in Switzerland. Once they were settled in a hotel, Princess Pierre remained behind with M. Bonnaud, Mimau, the tutors and servants. The prince led the rest on Alpine hikes. The group was still large: Aunt Jeanne with Pierre and little Jeanne; Jean, the prince's valet; Mimi; Antoine Leandri and his wife, Angèle. Le-andri had been second secretary to the prince since 1890. He was a Corsican and by far the handsomest man in the entourage. Angèle, his pretty Corsican wife, was only a few years older than Marie.

Despite the rigors of the hikes Mimi enjoyed them except for some moments of jealousy at having to share her father with her cousins, especially Jeanne. Mimi kept a diary with a matter-of-fact description of the trip. One incident she relates stands out.

In Maloja they were honored by the visit of Princess Letizia, the daughter of Prince Napoleon and the wife of the Duke of Aosta. She arrived accompanied by her chamberlain and lady-in-waiting.

---

* A letter dated July 28, 1973, from Professor Robert Vivian, member of the French chapter of the International Glaciological Society and director of the Institut de Géographie Alpine, to Princess Eugénie of Greece states that through knowledge of Prince Roland's publications he was "filled with ad-miration." Professor Vivian later wrote: "From 1890 until approximately 1905, one might see Prince Roland traveling the mountains of Savoy and Dauphiné, and the Pyrénées, marking the face of each glacier with a chain of markers, dated, initialled RB, and topped with a cross. Each chain was riv-eted at either end to the rock or some giant boulder. . . . Later the precious markers were found. Perhaps some are still in place. . . . But how far away from the glacier? If one wants to know the position of the glaciers in the French Alps at the end of the 19th century, it is usually Roland Bonaparte's writings that will provide the desired information. . . . He was the initiator of glacier-watching in France, and as such remains one of the great men of Alpine glaciology."

Like all the Bonaparte women she was said to be very fond of men. Mimi carefully observed her and her effect on the group. At the table the duchess kept up a ceaseless conversation in Italian with Leandri, of whom the chamberlain seemed to be jealous. Aunt Jeanne herself did not look pleased; as for Angèle Leandri, she was frantically pressing her handkerchief to her trembling and swollen lips. The enthusiasm of the Duchess of Aosta was such that she wanted to sing a duet with Leandri. "If my husband were ever to be unfaithful to me with another woman, I'd kill them," Angèle declared to Marie.

The return to Paris was more than usually difficult for Marie. She had spent more time than ever before with her father and did not want to give up this pleasure. She dreaded particularly the thought of returning to study with Mme Jéhenne. Despite all her efforts, she was incapable of understanding arithmetic as taught by this woman. Such a defeat was unbearable to her and undermined her carefully built defenses. Faced with the new scholastic year, she was seized by the violent despair of adolescents. She took to doubting her own intelligence, and even the need to go on living. Fortunately, her father had observed her more closely during their trip to Switzerland and when the crisis broke, he decided to get rid of a teacher who, as he admitted, was nothing but a "paraprofessional."

Two professional teachers, both of them with diplomas, who taught at the Lycée Racine, were chosen, this time with care, by her father. With them Marie quickly rediscovered her taste for study and her confidence in her own capacities. She knew at once that with Mlle Boutry, whom she liked "for her alert manner, and a forthrightness of speech that made her sound like a servant in a Molière play," she was going to learn spelling, grammar and composition.

Mme Grünewald, the science and mathematics teacher, entertained herself by solving mathematical problems while riding the train from Meudon to Paris—much to her pupil's surprise—but under her instruction Mimi no longer found it impossible to understand the elements of mathematics. This gave her back her self-confidence.

Something happened, however, that Marie would remember with indignation for the rest of her life: there was a standard rate for lessons given privately by teachers with diplomas, twenty francs for two-hour lessons. Without revealing the identity of their future pupil, M. Bonnaud, obviously acting on instructions from his employers, had haggled for a rebate of four francs.

Mimi was soon to be injured by another duplicity that disturbed her even more.

Having recovered both her drive to learn and self-confidence in her abilities, she was eager to measure herself against other girls of her age. Secretly she hoped that a succession of examinations might lead to her freedom, but she took care not to mention it.

Mimi was so pleased with her new life that she hardly noticed the iron brace to improve her posture, prescribed in February 1898. Mlle Boutry and Mme Grünewald compared her to their lycée pupils and told her that she matched the best of them. She assiduously prepared herself for the examinations. A week before registration day, Mimi was summoned by her grandmother, who received her ceremoniously in her bedroom and announced to her that since the name Bonaparte was cursed by most republicans, in order to prevent overly zealous republican examiners from failing her because of her name, the prince, in agreement with her, had decided that his daughter should not take her examination. "To spare you needless humiliation and disappointment."

This time Mimi understood immediately where the deception lay. They had agreed to let her study, to let her finally be tolerably educated, but from the beginning, they had decided against the examination. Why this fraud? "The curse of my name, of my social rank, of my money! The curse especially of my sex! Because if I were a boy, you couldn't have stopped me from taking the baccalauréat, in spite of my name, as Papa once did, and after all he didn't fail!" She had begun to realize that the marriage for which she was destined required a "modesty" of mind produced, in part, by ignorance.

July 2, 1898, was Marie's sixteenth birthday. Unlike the men she had loved before, her fourth love was closer at hand and dangerous: "4—the Corsican secretary, black hair, blue eyes, pointed beard—I was sixteen, he thirty-eight. I was ugly. He was handsome." That summer she must indeed have been especially awkward. Moreover, in a defensive struggle against her femininity and her sexual desires she sought to be as unattractive as possible and to resemble the sadistic father whom she loved.

She rigged herself out in a pair of useless suspenders to hold up her beige skirt; she refused a belt that would have made her waist, still constrained by the iron brace, look more slender. She walked and dressed like a Girl Scout, with heavy checked stockings and hobnailed shoes. Over her mop of unwashed hair, which she gathered in a short braid, she wore a man's floppy hat. The brim was not wide enough to hide the acne on her cheeks. Her appearance fooled her watchful guardians but did not protect her.

The summer was again spent in Switzerland with Prince Roland and his entourage, this time without the Villeneuves. Mimi followed the men, while the women remained behind. No longer sulking at starting off at dawn, she took pleasure in the mountains, mainly because of her father, and went into raptures over a vanilla orchid that he had discovered. After a picnic during which Mimi drank some beer, which went to her head, the Corsican demonstrated his skill by shooting the tops off the six empty bottles from their meal. He took the young princess for a walk among the daisies, and asked her to pull the petals off one of them while whispering the refrain: "I love him, I love him a little, I love him a lot . . . passionately . . . not at all." The refrain, as he wished, concluded with "passionately." Hastily they rejoined the others and later he hinted that she had accepted his love. Bewildered, Mimi exclaimed that she hadn't meant to say anything! But it was true that she had fallen in love with him.

Another day, on the funicular railway up the Kleine Scheidegg for a closer look at the Jungfrau, Leandri squeezed her hand under the blanket thrown over their knees, muttering: "The Jungfrau! The Virgin drives me wild!" (Not very sensitive or imaginative words, but sufficient to impress a sixteen-year-old.) This excursion was particularly memorable because they descended to the valley on foot, a long hike that ended by starlight. Years later, Marie spoke of it as one of the most perfect moments of her life.

The last weeks of the summer were spent in a hotel in Grindelwald, Prince Roland having contracted enteritis. In this confined atmosphere, Angèle Leandri sensed that something was going on between her handsome husband and the young princess. She demanded an explanation. "Like a true woman, I deny, I lie. I do not want to let my holy secret and my young happiness be wrested from me." For the first time Marie found herself living a lie, without seeming troubled by it. At sixteen instinct is often stronger than principles. However, for some time, she no longer dared to surrender her feet to Leandri's under the table. But soon these little pleasures were resumed, and as if by magic Angèle's jealousy calmed down.

Mme Leandri even became friendly; she invited Mimi to come to the couple's bedroom for nightly chats after Mimau had put her into nightgown and robe. Mimau encouraged this new friendship; the Leandris were Corsicans like herself and she liked Mme Leandri since she considered her a good Christian whose influence on Mimi could only be beneficial. She concealed these nightly visits from Prince Roland and his mother.

During these evenings in the hotel room in Grindelwald, there was a little furtive hand-squeezing, and once, standing behind the door, Leandri kissed her. She was quivering. "That evening, the Corsican could have done anything he liked with me." But Angèle did not leave them alone for more than a few moments. During another of these absences, instead of kissing her, Leandri asked Mimi for a lock of her hair and specified: "Wrap it up in a piece of paper on which you'll write that you love me, with that pencil, that pencil there. Don't forget to put my name—and write what the daisy said when you pulled off its petals. It would make me so happy!" She obeyed, retiring to the only place that could be locked with a key, and wetting the recalcitrant ink-pencil with the running water in the toilet bowl, she wrote: "To Antoine Leandri, from Marie who loves him passionately and will never forget him." Another evening, after a ridiculous scene in which he scolded her for her "unworthy" passion for Mounet-Sully, a "third-rate actor," she again locked herself in the toilet and, still using the same little pencil that he had given back to her for the occasion, she wrote to him that she had not loved Mounet-Sully with passion, she loved only him, the Corsican, and would give her life for him.

If Mimi had learned any caution, she was too smitten to use it. She had not the slightest idea that she was being made a fool of. Later she wrote of the experience: "I have had the habit, since my childhood, of always loving within a great halo of dream that hides the reality from me."

When the Leandris repeated the rumors about her mother's murder, Marie was not much affected. She loved her father and realized that she was jealous of her grandmother. She was all too aware of how these two had hurt her, but she kept their "crimes" at a distance. However, when Princess Pierre sensed a change in Mimi and sought to tighten her hold on her, Leandri urged: "Defend yourself! Show a little will power at last!"

Princess Pierre had urged Leandri on Prince Roland. The Corsican's past was dubious; having obtained a law degree and just begun a career in journalism, he had suddenly gone into hiding in the maquis. Rumor had it that he might have killed someone, perhaps a gendarme. His unsavory past did not alarm the dour old princess, and it might even have made him more attractive to her. Her husband, Pierre-Napoléon, had come to her with a much worse record. In any event, she saw other qualities in the man. "Corsicans are wild and temperamental but so devoted to us [Bonapartes]." For those who seek control, loyalty excuses a lot.

Prince Roland had given Leandri the post of second secretary and then, because he came to like his company, saw to his "rehabilitation" and admission to the bar. Leandri's desk was in the 100,000-volume library on avenue d'Iéna, next to the cubbyholes in which the slips filled out by all book borrowers were filed. Mimi and her tutor, Frifri, had often chatted with him when borrowing books.

Frifri had to go; she did not fit with the Leandris' plans. Mimi at their urging betrayed the girl who had been her closest friend by confessing to her father that Frifri had enlightened her about the mysteries of sex, without evidently giving thought to the consequences. Fräulein Frieda, who was on vacation at her home in the Black Forest, was asked not to return to Paris.

Once back at avenue d'Iéna, Marie found herself in a quandary. Much as she wanted to be near Leandri, too frequent visits to the library would hardly escape notice. She had to content herself with conversations with Angèle. The couple now insisted that she show her "will power" by demanding her rights in three apparently easy matters, tasks that were presented to her as "initiation rites." First, she was to demand to be taken to her mother's grave at Versailles; second, to be allowed to see her Radziwill aunt; and third, to insist that her grandmother stop dressing her like a pauper.

Mimi had lived in such isolation that she had no idea of what was customary outside her father's sway. She thought it normal for a daughter never to have visited her mother's tomb. As for her Radziwill aunt, Mimi had never seen her, for the quarrel between the Radziwills and the Bonapartes had preceded her birth at the time of her grandmother Blanc's death. She had felt no curiosity about this unknown aunt. While she had envied the clothes of others it had not occurred to her to demand fashionable clothes for herself. Now, as she began to claim her rights, grasping the simple logic of them, she was met by fierce opposition. Her response was startling: she sulked, she locked herself in, refusing to see anyone, while at the same time claiming that she was sequestered. She used a vocabulary never before heard from her. She provoked her father and grandmother during scenes in which she heaped them with reproaches, often just, but presented in a wholly new manner. This was her first open rebellion. Her attitude toward her Aunt Jeanne, whom she had always trusted, changed too.

Leandri had pointed out to her that everyone but Marie benefited from her money. Aunt Jeanne's allowance was 5,000 francs per month and her niece reproached her for it. However, it was Aunt Jeanne who had her measured for her first fine clothes and a satin corset from the best corset maker in Paris to replace the iron brace. The visit to her mother's grave was also granted, watched over by Princess Pierre, Aunt Jeanne and M. Bonnaud. But the meeting with Princess Radziwill had to wait.

Mimi was old enough now to be introduced to her social obligations. She was taken to pay a call on Empress Eugénie, to whom she much preferred the daughter of King Jérôme and the true niece of Napoleon I, Princess Mathilde, "more engaging and human than the dry Empress Eugénie." Divorced from a Russian prince, Princess Mathilde lived in Paris, surrounded by a court of artists and cultivated people. During the Second Empire, she had received all the famous writers: Renan, Flaubert, Théophile Gautier. The writers Mimi and her grandmother now met at her house were of lesser stature, but times had changed.

It did not occur to Mimi that it was her money that made her welcome in these salons from which her grandmother, who accompanied her as a chaperon, had been excluded for so long. Marie was not at all bothered when the Leandris told her so. Nor was she concerned when they mentioned the suitors who were beginning to make themselves known. Some belonged to the family. Prince Louis Murat, a descendant of Napoleon I's sister, paid a call in December, asking to be presented to Mimi, but was refused. Mimi was forewarned when he returned with his nephew, a young hussar, and barged in unbidden, to her grandmother's dismay.

When Mimi's request to meet her mother's sister, Princess Radziwill, was flatly refused, Leandri counseled her to insist on going to mass each Sunday at Saint-Pierre-de-Chaillot, the parish church of the Radziwills as well as of the Bonapartes. It was a skillful way of tormenting the nonbelieving tormentors. Leandri got in touch with Uncle Edmond Blanc, who served as a go-between with his sister. The meeting took place, but Prince Roland, furious, saw to it that there was no sequel.

It was difficult for Prince Roland to admit to himself Leandri's treachery. He seems to have had with his secretary one of those special relationships that for him were so rare. He liked the Corsican's turn of mind. Marie reported that her father and Leandri often laughed together. They shared male jokes and were both mountain climbers.

Prince Roland's response, however, finally came. The secretary was put on indefinite leave. He was to receive his salary but was forbidden the house on avenue d'Iéna, though his wife was still permitted to see Mimi once a week. For Mimi, it was a cataclysm. She wanted to die. The daily scenes she made to her father ravaged them both. Soon the prince, tired of being lectured by his daughter, put a stop to Angèle's visits, which only added to Mimi's fury and despair.

Nevertheless the crafty Corsicans found an ally within the house in the person of Hetty, the English tutor, who, though never liked by her pupil, now earned Mimi's gratitude for acting as a courier. The correspondence was soon established on a regular basis. Mimi was ordered to burn their letters and she asked the Leandris to do the same. It was mostly Angèle who communicated with their victim. In particular, she urged Mimi to protest against their eviction. They wanted to be reinstated.

To stop rumors spreading through Paris, father and grandmother were willing to show that Mimi was not kept in seclusion. On June 25, shortly before her seventeenth birthday, Prince Roland gave a grand ball for his daughter. "I am beautiful for the first time," she remarks in her notebooks. A photograph taken that evening shows her in a gown of pleated muslin, wearing a corsage. Her hair done in waves, the head poised on a rather long neck, she presents an attractive profile with delicate nose and chin. Her expression, grave and intelligent, is in arresting contrast with the hint of an anxious and melancholy smile: a serious girl, who appears older than her age, watching her guests with apprehension. Most of them she was seeing for the first time, but soon she discovered, by the way men and women appraised her, that she was not the unattractive person she believed herself to be.

Among the guests, singled out in her notes and memoirs, were the Grand Duchess of Mecklenburg; the Landgrave of Hesse, cousin of the German emperor, "a poor blind man but with the soul of an artist. He [talked] to me about his trips to Corsica, about oranges picked from the tree"; the cartoonist Caran d'Ache; the painter Carolus-Duran; Madeleine Lemaire, another painter; Bartholdi, the sculptor of the Statue of Liberty; Prince Henri d'Orléans, the explorer and geographer; scientists such as Darboux, Cailletet and d'Arsonval, who talked to her about liquid air, a recent discovery; Captain Gouraud, "who [had] just captured Samory, a black chief in Africa who so far had been unbeatable." Her father had invited 500 guests for the grand occasion.

Soon Marie showed signs of hypochondria. In her journal, she noted that around July 11, 1899, she had had "a slight difficulty in breathing, spat whitish then grayish mucus." In the same entry she wrote: "My grandmother . . . with her one eye and drooping lower lip, disgusting with a mouth that stank from false teeth that were never cleaned . . . a hard and authoritarian creature."

Before long she suffered from a psychosomatic illness, a so-called "hepatic syndrome," and Princess Pierre, who considered her an hysteric, once more called Dr. Josias. Professor Raymond, Charcot's successor at the Salpétrière, was consulted. On his advice, the family considered sending Marie as a boarding pupil to the fashionable girls' school of Sacré-Coeur. To separate her from her family was not a bad idea, and Mimi herself did not oppose it, but the studies offered by the nuns were not what she wanted. It was during this period, when she thought she might have contracted her mother's illness and would die of tuberculosis, that she started to dream of studying medicine. Aunt Jeanne, who, at her request, spoke to the prince about it, brought back his answer: he did not change his mind. This time, without discussion, Mimi bowed to her father's will.

Rather late in the day, Uncle Christian de Villeneuve, at the request of the family, investigated Leandri's background.* Far from being a romantic assassin, Leandri was revealed as a petty crook, who at one time had written, "I detest the Empire and the Bonapartes," and at another sought to join a pro-Bonapartist or-

---

* Christian de Villeneuve kept an extensive diary as a personal and historical record. It was entrusted to Marie and by her to the Bibliothèque Nationale in Paris, for publication after the year 2030.

ganization, had taken money for his good will and then attacked the giver, and had taken Angèle away from a man who trusted him.

Marie had a wretched summer. Her father's itinerary took her again through Switzerland, and every landmark was a bitter reminder. Although no longer allowed to see either of the Leandris, she was still secretly communicating with them through Hetty. Wearied by the constant scenes and having learned that Leandri had demanded the promise of a large sum (a half-million francs) to support the candidacy of one of Marie's suitors, Prince Roland decided to tell his daughter the full truth and himself took appropriate action: instead of remaining on indefinite leave, Leandri was fired.

The Leandris forthwith changed their tune and Marie at last understood. They made it clear that if she did not help them they would sue her father, alleging that he had dismissed Antoine only to cover up Marie's sexual indiscretions. They were prepared to use her letters as evidence, to the ruin of her reputation. Marie was too humiliated to go to her father. But what was a seventeen-year-old to do? The Leandris demanded 100,000 gold francs, suggesting that she secretly borrow the money from her uncle Edmond Blanc, with the promise to repay him when she was twenty-one. Marie rejected the plan, but accepted a compromise. M. Bonnaud was to pay the pair a monthly stipend of 1,000 francs until she reached her majority, at which time she would repay him the sum with interest. Bonnaud agreed and did not betray the secret out of fear of Leandri, but he declined to discuss the matter with the young princess. Marie, with no one to protect and advise her, knew that the demand for the full amount would be renewed the moment she came into her money.

She came to resent Hetty more and more, recognizing her role as the blackmailers' accomplice; to endure the Englishwoman's presence was a daily ordeal. Her would-be seducer had also wooed the teacher who preferred tennis to Keats and Shelley. Mimi's despair and disillusion brought her closer to her father. In one of her last notes to Angèle Leandri, she wrote: "I can't stand it anymore. I can't go on! I'm exhausted! I'm sick! And besides, I love my father, I can't go on hurting him so much." She was aware of her need to admire someone, which pushed her to reconstruct another idol. To her sense of guilt and shame, even her grandmother became an admirable character: "The plebeian woman from the lower class neighborhoods who became a princess reached this degree of social elevation by dint of courage and abnegation. . . . And if she was harsh toward me, it is because she is first of all harsh toward herself and knows no other way."

As to her father, Marie was even more guilt-ridden. His worries about her had caused him to abandon the book he was writing, *Geographical Ideas Through the Ages*, intended to be the major work of his life. Marie excused his stinginess as the result of his early poverty. She even sympathized with his weaknesses. It seemed to her childish that though people questioned his right to be treated as an Imperial Highness, he placed the letters H.I.H. before his title. He insisted that in 1815, in recognition of services rendered during the Hundred Days, Napoleon had finally raised his brother Lucien to this dignity, and he refused to acknowledge the decrees of Napoleon III whereby Lucien's branch of the Bonaparte family had been reduced to civil rank. A savant such as her father, she thought, a good, intelligent man, did not need embellishing titles.

But this attitude did not prevail for long. She persuaded herself that she was going into a decline, would become tubercular like her mother, and pine away little by little, dying by the age of twenty. It was her mother's story all over again. The heroine was different but the other two characters were the same. She was convinced that Dr. Josias too was lying to conceal from her the fact that she was doomed.

The image of her crabbed but admirable grandmother never reappeared. "Everything around [Princess Pierre] suffers and dies, as around large trees that are too strong," she was to write on November 15, 1903. And there were other equally harsh observations, while the relations between father and daughter underwent ups and downs.

At this juncture, Mimi once more turned to Mimau, but she did not confide the secret of the blackmail to her, knowing that Mimau was not capable of coping with it. At sixteen Marie had been allowed to make a will and had made a generous bequest to Mimau. Now at eighteen she revised it, leaving large sums for tuberculosis research and specifying that the will must be published in two newspapers with large circulation because she distrusted her father.

Marie was unaware of the convenience of her "illness" and the escape that the idea of dying before the age of twenty-one presented—the date when she would once more have to face

Leandri. Though she reproached her doctors with lying to her, she kept from herself the fact that her own lie barred them from understanding and helping her. Such are the workings of neurosis, and Marie was to remain neurotic for a long time to come.

Her pseudo-illnesses haunted her and spoiled everything; she found it difficult to concentrate on anything else. But each year brought greater responsibilities. On her eighteenth birthday, her father handed over her trustee accounts in the presence of the family notary, William Bazin, who had been the notary for the Blanc family. ". . . Papa has acted correctly, indeed scrupulously! Though he had me buy in my earliest childhood the house I was born in at Saint-Cloud, it is real estate that will remain in my possession. Though he sold for me, at the same time as for himself, my shares in the Monte Carlo casino, he acted properly. It was better to get out of that shady business, whose continued prosperity was doubtful anyway. Papa is honest and good, and it is with all my heart that I accept my trustee accounts as they stand and sign my name to them." She also received the jewels she had inherited from her mother. They were magnificent, of course, but her father called them "ornaments for savages." Since he despised them she did likewise, and the box containing them was sent back to the safe in the Banque de France.

1900 was the year of the Great Exposition, as Henry Adams noted, and of the Congrès International de Physique. Prince Roland was involved in both. He gave a big party for all the members of the physics convention, where Marie met many scientists: Lord Kelvin, "one of the greatest physicists in the world, a puny little old man with a white goatee . . . Graham Bell, the inventor of the telephone." Prince Roland also organized demonstrations in his home of the more extraordinary recent inventions—X-rays, the radio—and she saw Pierre Curie take out of his waistcoat pocket a tiny tube, which shone greenish in the dark. It was radium. . . . Enough certainly to interest a mind like hers.

Mimi's dominating need was enthusiasm for a great cause. She was ready to adopt that of the underdog Boers and dreamed of leaving for the Transvaal with a young Dutch cousin of her uncle Christian's but she got no farther than the dream. Her drive for action was counterbalanced by her love of literature. To read and to write, those two solitary activities suited her equally. She read the great nineteenth-century Russian novelists, then Diderot and Voltaire. After those worshipers of reason, Mimi rediscovered her affinity with Rousseau. Was he not, like herself, born on July 2? "And as he was born, he had cost the life of his mother!" In the journal that she later dedicated to her daughter, the entry of January 27, 1901, reads: "Rousseau stirred me completely, though I would not say he changed me; he merely awakened everything, everything that was in me. . . . My Jean-Jacques, I would love to be warm and eloquent like you, I would love to be like you, I would love to stir up people and the world as the wind stirs up a heap of dry leaves, as you did. I would love to have genius like you, I would love, I would love . . ." (Freud, when she sent him this page twenty-four years later, remarked that this was a narcissistic kind of love.)

The Bonapartes spent the summer of 1901 at Saint-Cloud. It rained a good deal and the house was sad. Marie occupied the bedroom in which she was born and where her mother had died. She used to read late at night during this summer. There was still no electric light, and an oil lamp burned on the table at which she was reading, acutely aware of the silence, the shadows, as she immersed herself in the tales of Edgar Allan Poe. Her father, by no means a lover of fiction, found these earliest detective stories entertaining. On his advice, Marie read first *The Murders in the Rue Morgue*, then *The Purloined Letter* and *The Gold Bug*. She was thrillingly frightened by them and wanted to read more of Poe. *The Masque of the Red Death*, because of the drops of blood on the corpselike masquerader, made her think of her mother's hemoptyses.

One night, she chose to read *Ligeia*. "But having begun *Ligeia*, a tale my father despised, I was gripped by such dismay at the description of the living and vengeful corpse of the woman that I don't believe I was then able to finish the story. I soon abandoned the terrifying book. . . . And for twenty-five years of my life, I did not open any book containing a story about ghosts—especially about ghosts of women."[4]

The following autumn, she had nightmares about the skeleton of a Hindu woman, dead of tuberculosis at the age of twenty, which hung in her father's library, near the desk where Leandri once worked. She saw herself searching for a book on the shelves without the librarian's assistance, which was forbidden, and suddenly she heard a clicking of bones. "It was the skeleton, which had detached itself from its hook and was walking. I turned around, I saw its grinning rictus, its arms extended toward me. I woke up terrified." She was fervently studying anatomy with Mme Grünewald at the time. The association with her dead consumptive mother was not clear to her and she believed that she was simply afraid of skeletons. She asked her father to let her borrow the skeleton in order to overcome her fear. For days she was to keep the object of her fright in her study room, "installed in the corner near the window, to the left of the smoking fireplace."

About her physical health she was not brave at all. She was constantly watching for symptoms of her "latent tuberculosis," ignoring the doctor's contrary verdict. Whenever she had a cold and felt feverish, she stayed in bed. Her fantasies of death had gained control over her.

The following year, 1902, she spent the whole summer in Touraine, at the château de l'Aubrière, taking long walks, always a pleasure for her, and reading *The Kreutzer Sonata* and *War and Peace*. That summer, Colonel Gabeau, an old friend of her father's, whom she had known since childhood, attempted to seduce her. He and his wife were the Bonapartes' guests. Marie took this in her stride and indeed permitted some mutual fondling, but he was even more daring in speech and Marie, who knew how to ask questions, learned a great deal from him.

As soon as she returned to Paris, Mimi came down with a sore throat, lost weight, turned yellow, and was more deeply convinced than ever of her mortal disease. Dr. Josias diagnosed only anemia and recommended her departure for the South, mortifying Mimi, who felt that he did not take her illness seriously, though the doctor's advice was acceptable to her.

She liked the Villa Magali, a large yellow house in Valescure, from which she could see Saint-Raphaël and the sea. The mimosa was in bloom and the garden overflowed with it. Prince Roland came to join her. Life immediately intensified. Father and daughter visited Roman ruins together. Since the prince had given up geography for botany, they collected plants. In spite of the excitement and the joy of having her father with her, she continued to worry. In the morning Mimau, too, coughed and spat, a discovery that of course terrified Mimi; she feared that she had infected her old nurse. There was no way to restore her to reason—she refused to believe anyone; they were lying to her, she thought, in this as in many other things before. The diary she kept at the time is entitled *Journal of a Young Consumptive*.

Returning to Paris put Mimi in a state of fright. She was afraid of getting sick there, and there were few occasions to cheer her up. Fortunately, her uncle Christian attached himself to her. He was probably the first to recognize the originality of Mimi's mind. For her, he was someone to listen to, but not someone to whom she could talk of herself. Their relationship was more intellectual than emotional, and remained so. He introduced her to the German Romantics, made her read *Thus Spake Zarathustra* and read Plato to her in his warm voice "warmed still further by his slight southern accent." She credited him with opening up to her "the pleasures of the mind" extolled in *Phaedrus*.

Marie was invited, with her grandmother, to the Saturday dinners at which the Villeneuves assembled artists and writers rather than duchesses. It was also at her aunt Jeanne's that she heard the *Dichterliebe* cycle, sung in German, "the verses of Heinrich Heine on which Schumann embroidered songs as eternal as those cries of love and distress. *The* voice laments, *the* voice sobs, and so do I. Hiding my face in the shadow, I weep, I weep hot tears that run from my closed eyes! . . . Why was Heinrich Heine's beloved so miserable? Probably because she did not know how to love. . . . He is rich with the strength of life, with the splendor of his love. The same for me! It is not Petite-Maman's jewels in their box that are my true wealth, it is my heart, it is my mind. And whether I am loved or not, I know how to love!"

But there was nobody on whom to focus her love. Every Sunday afternoon, in the blue drawing room of her father's house, she was present to receive visitors who came to see her grandmother, some of them introducing suitors, among them a Hungarian knight, an Italian duke, a Prussian junker and two princes, one an Austrian, the other a Rumanian. Uncle Christian had his own candidate, Don Jaime de Madrid, the son of his hero Don Carlos de Borbón, for whom he had fought in Spain. All those suitors seemed more interested in her fortune than in herself. "I am nauseated by all this greed, especially when it pretends to be love." The only disinterested suitors were old gentlemen, some of them distinguished scientists, such as Jules Janssen, a man almost eighty. He offered to give her lessons on the movements of the stars but instead of teaching her Newton's laws, he told her about Héloïse and Abélard. " 'Nothing is more beautiful, more lofty,' he says in a voice trembling with enthusiasm, 'than a love that has grown under the constellation of science.' " In view of Janssen's exalted position in the scientific world, Marie had reason to be flattered by his attentions, but they were also verging on the ridiculous. Unfortunately, Mimi's mind was not disposed toward gaiety. She was tense, worried. Her successes with old men were not exactly reassuring to her.

What is more, some of her cousins who were her contemporaries got married without difficulty. It was on the occasion of the wedding of her cousin Loche Radziwill that her father and grandmother finally had accepted a reconciliation. Mimi soon met Loche's sister, her cousin Lise, married to the son of the Duc de Doudeauville, a pillar of legitimism. But the French aristocracy did not tempt her; she felt inferior in manners and superior in mind. She was bored at La Vallée aux Loups, the estate of the old duke.

On July 2, 1903, she celebrated her twenty-first birthday. A few days before, she received a letter postmarked Ersa, in Corsica. She knew its contents before even opening it. Leandri had not forgotten. Bonnaud, who had sent him his "wages" for three years, had slipped up on the fourth year. Leandri assured her that this did not matter since she would soon have control of her money. He gave her a choice: he would accept 12,500 a year for life or 200,000 francs outright. Of course, there was a threat: Leandri was ready to use her letters to him. Mimi was appalled, and ashamed of her past stupidity. The only person she felt she could approach for advice was her uncle Edmond Blanc. She decided to show him the blackmail letter, with no comment. He told her that her father had to know. How difficult it was to confess such a thing to such a man! Prince Roland, however, showed no outward signs of emotion. There was only one thing to do, he said, keep the letter and wait for the next one.

Soon after, Mimi left again for the château de l'Aubrière. She was much too tormented to enjoy the meadows, the flowers, the butterflies, the woods, as she had done the year before. Her old suitor, the colonel, was again a visitor, eager to please her. She longed for the winter months and another long stay in the South. As she dreaded the mistral, which blew strongly on the Fréjus plain, a villa, the Albertina, was rented in Cimiez, above Nice, for the winter of 1903–1904. The garden was "a jumble of eucalyptus and palm trees." Aunt Jeanne came to spend a few weeks with her, and Uncle Christian arrived in his turn. His journal contains some curious descriptions of the condition in which he found his niece.

"Tuesday, December 29, 1903. For five minutes I saw Mimi, bundled up in old-womanish clothes, living in a room without curtains for fear of microbes, without a fire for fear of the lack of oxygen, etc., etc.

"I talked with Jeanne for a moment: Mimi leads the oddest life imaginable, lives in terror of microbes, does not enter a drawing room when there are several people, for fear that the air might be contaminated, would consider herself lost if she were outdoors after four o'clock. Her father is very upset about it, declares her to be unmarriageable, and I agree with him. A husband—no matter how patient—would not put up with such nonsense for two weeks. Mimi admits that this life is painful for her." Nevertheless, she looked better, she thought, than she had in Paris. The pain in her chest, the alarming cough and the redness of her throat disappeared for a while in this balmy air. A physician recommended by Josias, Dr. Gaston Sardou, gave her a treatment of which he claimed to be the inventor: opotherapy. She was willing to swallow anything, even these capsules containing pulverized pork pharynx. She and Dr. Sardou had literary conversations, and he tried to persuade her that she had never been tubercular. Deep down she knew that what was wrong with her was the fear of the Corsican.

After the agony of waiting for the unknown, Marie almost felt relief when the letter that she dreaded so much arrived. It was postmarked Nice, dated from the Hôtel des Etrangers. So he was there! He wrote that he was free of all other concerns and could devote himself entirely "to our business." He would not budge from Nice without an answer from her.

The following day brought another and more violent message, ending: "If it is war you want, you'll have it, and without mercy." Mimi could not bring herself to speak to her grandmother. Fortunately, Aunt Jeanne was still there and could act as intermediary. It was decided to send for the prince, against the advice of the grandmother, who feared that the Corsican might attack her son. Upon his arrival, Roland put Edgar Demange, an attorney, in charge of the case. Demange had been involved in the Bonapartes' history before. His first case had been the defense of Prince Pierre in the trial in Tours after the murder of Victor Noir. He had also been Alfred Dreyfus's lawyer. "He is a heavy old man with white side-whiskers, blue eyes, a kind expression, a slow step." His tactic was to make no move and to wait for the Corsican to file suit. He advised Mimi not to "worry too much."

But Mimi had good reason to worry. Her father suffered from terrible neck pains, chronic fatigue, intestinal disturbances. She was mindful of the uncompleted manuscript in the desk drawer on avenue d'Iéna. And she missed Pascal, who was away. Apparently he had gambled at the races with money intended for the suppliers of the stable. Horses had always been his passion as much as women.

Her piano was her means of escape. After dusk, when the drawing-room curtains were closed, she played *Parsifal*, the plea to the Heavenly Father. One evening, already seated on the stool, she leaned forward too abruptly and hit her nose on the edge of the piano. She did not break it but there was a deep cut at the base, an open wound that would leave a mark, Aunt Jeanne predicted. ". . . I turned against myself a latent but violent aggression that would have been better directed at the real object who deserved it, the Corsican from the maquis," she later wrote.

The suit was finally filed. The bandit had reduced his demands, asking for only 18,000 francs in compensation for a position lost on account of Marie. "He unmasked himself," was the comment of the prince, who was against paying up. Demange also advised letting things take their course. Marie clung to her attorney, who had become a father figure to her. When she learned that Leandri had chosen a Corsican lawyer of good reputation to represent him, she was shocked. How could any honorable person agree to advocate such a cause?

The date of the hearings was set for the beginning of July. In the first days of May, Marie was back in Paris and Leandri began a new offensive. He demanded 100,000 francs, as Demange soon found out, and refused to settle for less.

On the day before the scheduled trial, Mimi was made to participate in an odious scene. She waited alone in her father's large blue drawing room with 100,000 francs in cash. Demange was shown in with a heavy package in his briefcase: Mimi's correspondence with the Leandris. A court clerk entered in his turn. He was to deliver the 100,000 francs to the bandit. Mimi noticed that the banknotes made up only a thin bundle, and then added: "I am freed! My peace of mind was well worth one hundred thousand francs! Money has never been very important to me. Its only value is to buy freedom."

She immediately reimbursed M. Bonnaud, whom she owed 36,000 francs, plus four percent interest. Maître Demange refused to set his fee. Someone suggested 10,000 francs. Once again the prince was indignant. Mimi reacted differently. "As for me, I think that the old lawyer's services were well worth that amount. But since I paid my debt to him in cash, I no longer pay in love. I like him much less. I detach myself from this fictitious father."

She had always known that her father was miserly. As one reads what she wrote years later about Edgar Allan Poe's adoptive father, the association imposes itself: "But this parsimony which so tortured Edgar, like all parsimony, it must be remembered, is *related to somebody or something*."[5] She revealed that Edgar suffered from it just as she had, in the hidden knowledge that for the unconscious the gift of money is the equivalent of the gift of love. She could not accept this fault in her father.

For more than four years she had kept to herself the secret of the blackmail. She was used to hiding her feelings and even Mimau did not realize how deeply wounded she was. The relationship with her father was particularly painful. She was, as she wrote, again "completely submissive" to his will. His main concern now was to find the right husband for her. He still had the highest expectations but at the same time he was able to tell her ("rather brutally," she remarked): "If I saw you in a brothel, you are certainly not the one I would pick."

Most of the time she forgot that she was young, in her early twenties, though unsuitable suitors seemed to follow her everywhere. During the summer of 1904 some pursued her to Touraine, where she stayed at the château de La Branchoire. The winter of 1904–1905 brought other suitors to Cimiez, where again a house had been rented for Mimi, higher up on the hill. Her thoughts returned to her old companion, death: "The sounds of the bells entering through the open window, the sound of voices, the white light of the sky, everything makes me sad. Death is everywhere, but some see it and others forget about it."[6]

In the summer of 1905 she was back in Touraine, at La Branchoire, with her Villeneuve cousins. This time, the limelight was on her cousin, who was wooed by the young owner of a château in La Sarthe. He was a good match for little Jeanne, by now prettier than ever and enchanting everybody. Mimi observed her cousin's maneuvers with irritation. Here too she discovered falsity.

Another event took place that disturbed her more. Toward the end of the stay at La Branchoire, Princess Pierre suffered her first attack of angina pectoris; unaware of the true nature of her illness, she blamed it on indigestion. When the terrible pain was over, she seemed to have put it out of her mind. Soon after, however, Princess Pierre summoned Mimi to her room. She wanted to talk to her, to tell her "her truth." As soon as the young woman had settled in an armchair beside her grandmother, she heard for the first time from the old lady what the servants had whispered about for years. The old princess, always so vain about her name and title, confessed her humble background. She also talked about living with her prince when she was nineteen and very beautiful. He had not been able to marry her because of his cousin Napoleon III. Mimi now also heard from her that the two children who survived out of five, Roland and Jeanne, had been illegitimate and could not bear their father's name until 1871. The old princess still felt guilty about her life, and mumbling that she had always been an honest woman loyal to Pierre, she begged Mimi's forgiveness.

Suddenly, mother and son seemed more human to Mimi, but in spite of this confession, the relationship between grandmother and granddaughter remained unchanged.

Back in Paris, after dinner on Friday evening, October 13, 1905, Princess Pierre had a violent argument with her reader, Mme Proveux, but since such scenes were frequent between them, no one gave it any thought.

Mimi went to spend the evening in her father's study. Their talk was suddenly interrupted by a knock at the door. Juliette, the seamstress, summoned them urgently to the princess. She had fallen in front of her armchair in the little dressing room, struck her nose on the low table, and was bleeding profusely from a deep cut. Anna the chambermaid had fled in terror. Father and daughter carried the stricken woman to the chaise longue in her room, where they tried to warm her with hot-water bottles and massaged her arms and legs, but when the doctor arrived, he pronounced her dead. It was Mimi's first face-to-face confrontation with death. The old princess whom she had always seen fully dressed was now almost naked. Mimi looked at her legs, her thighs, her belly. "Her skin is white and beautiful. The words of the doctor [after examining Princess Pierre] reported long ago by Gragra, came back to me: 'It is not flesh, it is marble.' "

Prince Roland was stunned, unable, at first, to measure his loss. Marie observed: "His mother was the greatest love of his life." She, too, slowly came to know the importance of Princess Pierre in her formative years.

4

A FALSE HAPPINESS

*"My fiancé's age and position allowed me to make
the transference of my love for my father to him."*
MARIE BONAPARTE,
Psychanalyse et anthropologie, p. 106

FOR THE FIRST TIME MARIE, WHO HAD SPENT SO MANY YEARS
of her youth preoccupied with the idea of death, was faced
with its reality. Society in those days was not evasive about
death, quite the contrary. Marie was fascinated by the mortuary
rituals surrounding the corpse, which remained in the house until
taken to the church for the requiem mass. On the day of the burial,
she was swathed in long black veils and streaming with tears.

Later, her foremost feeling was that of deliverance. "They seem
to have buried Death with Grandmother. Only life remains, life
free at last, without that single black eye watching over me." She
soon realized that Princess Pierre's death had not brought her
closer to her father. Her dismay at her father's grief destroyed
her feeling of liberation. Once more her neurosis overwhelmed her
and she again became obsessed by death. Now it was Mimau's
death that she dreaded. She could not face any form of independence and was unable to discern that the old woman was getting
more and more paranoid. She felt quite lost and contemplated
suicide.

Worried about her, Colonel Gabeau and his wife, Laure, offered
to give up their country life in Touraine to come and stay with
her. It was a generous gesture and Mimi accepted gratefully. She
took comfort from their presence. The old colonel's continuing
attentions cheered her up. The kindness of Laure Gabeau, now old
herself and with a heart condition, was equally consoling.

Life in the big house at 10 avenue d'Iéna was unchanged in its
austerity. Marie gives many examples of it. In one of her notebooks, she describes a typical day a few months after her grand-

mother's death, heading the entry: *The Dismal Day of January 9, 1906:*

"Up at 6:30—bathroom at 7, Nelly the chambermaid comes, shower, breakfast, wash and do hair until 9—letters 2 hours—then tradesmen brought in by Jules and Michel. —Then Gabeau at 11:50, must get ready for lunch, which Adrien comes to announce at noon. In the drawing room with the Gabeaus, then my father, and we go to the table. My father, head in his hands, answers in monosyllables, devours his food. —Later, in his room, my father sermonizes me while walking back and forth. He makes a business out of being a galley-slave, he has no time to work since his mother died. He also complains about the unstable political situation and ends by advising me not to waste my money.

"At 1:30 I go to the Bois with the Gabeaus. Both are old and the walk is ominous. I go home, receive one or two ladies [acquaintances of her grandmother's], then go to see Mimau, who tells me how 'Old Faithful' [Bonnaud] is persecuting the servants. Later on I receive Bonnaud in my study room.

"Dinner with my father, and afterward the same sermon. In addition: 'My daughter doesn't love me.' I reassure him and go to bed."

This period was dominated by her relations with her father, and Marie could hardly accept them with equanimity. Prince Roland was not cut out for intimacy. His daughter, however, insisted on calling him by the familiar *tu*, while he addressed her as *vous*. He never forgot their social rank. Often he employed a more disquieting form of expression, using the third person in speaking of himself or of her. "Papa is so anxious when he sees his Mimi go out," he would say to his twenty-three-year-old daughter. Still, this astonishing baby talk did not keep him from discussing the question of money. Like his mother, he never tired of the subject. He complained about expenses, and kept repeating that spending a sum of 1,200,000 francs a year was too much. It was indeed a large figure for that time, but he was so rich that Marie was not disturbed by this statement.

What upset her was his request that she draw up a will in his favor, "to set matters straight," as he specified. He did not relish the thought of having to argue with Edmond Blanc or the Radziwills, who would be in the line of inheritance should something happen to Marie. She remembered that her mother had been urged to draw up a will. She had heard this talked about all through her childhood and she rejected this form of identification with her mother. When he said to her repeatedly that "Mimi should send for Bazin [the notary] so that her father, who loves her so much, will have a little peace of mind," she took care not to protest, but she did not give in. "And that will was never made."

Could they speak of no other topic but money? Marie asked herself. In her presence, her father always seemed ill at ease. So she did not dare to speak to him freely about her personal concerns, as she would have liked to do. Nor did he speak of himself, except for a few cries wrung from him by his suffering over the death of his mother.

Dominated by his mother, the prince showed little interest in women. Yet Princess Pierre had shrewdly avoided keeping him tied too much to her apron strings; she had even urged him to attach himself sexually to a woman, a stout lady with whom he never appeared in public. "Eugénie Baudry, my father's mistress," Marie wrote on the back of a photograph dating from 1910, which shows a woman of middle age, neither beautiful nor displaying any particular character, and certainly a woman of simple origins. There was also another friend, with a Flemish name, with whom the prince made trips to Switzerland. She drew an amusing caricature of him and seems to have been more sophisticated than Mlle Baudry. But Eugénie Baudry was the only one the prince ever mentioned, the only one who came to visit him during his long illness and who came back to see him on his deathbed. Nevertheless it is certain that this attachment, though of long standing— Marie Bonaparte believed that it predated her parents' marriage —could not have occupied a large place in the heart of this dissatisfied and limited man.

Marie still suffered from too much solitude. She still knew very few people of her own age, nor did she see much of Geneviève Ollivier. The way of life maintained by her father made her conscious of being subject to rules that did not apply in other families.

The only social life expected of her was fulfilling family obligations. She paid visits to the former Empress Eugénie, then eighty years old and still beautiful; or Princess Letizia came to lunch. Of these visits Marie remarked: "We do not enjoy seeing each other but would be unhappy if we didn't."

Marie was almost twenty-five when she went to her first ball in somebody else's house. It was at Princess Murat's, and she wore "an Empire gown all spangled with mother-of-pearl, with a diadem of white egret feathers." She did not know whether she looked pretty or not but thought she was "sufficiently admired." She had not forgotten how her grandmother's entourage used to tell her that with all her money she would always be liked. Not only did she lack the unquestioned beauty and charm of her cousin Jeanne, with whom she continued to be compared, but she was unable to enjoy herself spontaneously as Jeanne did. It was not in her character to take things lightly. Most certainly she did not pride herself on being a rich heiress. She was too unsure of herself and cared too little about society for that.

For the time being, Mme Gabeau was her chaperon. To her at least Marie could talk. She recalled a conversation they had, in January 1906, on the subject of marriage, at which the name of Prince George of Greece was mentioned.

Mimi's father had carefully examined the credentials of the more prestigious candidates, among them Prince Hermann of Saxe [Weimar], perhaps the future Grand Duke of Saxe-Weimar, and Prince Louis of Monaco, who was not really interested but whose candidacy had been put forward by the Church, through Mimau, of all people. Prince Roland had chosen Prince George of Greece as his favorite. Such an alliance would fulfill his wishes for social success. But Mimi, though she had not forgotten how dashing the prince looked in a photograph she had seen some years before in the *Graphic*, was not interested. She did not like the idea of living abroad. She preferred Monaco, which was closer, and Mimau's candidate had the further advantage of being very rich, which gave her the assurance of not having been picked solely for her money.

The next month, February, she left once again for the South, where she hoped to meet Prince Louis. Like the prelate in Monaco, the bishop of Nice wished to see the prince married, to save him from a sinful life. The bishop came to lunch, but the prince was not ready to listen to pious advice. Fortunately Mimi's relationship with Mimau consoled her to a certain extent. They continued to be close.

In 1906, the young princess spent her third summer in La Branchoire with her aunt Jeanne, Mimau and the Gabeaus. It was a period during which, in the solitude of nature, she was questioning herself anxiously about the future. She did not know how to plan it, and had no idea how deep her neurosis was, or how her uncertainty would affect her choices and reactions. She returned to Paris earlier than in previous years because her father wanted her to be there in September. He was assiduously campaigning for election to the chair of the Académie des Sciences that he had long been coveting, willing to postpone his work in order to pay the customary calls. But this did not mean neglecting his plans for Mimi's marriage.

That September, King George I of the Hellenes was to visit Paris, and Prince Roland decided to give a formal luncheon in his honor. The prince had surrounded himself with the trappings of Napoleon's myth—paintings, engravings, and Empire furniture— down to the household linen with imperial bees woven into the fine cloth. This carefully constructed environment did not really protect him against the consciousness of his own questionable birth or shield him from the contempt of the older nobility for the Bonapartes. Rather, his position intensified his interest in gene-alogy.

King Christian IX of Denmark, the father of King George of the Hellenes, was not descended from a line of Danish kings; he was a German prince of the house of Glücksborg, a branch of the house of Holstein. His wife, Louise of Hesse-Cassel, niece of the heirless King Frederick VII of Denmark, brought him his claim to the throne, which was recognized by the Protocol of London, signed on May 8, 1852, by the five great powers—Austria, France, Great Britain, Prussia and Russia—plus Norway and Sweden. The docu-ment was a compromise concerning not only the question of Danish succession but also the rival claims of Denmark and Prussia to Schleswig-Holstein.

Christian IX, the "protocol king," pursued a matrimonial policy which later earned him the sobriquet "father-in-law of Europe." His eldest son, who ascended the Danish throne as Frederick VIII in 1906, married a Swedish princess. Alexandra, his second child, married the future Edward VII of England. Princess Dagmar, his fourth child, married Czar Alexander III of Russia (she was the mother of Czar Nicholas II). Princess Thyra, next in line, married the Duke of Cumberland. The youngest, Prince Waldemar, mar-ried Marie d'Orléans, granddaughter of King Louis-Philippe of France.

George I, king of the Hellenes, who was to be Prince Roland's luncheon guest, was Christian IX's third child and second son. He had married the Grand Duchess Olga of Russia, granddaughter of Czar Nicholas I. Prince William George became the king of the

Hellenes in 1863, following the overthrow of Otto I, son of Ludwig I of Bavaria, king since the recognition of Greek independence from Turkey in 1832. King George's crown was his, just as his father's was, thanks to British support and international agreement.

Some fifty guests were invited to the luncheon in the king's honor. Marie was seated to his right, and her diary tells us: "I like him, I am charmed by him, he is one of the most attractive men I have ever met." But when her father solemnly informed her that the king would be willing to accept her as a daughter-in-law, wife of his second son, Prince George of Greece and of Denmark, she was panic-stricken. She insisted that she did not want to leave Paris. She was especially convulsed at the idea of giving in to a wish of her father's. Although she proclaimed that she wanted to change her life, she was terrified at the thought that this was about to happen. Her relationship with her father was too neurotic to be easily severed. But the prince was too close to the goal he had set for himself ever since his daughter was in her cradle to relinquish it now. "You're wrong, my father tells me. You're a child. You'll never again find such a match. In addition to his social position, Prince George is a serious and charming man, just what every father would want for his daughter."

Who was this prince, who, said Roland, "has just left his post of High Commissioner of the Powers in Crete and was traveling in the Far East"? Mimi seems to have forgotten how handsome she had found the dashing naval officer in a photograph in the *Graphic*. She had not forgotten that her maternal grandparents, not to mention Princess Pierre Bonaparte herself, had come from the people. And her favorite quotation from Napoleon I was: "A man's failures are his alone." Her belief in the quality of individuals never left her.

She agreed, however, not to go to Touraine in the summer of 1907, since Prince George would be visiting Paris. She had long given up any open struggle with her father; when she had opposed him it was because she had been urged to do so by Leandri.

July 19, 1907, was a torrid day, and Crown Prince Constantine and Prince George of Greece had agreed to pay a visit at four o'clock in the afternoon to the house on avenue d'Iéna. For good measure, "my monthly indisposition was twisting my insides," Marie noted. She looked greenish and would have liked to stay in bed. Her father had asked her to make an effort and himself had gone outside to wait at the door for the royal visitors. Marie was to welcome them in the blue drawing room, in the company of Aunt Jeanne.

Prince George turned out to be a Scandinavian giant half a head taller than the crown prince and Prince Roland. "Slim, fair, with a long blond mustache like his father's, a straight nose, and smiling blue eyes. Not much hair, though, he is bald. Who cares? He is tall, handsome, blond, and above all he seems so kind, so kind. What's more, he looks a little ailing, this handsome giant, which makes him still more touching, more likable. . . . He has lost weight, a lot of weight. Pale, his features drawn, one would say that he is recovering from typhoid fever. . . ."

The princes stayed two hours, and Mimi found George charming. She regretted that he lived so far away from Paris but did not mention this to anyone and became again absorbed by her menstrual cramps.

Next day, while she was still in bed, Mimau brought in an enormous array of orchids on a bamboo trellis. On the same day, Roland went to pay a visit to the Hôtel Bristol, where the princes were staying. Soon after, the royal princes, the Bonapartes, the Villeneuves and the Greek minister in Paris, Delyannes, visited Versailles and the Trianons, stared at by tourists.

Another day, the courting couple went for a stroll in Bagatelle accompanied by Aunt Jeanne, the crown prince and the Delyanneses.

Soberly, Prince George warned Marie that though he knew she wished to remain in Paris, his royal obligations made this difficult to promise and perhaps impossible. If he were needed in Greece or Crete he would have to go. He aspired to a life of bourgeois privacy with his wife at his side. Furthermore, he was a devout Christian. Then he proposed. "Mimi was surprised by this conversation and completely disconcerted. It has given her considerable respect for Prince George, but she dreads the thought of living in Athens," Christian de Villeneuve noted.

Aunt Jeanne tried her best to put pressure on Mimi, and her husband reports: "I advised Roland to tell her he would give her a specific sum for every month she stayed in Paris. This would probably be a way of making her husband stay here longer."

Mimi, with Mme Gabeau, went to see Princess Sophie [wife of Crown Prince Constantine and sister of Kaiser Wilhelm II of Germany], who told her about life in Athens, which was not very lively and where society consisted mainly of the wives of tobacco merchants. But she added that Prince George had almost no official obligations and that he was perfectly free to make long visits to Paris.

To escape the curiosity of journalists and society people, while giving her a chance to become better acquainted with the prince, Marie and George saw each other every day at the house of her aunt, the Marquise de Villeneuve. Mimi arrived, escorted by old Colonel Gabeau and his wife. They all had tea together, and then Aunt Jeanne and the Gabeaus withdrew, leaving the young couple alone in the large drawing room. "The prince and I chatted, sitting on a high Empire sofa covered in old faded pink silk. Four swans, greenish and gold at their curved necks, formed the corners. It was an awful piece of furniture and quite uncomfortable. What did it matter? We were there to get to know each other and not to admire the furniture." Marie had already developed a horror of the Empire style, which stayed with her all her life. Later she always managed to keep at least her bedroom and study free of this style, which had spread all over her father's house, including many invaluable Napoleonic memorabilia. George did not share her taste. He liked what was old: furniture, pictures or objects. He had no taste for art in general and told her so simply. Nor did he care for poetry and novels. Shakespeare seemed to him "bombastic." He liked history and "factual matters." Marie accepted this declaration, which ought to have put her off, without passing judgment on it. He had reached her heart by the story of his misfortunes. She did not have many points of comparison, so few people having ever confided in her, but she believed what he told her and sympathized with him in his unhappiness. For her first impression had not been false, as she was soon to learn. The prince had suffered some serious sorrows that had scarred him deeply. She knew how to listen.

George had been born on Corfu, on June 25, 1869, and had been raised in Athens. When he was fourteen, his parents had taken him to Denmark to be enrolled in the naval academy in Copenhagen. He was slated to become a sailor. They had entrusted him to his uncle Waldemar, ten years older and an admiral in the Danish fleet. At the moment of his parents' departure, he was with his grandfather, King Christian IX, and his uncle, standing on the pier where the ship was moored. Suddenly a feeling of being abandoned overwhelmed him. His uncle realized it and took his hand. Together they walked back to Bernstorff, the prince's residence, and Marie quotes George as saying: "From that day, from that moment on, I loved him and I have never had any other friend but him." Prince Waldemar soon married a Frenchwoman, also named Marie. Prince George vaunted his friend's upright character. Nowhere else did he feel so happy as when he was in Denmark with this good, this honorable man. "You will love him too," he concluded, "when you meet him."

In 1891, not yet twenty-two, George had accompanied his cousin Nicholas, the czarevich of Russia, on a trip around the world as a lieutenant in the Russian navy. On the cruiser *Azov*, escorted by three other Russian warships, they went to Ceylon, Singapore, Java, Siam, Cochinchina, China, Japan. They visited temples and many ancient monuments; they hunted tigers, elephants and crocodiles. On May 9, the ships entered the port of Kobe. From there the czarevich and his cousin went to Kyoto, and then to Otsu by train. There, in a narrow street, one of the policemen standing guard drew his sword and, running up behind the rickshaw, struck Nicholas twice on the head, which fortunately was protected by his bowler hat. George, whose rickshaw was behind his cousin's, jumped out and with his cane felled the attacker, a disgruntled samurai who had become a policeman and hated Westerners. The czarevich's wound was tended to and the visitors took the train back to Kyoto.

A false report was sent to Saint Petersburg by the czarevich's entourage. George, the rescuer, was accused of provoking the attack. In one version, he was said to have dragged his cousin into places of ill repute; in another, that he had encouraged him to violate the sanctity of a temple by entering without taking off his shoes. Marie, who tells this story in her memoirs, adds a quotation from the journal of Nicholas II, dated October 8, 1891, when the two cousins met again in Denmark, on the occasion of a family reunion five months after the drama: "I am incensed by the rumors that are floating around. It seems that Bariatinsky goes so far as to say that it was not Georgie who saved my life. I don't understand what he hopes to gain by it. Is he trying to excuse himself? (But who accused him of not doing anything?) Or to blacken George? But why? In my opinion, it's just simple baseness." The journal was published along with other documents after the October Revolution.

George, in disgrace, had to leave his cousin. On his arrival in

England Queen Victoria at first refused to receive him, but his uncle, the Prince of Wales, questioned him and, struck by his truthful tone, convinced his mother of the young man's innocence.

The prince did not seem embarrassed in telling Marie of the wrongs he had suffered, but he did not conceal from her that his experiences had made him melancholic and bitter, affecting him physically as well as morally. He had been much heavier in the past, strong as a horse, a champion sportsman and eater. Once dared by King Christian, he had consumed eighteen cutlets.

Prince George was on active duty with the Greek navy before and during the Greco-Turkish war of 1897. Peace was signed on December 4, 1897. Crete was declared autonomous and the Great Powers agreed to appoint a high commissioner to supervise the island in the name of the Sultan, who kept his sovereignty over the island but had to withdraw his troops. Prince George was chosen.

It was a difficult job from the beginning. For the Great Powers —France, Great Britain, Italy and Russia—he was a figurehead, at best. For the Greeks on Crete, he was the representative of the hated Turks. Another man might have realized the necessity of bending one way or another but George clung to his duty to the Sultan. He complained of little support from Athens and told Marie how he had lived in isolation, "crying like a homesick child on Christmas night the first year, alone in his little house far from his family."

The Greeks on Crete, led by Venizelos, agitated for union with Greece or, failing that, complete independence. When George opposed him, Venizelos denounced the prince as a tyrant, and was forced underground, only to emerge triumphant with the armed revolt of 1905. The union of Crete with Greece was proclaimed. Prince George's opinion did not change despite these events; he resigned on July 23, 1906, and secretly left from Canea, on September 25. He had lost 75 pounds in six months. His failure discouraged and demoralized him; he could not accept defeat because, as he repeated to Marie, he was a navy man and a man of duty.

Marie liked the tall prince, blond as a stick of barley sugar ("Sucre d'Orge" was the nickname she was soon to give him), but she still had difficulties in making up her mind. There were things she would have liked to tell him about. He ought to know of Leandri's blackmail, for instance; it would be dishonest to hide it from him. But each time she tried to broach a subject that concerned her, he wasn't listening. It was as though he were not interested in who she was. Were all men like this? she asked herself.

Marie hesitated for twenty-eight days and then accepted George's proposal, only conditionally, however, since the marriage contract had first to be drawn up and agreed on. Prince Roland saw to that. The prince, assuming that George and the king were like himself, foresaw problems with the financial arrangements. There were none. George wished to marry with complete separation of assets, waiving rights of inheritance. Subsequently, he accepted limitations on the manner of investing Marie's capital—a clause written to prevent her money's use for political purposes outside France—and refused a donation from Prince Roland. Marie's suspicious, parsimonious father was astonished at such simplicity and disinterestedness.

The day came for Prince George to make his formal request to Prince Roland. The king arrived soon after. Mimi and George waited for him at the top of the grand staircase, and Mimi told him she was happy to become part of his family and that she loved his son very much. The king kissed her and asked her to call him "Father." The newspapers published photographs that Marie looked at with childish vanity, thinking of the hundreds and thousands of young girls who might envy her "the noble, kind, and handsome blond prince."

The following Sunday, September 1, a *Te Deum* was sung in the Greek church. Aunt Jeanne was in charge of negotiating the question of a Catholic marriage with Abbé Odelin, but there were obstacles that only the Pope could lift, and it was necessary to apply directly to Rome.

An atheist like her father and Princess Pierre, Marie refused to abjure a faith she did not have and to take an oath that she would not keep regarding the religion of her children. Her fiancé was deeply religious, as he had told her. He was Orthodox like his Russian mother, while his Danish father was a Lutheran, something surprising for a king of the Hellenes.

Since Pius X proved inflexible, she was to be married without his permission, in the Orthodox rite; this was a valid marriage, in view of the recognized equivalence of sacraments in the Orthodox and Roman Catholic churches; however, "for disciplinary reasons," she was still subjected to the "lesser excommunication," which troubled her father, not on religious but on social grounds.

Aunt Jeanne, a practicing Catholic, and Mimau, of course, were affected for different motives.

Marie's life changed immediately. She was kept too busy to withdraw into her shell, and the engagement ring, a cabochon ruby set in diamonds, was a constant reminder of the unknown and imminent life in Athens, which she was beginning to dread when finally she found herself alone at night. She thought of what she was about to give up, and all of a sudden it became precious to her. For someone like Marie, change was a threat. The defenses she had so painfully constructed were in jeopardy. Again she brooded over loss and death.

An attractive photograph shows the engaged couple: Prince George, in an admiral's uniform, is seated in a kind of neo-Gothic stall; standing beside him, Princess Marie rests her hand on his shoulder. Over a dress of light muslin, with embroidered blouse and skirt, she is wearing the string of pearls and rubies that George had given her a week after their engagement. What is especially apparent in this double portrait is the melancholy of the beautiful face with its dark eyes, in contrast to the serene assurance of the prince, his frank gaze and air of placid benevolence.

George seemed better adapted to the situation than she. He was used to being on display and with people. Solitude had never been his lot; he had seven brothers and sisters.

George was less than a year younger than Crown Prince Constantine, who had married Princess Sophie of Prussia, granddaughter of Queen Victoria and daughter of Kaiser Friedrich III and Kaiserin Victoria of Germany. His sister Alexandra had married the Grand Duke Paul of Russia. Prince Nicholas of Greece, whom Marie had already met, married the Grand Duchess Elena of Russia. Two more sisters followed: Marie, wife of the Grand Duke George of Russia, and Olga, who was born and died in 1880. Then came two brothers: Andrew, born the same year as Marie, was married to Alice, princess of Battenberg, another granddaughter of Queen Victoria and sister of the queen of Spain; Christopher, the youngest, born in 1888, later married twice; his second wife, Françoise, was princess of Orléans, daughter of the Duc de Guise and sister of the Comte de Paris, the Bourbon pretender to the French throne.

Prince Roland had played his cards well and was enchanted with Marie's royal relatives. She, free of his snobbishness, was less impressed. According to his daughter Anna, Freud later remarked that one never knew whether Marie was talking about a dog, a servant, a commoner, or a prince when it was someone she liked.

The first days of the engagement were spent in making the customary calls. Marie was curious about the people she was going to meet and just as curious about the reactions of those she already knew. She took George to see the Radziwills. Uncle Constantin Radziwill did not conceal "his scorn for anyone not descended from Lithuanian princes, in particular for the great-grandniece of 'the Usurper.'" George immediately nicknamed him *"le grand seigneur."* George, in his turn, took Mimi to the Hôtel Bristol, where the Greek family was staying, to meet his sister-in-law Elena, the Russian grand duchess. Mimi found her superb, but added: "My future sister-in-law scared me a little by her beauty and her pride."

The young couple had also to think of the house that she would live in in her new and unknown country. She and George ordered their furniture and cars. On September 29, George left her to go to Denmark, where he was to remain until November 10. Her "Sucre d'Orge" often traveled to the North.

Nothing in her notebooks of this period indicates her feelings at his leaving. During the month that their engagement had already lasted, they had spent their evenings alone in her former study room. George already did all the talking, speaking primarily about politics, endlessly going on about his quarrels with Venizelos, and inducing in Marie a drowsiness that made it hard for her not to send him away before eleven. Their engagement had nothing in common with that of her cousin Jeanne, who had kissed her fiancé freely in every corner of the house.

Her future mother-in-law set the date of the wedding in Athens for December 12. To avoid his enemies, the Greek politicians, George would have preferred to get married in Paris, but the king was of another mind. The idea of marrying the son of a king in Athens enchanted Marie.

Since her grandmother was no longer there to interfere with her spending, Marie ordered a fabulous trousseau: dresses, shoes, hats, lingerie, household linens. The house of Drecoll, which supplied her wardrobe, and the other firms asked her permission for a joint exhibit of all the things they had made to her order. She was naïve enough to agree, and the exhibition was held on November 3 in the large hall of the Hôtel des Modes. Only when she entered and saw all the mannequins and the piles of linen in the showcases did she realize the number of dresses, hats and pairs of shoes she had ordered. "The whole thing offends and oppresses me," she writes.

It was done out of revenge, revenge which others were unable to understand. Marie was harshly criticized. Her father lectured her for having paid invoices in excess of 500,000 francs, including 40,000 francs to Cartier's and 210,000 francs for "*toilettes*," as women's outfits were then called. Having only 5,000 francs left she was to feel strapped for several months. At this time she had an annual income of 800,000 francs, and her father had promised to make over to her the life income of 250,000 francs that he had been receiving up to then under the terms of the will made in his favor by Marie-Félix.

The civil marriage took place on November 21 at the municipal hall of the sixteenth *arrondissement*, in which avenue d'Iéna is situated. Marie's witnesses were her two aunts, the Marquise de Villeneuve and Princess Radziwill; George's were Delyannes, the Greek minister, and his brother, Prince Nicholas. The bridegroom left for Greece immediately after.

Marie left Paris on December 5, in the company of her father, the Villeneuves, Mimau and Nelly the chambermaid. George himself had invited Mimau to live with them in Athens. He did not seem to fear the presence of this sort of mother-in-law, who had already proved to be rather despotic toward him. Mimau was delighted. She did not mind leaving Paris. All she wanted was to live with her Mimi, wherever that might be. Mimi was wishing she could resign herself as easily. She loved her prince, already her husband in the eyes of the law. Soon she would be his wife in the fullest sense. They would probably very soon have children, since that was what George wanted. He had told her so. It was his way of talking of love, she thought, but she was already afraid of dying in childbirth, or shortly thereafter, like her mother. She was anxious without knowing the reason.

In Brindisi, the royal yacht *Amphitrite* was waiting for them. A fanfare welcomed them on board, and the sailors presented arms. Marie had never before made a sea voyage. She was seasick the first day. Next day the sea was calm and the *Amphitrite* sailed toward the Gulf of Corinth. Marie as always was sensitive to the beauty of the landscape, which she described with feeling: "The scent of the Greek underbrush becomes more and more inebriating as the ship proceeds. The coast becomes closer. . . ." The expanse of starry sky over the canal fascinated her. She had trouble falling asleep after so many new impressions. Next morning she was awakened at eight o'clock by the cannons of three warships. Mimau and Nelly dressed her in a white silk dress with a blue sash, the Greek colors. Her hat was also blue and white. This outfit did not suit her, but she didn't mind. She felt she was performing a duty and went up on deck. At the stroke of noon a motor launch approached. It was George coming to meet her. In his admiral's uniform, his cap set at a rakish angle, he looked like his picture in the *Graphic*. "His blue eyes smile at me and all the sea and all the sky suddenly seem brighter, as though his beloved fairness had irradiated them too." Small craft surrounded the *Amphitrite* and Marie was acclaimed.

Her in-laws were on hand to welcome her to Piraeus. They all came by motor launch and boarded the royal yacht. The king, too, wore the uniform of an admiral. "How alike the two look," Marie noted, "but coming in different sizes! One could be the case for the other." Her mother-in-law, with "tender, blue, near-sighted eyes" and "a sweet refined face," kissed her while making the sign of the cross over her forehead in Orthodox fashion. Her sister-in-law Elena seemed to her as resplendent as before, and her other sister-in-law, Alice, "a beautiful blond Englishwoman with ample flesh, smiles a lot and doesn't say much since she's deaf." Princess Alice's husband, Prince Andrew, even taller than George, "looks like a thoroughbred horse." Christopher, "twenty years younger than his eldest brother[, is] nice and fat and smiles pleasantly." The person to whom Marie obviously paid most attention was Prince Waldemar, the uncle about whom George had spoken so enthusiastically. "Rather tall, slender, and elegant, a pointed chestnut beard completes his face with its gray nearsighted eyes behind a pince-nez placed on a nose that is slightly tilted upwards. Czar Nicholas II and George, the Prince of Wales, are blond versions of him. Waldemar smiles and speaks kindly to me. I am happy to meet the great friend of the man I love and to see that he likes me." The journey from Piraeus to Athens was made in a railway carriage, then in an open car, with throngs of people acclaiming her. The Greeks had adopted the Duchess d'Abrantes's fable inventing a Greek origin for the Bonaparte family. Streamers bore the name of Bonaparte in Greek: Kalomeri.

"The streets were planted with poles from which banners with the Greek and French colors flapped in the breeze, garlands of foliage were dotted with red, blue, and white flowers," reports *Le Figaro* of December 10, 1907.

Marie, her father, and the Villeneuves were lodged in the royal palace, "a long and heavy building in pseudo-classical Bavarian style built by King Otto," a Wittelsbach. Their rooms were on the second floor, and she had difficulty orienting herself in this huge palace with its numerous corridors.

In the evening, in the enormous room where she was alone for the last time, Marie brooded that on the following day "by all the telegraph wires on earth, reports will be transmitted of these ceremonies, which after all merely celebrate the fact that a man and a girl, she having long been fettered, are finally about to fulfill the simple law of nature, which wants to perpetuate the species."

Front page news was scarce at the end of the year 1907. No serious threat hung over the world. The Anglo-Russian accord signed in the month of August had ended the rivalry of the two powers in Asia and weakened Germany's position in Europe. The newspapers thus had a good deal of space to devote to the event, both political and social, that this wedding represented.

Familiar faces from Paris were reassuring before the ceremony. Marie's hairdresser, "my old friend," Loisel, had come, so had Mme Annette, her saleswoman from Drecoll's, to adjust the wedding gown of white satin with its pattern of silver roses. "How lovely you are!" exclaimed Mimau. She too had made herself beautiful. With tears in her eyes, she kissed her Mimi and left for the cathedral, where "the choice seat she deserved for all her years of love" was reserved for her among the guests.

The king's gilded carriage took Marie and the queen to the cathedral, where the king and his sons, on horseback, awaited them at the entrance.

In accordance with the Orthodox rite, the religious ceremony was long, and Marie had trouble staying on her feet. Waldemar and the queen were "what they call in Greek the *Koumbaros* and *Koumbara*, a sort of godfather and godmother of the couple being united." It was they who put the rings on Marie's and George's fingers. Next, the brothers-in-law and cousins came forward carrying large gilded crowns at the end of long poles; they followed the bride and groom, who walked around the table that was surrounded by candles and on which the Gospels lay open. These movements symbolized the journey through life that the newlyweds were to undertake together. Then the priest in his golden robe gave them red wine from the same cup. The crowns were heavy to carry and the men of the family took turns; the chants died down, then resumed; Marie was about to faint. Finally she was on her way out of the cathedral on the arm of her husband. Later, before the family luncheon, she still had to appear on the palace balcony.

In the evening, a grand banquet was held in the palace for all the notables of Athens and the young couple ranked first, sitting at the center of the table. "On this great day, we had precedence even over kings," wrote Marie Bonaparte.

In a notebook entitled *Le vieux compagnon* (The Old Companion), dated Copenhagen, January 1939, Marie Bonaparte retraced thirty years of life shared with Prince George. "We were of different races. Not only by complexion and the color of the hair, but by the reverberations of mind and heart," she starts the pages that George most likely never read. She wept during the marriage ceremony, and she also wept at night in Paris after his departure. He had talked to her about the Friend (Waldemar) and the Enemy (Venizelos), but he had not once taken her in his arms. She had attributed his perfect chastity to his religious beliefs. She had wished he would kiss her. She was in love but so disconcerted that more than once she had wanted to break the engagement.

On the wedding night, in Athens, when he came to her room, he was coming from his uncle Waldemar's, and "you needed the warmth of his voice, of his hand, and his permission, to get up your courage to approach the virgin. . . . You took me that night in a short, brutal gesture, as if forcing yourself, and apologized, 'I hate it as much as you do. But we must do it if we want children.' "

Two days later, they left on their honeymoon, on the *Amphitrite*. Waldemar sailed with them. They spent three days together. George cried when they parted from his uncle in Bologna.

During the honeymoon and after the return to Athens Marie exchanged letters with her father. She immediately adopted an impersonal tone with him and filled her letters with vignettes of royalty: Kaiser Wilhelm, King Victor Emmanuel II and comments on court life: "To start with, everybody is very nice to me and the King and Queen are so good! The lady in waiting is not too hard to put up with. I see very little of her." But her feelings Marie kept to herself.

Actually she already knew that this life did not suit her, but she could not imagine another. She was disappointed with the sexual side of her marriage and wrote that in March 1908 she "felt like leaving Athens and never returning," or ever seeing George again; but she stayed. The following month, it was too late. She was pregnant.

At the start of her pregnancy, she returned to France; it was understood that, as she had wished, she was to have the baby in Paris. George accompanied her. They lived together in the house on avenue d'Iéna, from which formerly she had so often wanted to flee. Ever since becoming pregnant she had felt threatened. She did not succeed in dispelling the memory of her mother's dying a month after giving birth. Mimau contributed to her fear of death by frequently speaking of her own death: "The only grief I'll ever cause you, my daughter, and I can do nothing about it, will be when I die." They wept together during such conversations.

There were days, however, when Marie hoped that this marriage would make her freer. "It takes plenty of love, a simple mind, a tranquil heart, and no imagination to be happy to love and obey the conjugal yoke," she wrote later. She had this experience of the conjugal yoke immediately. Though George was not a tyrant by temperament, he had a set number of habits to which he found it natural that she should submit. For instance, he spent every summer in Denmark, at Bernstorff, his uncle Waldemar's castle near Copenhagen. Pregnant or not, he wanted Marie to meet those members of his numerous family whom she did not yet know.

Frederick VIII, the Danish king, was King George's eldest brother. "Pleasant and mocking," he immediately became Uncle Freddy to her. The queen, a Swedish princess, was nicknamed "the Swan" because of her long neck and swaying body. Marie continued to keep a daily journal of impressions and events. It begins on August 13, 1908, with an evocation of "slow and dreary evenings after dinner at Uncle Freddy's, in the cold palace that Marguerite de Magenta calls the Palace of Desolation." But she also speaks of life at Bernstorff being "lit up by that vibrant and enlightened woman, Marie-Waldemar." She had been immediately taken with Waldemar's French wife, who seemed to her to have both character and imagination, and was a painter to boot. Marie sensed in her a human quality to which she responded, an aristocracy of mind and heart that she loved and found so rarely. She also liked Marie-Waldemar's children. "Aage, 20 years old, handsome, large bright eyes in a tanned face, cocky; Axel, 19 and handsome; Erik, 18, looks like 14, soft and taciturn; Viggo, 14, intelligent and spirited monkey; Baby (Magrethe), 12, blond and fresh, decked out like an urchin, lively and intelligent."

The entry of August 23 describes a day at Bernstorff: She was ready at eleven o'clock (having risen, bathed, dressed and done her hair), when she joined George, who had been with Waldemar since seven in the morning. They had been for a walk together or reading in Waldemar's room. She called them her "two husbands," and went for a walk with them, kissing now one, now the other, until it was time for lunch. Then she wrote while Waldemar and George went into town. Around four o'clock, she heard the back-firing of motorcycles under her window; George and Waldemar were returning. They all had tea together, and if they were not invited to the royal palace, they dined at Bernstorff, where they spent the evening in the "deep sweet joy of a *tête-à-tête à trois*, George, myself, and sweet Waldemar."

The next day, she noted down what she called an evening scene: Waldemar and George were in her room, where she was lying on a chaise longue, Waldemar kissing her and George refusing to kiss her the way his uncle did.

All this is casually written. During these first weeks of her stay in Denmark, her writing for the first time reflects a slightly acid *joie de vivre*. Marie seems younger, younger than she actually is. She appears to be a slightly perverse ingénue rather than a young woman developing under the influence of love and approaching motherhood. The amorous games with Waldemar surely had something to do with this.

The Duke and Duchess of Cumberland came to visit Bernstorff. Ernest, the duke, whose father was king of Hanover before being expelled by Prussia, was Waldemar's brother-in-law, having married Thyra. They arrived by special train, with ten domestics and fifteen trunks. Aunt Thyra had the look of a white mouse, with beautiful white hair, large gray eyes, a small simian face and very gentle movements. Uncle Ernest, inimitable in face and costume, was tall, thin, with a broken nose sunk in his broad flat face, thick glasses, small eyes, bald skull, thick neck, batiste shirt without a collar, thick lips. He liked to tell dirty jokes. He was pleasant and amusing, but when "the others annoyed him, he didn't say a word." He and Marie-Waldemar stood out "in the family like two lighted candles among extinguished ones, peculiar but interesting.

The mentality of the others lacked that strong imprint provided by the presence of a will. Soft, indecisive, tame . . . the czar was unable to decide which of two parties to turn to for the good of the empire; and Waldemar was unable, before going out, to decide between two overcoats: 'Georgie, tell me what I shall put on.' "

The dowager czarina of Russia, another of George's aunts, stopped on her way to visit her sister Alix, Queen of England, in Christiania, on board the yacht the *Polestar*, where they all went to dine in Romanov splendor, on August 28, 1908. Aunt Minny was "a small slender woman, with a dark wig coming down to her eyes, wrinkled face, very upturned nose, harsh and serious voice." Marie was willing to please her in-laws and to give them the image that was expected of a Royal Highness.

When alone Marie and George often spoke happily of the child they were expecting. Marie enjoyed the summer at Bernstorff, where there seemed to be no set rules to restrict their desires. This discovery of free and easy ways was new for her, brought up as she had been by her austere grandmother and father, and by Mimau, who saw and denounced vice everywhere. In her journal she addressed George: "I would need to take refuge from the whole world, to nestle in loving arms. O my darling, understand this, open yours to me!" But there was no chance he would do so. George was not tender toward her, and she was realizing it more and more.

As the date of departure from Bernstorff neared, her husband's mood threw her into despair. She did not know how to cope with it. Everything became a source of pain. George began to denigrate Marie-Waldemar, saying that she was compromising herself with Riss, the riding master, and that she had episodes of drunkenness whose ill effects she was unable to hide. It did not occur to him that Waldemar might be partly responsible for all this. Marie at first believed that if she and Waldemar could only talk things over, they would arrive at an understanding and many problems would be resolved. But when she tried to talk to him "he goes away, too selfish." She cried and again felt chilled, wishing for death. Her husband seemed "as naïve as a child." Besides, "poor George" had nothing to occupy him, which was not good for anyone. She must have wondered how they were going to live in Paris.

On the train that was taking them back from Copenhagen toward France, she wrote: "My George, near his Waldemar, is like a day lit by the sun, and away from him like a day of fog. . . . The day before our departure, Marie came to see me while I was in bed. 'They're down there. It's the same scene every time when there's a departure. George is crying. Waldemar is as green as an apple.' " The two women conferred. Nothing could be done about it. Marie-Waldemar was used to it. She had understood for a long time. Waldemar accompanied them on the train as far as Gjedser, the border of Denmark. Finally the train was put on the ferry. Waldemar remained on the upper deck of the boat, while George returned to the railway carriage and went to sleep. He awoke shortly before Berlin. "Now they are sitting down at the table," he said, taking out his watch. His thoughts were in Bernstorff.

At the station in Paris, they were welcomed by Lépine, the prefect of police, accompanying Prince Roland. Marie was back with Mimau, my "Zinzin," who caressed her belly. Her old nurse was the only dispenser of genuine tenderness she had known so far.

Daily life began again in that large and overly solemn residence, forever her father's house, where George easily found his place. Turned in on himself and the past, he projected a sort of nonlife around him, which Marie had already learned to dread.

Her father-in-law, the king, spent the month of November in Paris, at the Hôtel Bristol, getting ready to go to Vienna, where early in December the jubilee of the Emperor Franz Josef was to take place. He often invited them to lunch in the small salon of his hotel suite. All his talk turned into banter. Father and son avoided talking to each other, and the king eschewed any mention of Crete, which had just proclaimed itself Greek.

Marie focused her attention elsewhere: on the proclamation of Bulgarian independence (she found the Bulgarians "interesting" because "they do something while we poor Greeks will never do anything, absorbed as we are by the internal quarrels of individuals"), on Aunt Alix (wife of Edward VII): "Sixty-three years old, surprisingly young, enameled skin. Disturbing when youthfulness covers an old skin. She seems kind and friendly, but also insignificance personified."

Marie tried by every means to get the better of her apprehensions, which increased as the time of delivery approached. Mimau had a slight attack of angina pectoris; to see her suffer and to know her threatened was deeply upsetting to Marie. How would she live through the impending ordeal, with its implied danger of death, without Mimau by her side?

Her diary, in a section entitled *My First-born*, reports: "On December 3, 1908, I wake up at 6:40, soaked in very warm water, and I awaken 'Sucre d'Orge' who was sleeping beside me. He puts on his beige bathrobe and turns on the lights since it's dark out-side. Mimau soon arrives, covered in shawls. The doctor suggests chloroform but I refuse. Oh no! it was beautiful, it was grand thus to feel oneself giving life to a new being! After the cannon shot at the Eiffel Tower, at 12:05, the doctor said: 'At the next pain, I'll deliver you.' Six endless minutes went by. Finally the pain came. 'Don't push any more,' the doctor said, and he pulled out something weighty that looks to me very long." Prince Peter of Greece was born. Marie was elated to have a son.

A few days later, she started to cry; fear gripped her again, fear of losing her child, fear of not having other children. She had need of God and envied George his faith.

It was during this crisis, which was hardly characteristic of her since she had never felt a need for God, or had even been willing to search for an understanding faith, that she received a visit from Monseigneur de Curel, the bishop of Monaco, who brought her the absolution of Rome. Before his arrival, she had thought that perhaps she was to hear "through the word of man a very far echo of the word of God." She was in bed, he, fat and red, sat down at her bedside, glancing at the baby in his bassinet, and the words of this priest "as always, alienated me even more from religion."

His first attempt having failed, Monseigneur de Curel had agreed to go to Rome a second time in order to intercede in favor of H.R.H. Princess George of Greece and Denmark. From Athens, King George I had contributed valuable support by threatening, should the lifting of minor excommunication not be accorded his daughter-in-law, not to "tolerate" any longer the presence of a Roman Catholic bishop in Athens, where he was indeed only tol-erated. "So went the world in Rome," Marie noted. It had been agreed that the excommunication would be lifted in return for cer-tain financial considerations.

The decision had been slow in coming and Marie had sent and received many letters. George had asked her several times why she cared so much about having the excommunication lifted and also why she was going to mass every Sunday when she was in Athens. She admitted that she was going to mass in a spirit of bravado, but her insistence on seeing the excommunication lifted was of an-other nature. It was very important for her aunt Jeanne, and even for her father. She was told that without it she would be denied burial by the Catholic Church. She was doing it for them. Otherwise, "the Greek Church would be charged to bury me as well as to marry me." This painfully obtained absolution terminated her relations with the Roman Catholic Church.

Her diary entries through December 1908 center on her son. She was dazzled and fulfilled by her motherhood. During these first weeks, she and George enjoyed a sense of union they had not known before. George was as happy as she was. He loved his son so much that he envied Marie for nursing him. He took pictures, he walked back and forth in the room with little Prince Peter in his arms, singing him a lullaby in Danish, which he himself was to copy down on December 7, 1951, and sign with his initial G, still remembering the words.

Marie was to get up only two months after giving birth, when it was time to depart for Greece. She was in excellent physical condition, healthy and radiant. The couple returned to Athens on February 6, and the baptism of the little prince took place on the 20th. The joy of motherhood could not satisfy her for long, however. She felt again lonely and her life bored her. George's interests were far removed from hers. He was giving all the gymnastic exams in the schools of Athens for the Panhellenic games, while she was "suckling Peter."

Athens did not suit her. Its intellectual life lacked intensity, and her rank in society prevented her from mixing in what little there was. But that came as no surprise to her. She was too sensible not to accept the consequences brought about by her choice, though she may not have foreseen how much this idle life would weigh on her and may not have measured its emptiness in advance. "Four months spent with family gatherings three times a week. It's too much for me. Last week there were the visits of the aunts from Russia and England. All royal bourgeois, these Danes, bourgeois virtues and defects, united, honest, good, simple, kind, desperately the common path."

Weighty events were taking place in Greece, and Marie commented on them with the same detachment. She communicated her observations on the development of the political situation in the Balkans to her father: "One sees nothing but fezzes in the streets [of Athens], poor fezzes taking refuge here for fear of being hanged." In Turkey, where revolution had broken out a year earlier, unleashed by the "Union and Progress" movement launched by the Young Turks after previous failures and the temporary rise to power of counterrevolutionaries, the Young Turks had finally succeeded in deposing Sultan Abdul-Hamid in April 1909. The whole East was in an uproar. "Do you think these Young Turks will do something?" Marie asked. "Will they be able to rejuvenate Turkey? . . . I find them interesting."

Following the model of "Union and Progress," a military league formed in Athens in May 1909, demanding the reorganization of the army and navy. In a letter to her father Marie mentioned the recent fall of the Greek government and named several politicians, Theotokes, Rhalles, Dragoumis, who did not care to take the risk of forming a new cabinet. "We don't know where to turn," she wrote, without seeming to foresee the coup d'état that was to take place in August.

That summer, spent again in Denmark, she became involved with Aage, the eldest son of Marie-Waldemar, who kissed her in corners and told her about his Paris flings. She had no illusions about him; Aage was shallow and allowed himself to be pampered, but he had the advantage of being young like herself. "We never find the total object of love. So let us gather the beautiful fragments. I have found a beautiful fragment," she wrote. Angrily she wrote of Waldemar: "He does nothing from morning to night but slumber over the same newspaper, inactive, indolent, interested in nothing and incapable of having an interest, limited by his lack of intelligence." The summer went by slowly. The Greek situation was not promising.

"Poor Crete is in bad shape. The officers have rebelled, and the king has yielded and granted them amnesty. The cabinet has fallen. The new one (of which Mavromichalis is prime minister) has promised the military everything they want . . ." Marie recounted in her journal. "But to give in is the method of government of my father-in-law and the whole family." The military league summoned Venizelos to Athens, and the princes had to leave the army. "Tino" [Crown Prince Constantine] was in Kronberg, where George met with him. He had been able to leave Greece in order to join his wife, but had received a telegram not to come back for several weeks at least, as Marie informed her father on September 18, and thus George was not to go to Greece either. "Very good," she added. She was obviously happy at the thought of not having to spend a third winter in Athens. On September 27, she asked her father to have the rugs put down for her return. She would probably be heavy and was afraid of falling.

Marie remained very late at Bernstorff, while George and Waldemar went hunting at the Cumberlands'. She was back at avenue d'Iéna, with George, only a few days before November 12, when Waldemar and his three sons left for Siam. But they were to return to Denmark earlier than planned. On December 5, 1909, Marie-Waldemar died, at the age of forty-four. The travelers were in India when the news reached them. Returning, they took a large British liner instead of the small Danish vessel on which they had set out. Aage had a carefree time on the English ship, as Marie was to learn with no surprise. "He is weak. He has not inherited his mother's character." Marie was saddened by Marie-Waldemar's sudden death.

At this time a friendship began to flourish that up to her meeting with Freud was to be essential to her. Gustave Le Bon was one of the father figures whose affection, guidance and encouragement in intellectual endeavor she was forever seeking. Close to seventy, famous, voluble, overflowing with energy, he was a doctor, sociologist, a great traveler, and had written several books that had brought him fame. Some of his works had achieved a wide circulation. *La Psychologie des foules* (*Mass Psychology*) and *Les Lois psychologiques de l'évolution des peuples* (*Psychological Laws in the Evolution of Peoples*) presented his ideas on what he called "collective psychology" and gave him a reputation as a thinker to which he was not insensitive. In his Paris apartment on rue Vignon, near the Madeleine, or in his house in Marnes-la-Coquette, near Saint-Cloud, his Wednesday luncheons and Sunday dinners brought together a brilliant company of artists, writers, politicians, scholars and society people.

Prince Roland Bonaparte introduced him to his daughter. The old gentleman was not without picturesque qualities with "his pink and fleshy face, bristling with hair discolored by the sun of the Orient."[1] During the summer of 1909, Marie had written him every other day from Bernstorff. "He gave me confidence in myself and courage, and showed me—reassuring truth—that the mind comes *first*. . . . Superiority in the woman humiliates the man and must be displayed only to equals or superiors." She submitted with joy to this father, who brought her at last what her real father had always denied her. More than ever she needed to be both reassured and urged to undertake something on her own.

On February 10, 1910, at 11:14 P.M., her second child was born, a daughter, Princess Eugénie of Greece. The labor pains had started early in the afternoon, but Marie was still arranging papers at seven in the evening. She gave birth easily, but later she was to suffer from a double sciatica and be haunted by the thought that her breasts were disfigured from nursing. She only partially nursed her daughter, who was also given donkey's milk, one feeding time out of three. "I spent one month in bed reading all the works of Maupassant, without a moment of idleness or reverie, which might have opened the door to the terrible attack of philosophico-religious, puerperal psychosis from which I suffered after Peter's birth." This is an overstatement characteristic of the princess, for her brief depression and religious ruminations were hardly a postpartum psychosis.

This time Prince George did not share in her rejoicing. Their daughter was admired by the whole household, but he would have preferred a second son. He did not hide his disappointment and was preoccupied by other things. He was going through a period of resentment over the policies of his father, who had not valued his abnegation in Crete and was to allow the election to Parliament, on April 8, 1910, of his personal enemy, Venizelos. Nevertheless George would have liked to return to Athens, to the house on Academy Street, which Marie refused to equip, fearing they might be expelled from it—precisely by Venizelos. George then decided to go to Denmark to keep Waldemar company for a time. He had not seen his uncle since Marie-Waldemar's funeral, which Marie had not attended because of her pregnancy.

Thanks to Le Bon, this Parisian spring was still to be pleasant. "I love intelligence and understanding above all," wrote Marie in connection with the man whom she calls l'Ami—the friend. For a long time she had dreamed of drawing to her house the intellectual élite. Le Bon, "sparing no effort, brought to my house the finest and rarest minds of France. My little weekly dinners were a delight for me and [I experienced] a joyful pride in feeling that I pleased such minds." Poincaré and Tardieu (a president of the Republic and a prime minister) were among the first guests at these dinners, which she started in April 1910.

But Mimau was making constant scenes about everything. She accused Marie of neglecting the house. The servants had become her obsession. "And the good Lord, who is making me get old, should make me younger so I can look after you." On May 10, George returned from Denmark and Mimau began to have suspicions about him, just as she had after Peter's birth. Again she was convinced that he was betraying Marie with a little nurse, and made a scene in front of the other nurses. Finally she decided not to stay any longer. For Marie, this was a disaster; one more time her precarious sense of security was shaken. Changes were unsettling, and Mimau was most precious to her. She did not want to relinquish her, but she realized that the poor woman had become completely paranoid and was unable to cope with so many people, who made her spin all kinds of frenzied stories. Mimau left to settle in Monte Carlo, where one of her nieces was to take care of her. From time to time, she came to stay with her Mimi, or Marie went to see her with the children.

The summer of 1910, which like the previous ones she spent at Bernstorff, gave Marie little happiness. She realized to what extent the charm she had once found in the castle was owing to the imagination of Marie-Waldemar, that clear-sighted and unhappy woman. Another death affected her greatly. "Aunt Jeanne died yesterday [July 25, 1910], following an operation. Pioche [Prince Roland's secretary] sent a telegram. George opened the envelope and delayed the blow for a few seconds by saying, 'You know, your Aunt Jeanne is very ill.'" Marie was overcome with remorse because she had not visited her before their departure. She reproached herself for being "inconsistent in the manifestation of my love. Doomed to blaze up, followed by a long smoldering under the ashes, where I look in vain for the spark." After hearing the news, she felt unable to join with the other members of the royal family in a visit to a British ship, nor did she appear at dinner at the king's. "And George, whose heart constitutes his greatness, is staying with me."

In spite of this laudatory remark, George was unable to give her the consolation she needed after this death. She dreamed of the dead woman, "my Aunt Jeanne whom I loved so much." She could not attend the funeral because she was nursing Eugénie and did not want to wean her. Once again she was alone. Mimau was not there to love her.

Rendered more sensitive by her grief, and also because Marie-

Waldemar's absence made certain things clearer, Marie realized that the relationship between George and his uncle was not what she had imagined. "Your body adverse to female bodies, your body like your soul devoted to man, chastely but ardently fixed on the one Friend."[2] It was while looking at a book on Michelangelo and comparing it to the drawings of athletes that adorned her husband's dressing room that she understood. George, "upright in soul as in stature . . . a being with abnormally strong and fixed passions . . . loved only one friend at the age of fourteen. Ten years his senior and like him devoted to the sea." But who then was Waldemar, toward whom she now began to feel a nagging jealousy? In this text, we see the image that had already faded in 1909 deteriorate still further: "A very ordinary creature, neither very handsome, nor very intelligent, nor very generous, and often unpleasant, especially toward his children." But Marie recognized that he had been able to inspire in George "one of those great passions that, according to Rousseau, are as rare as great genius." Discovering this shook her to the core. The period was anything but open about such strong attachments, and her upbringing had been more restrictive than most. On the other hand, there had been the precedent of Uncle Christian, who had strange accidents and disappearances and was the subject of Mimau's, Gragra's and her grandmother's gossip. Although she remarked on Uncle Christian's searching for young men of classic Greek type when in Athens, it is by no means certain that she understood about his predilections. She was confused about those matters. Early in her adolescence Frifri had provided some information but Marie does not seem to have felt, even toward her, who was certainly the closest of her girl friends, the crush that many girls experience for someone of their own sex at the time of puberty.

The only remedy was to find other partners for her female role. In the notes entitled *The Men I Have Loved*, the next in line, number five, is described as follows: "Haunted by Shakespearean memories and by *Pelléas and Mélisande*, which had me sob when I was eighteen, I was ready for a banal adventure. Only incest would do. I took as Pelléas the young and vulgar ruffian, five years after having met him and having lost sight of him in the interval. . . . Pelléas . . . fled. His wife, abandoned for six months, thought of killing herself. Drunken and coarse," she concludes. Nevertheless, she enjoyed "some orgiastic days" with him, but they were merely an interlude in the events she had to face.

Her aunt Louise Radziwill died on February 14, 1911. Marie attended the funeral, which took place in Ermenonville, a château near Paris belonging to the Blanc family. On March 24, she went to Wiesbaden to see her mother-in-law, and stayed there for a week with George and two of her brothers-in-law, Constantine and Andrew. By March 30, she was back in Paris by herself, while George stayed on with his family for a few more days.

On June 22, Marie accompanied George to London. He was there to represent his father at the coronation of George V. "We will produce the third child afterwards," she added, ". . . I am being especially noticed by the envoy of the republic of Panama. . . . I am crushed by the beauty of Marie of Rumania. Le Bon guessed, seeing my sadness on my return."

Le Bon did his best to give her self-confidence, but Marie was incurably doubtful of her physical appearance and her powers of attraction. Her marriage could not have reassured her, nor had her recent amorous experiences. She tried not to let her anxiety show, and did what was expected of her.

During the previous fall, her friend Geneviève Ollivier had married Dr. Jean Troisier, a young and promising physician. She seemed fulfilled by her marriage, and Marie must have compared their fates. For some time she had been wanting to undergo a small surgical operation in order to get rid of the slightly puffy scar at the base of her nose caused by hitting it against the piano during the Leandri crisis. She was obsessed by this scar, which, she thought, disfigured her. Of the various operations she decided on in her life, this was the first. It was at this time that she had secret trysts with Lembessis, her husband's aide-de-camp. They met at Bagatelle. "Scenes in my room during the night. Ej. praecox." Her love affairs were decidedly unsuccessful.

Except for her children, who were developing normally, her life was under a cloud. On November 11, Laure Gabeau, half-paralyzed since the time of Marie's and George's engagement, died at her home in Touraine. Marie and George attended her funeral in Fontaines-les-Blanches. "Desolate visit," Marie recorded.

In November of that year, 1911, *La Gazette des Hôpitaux* published the first article in French on *Le Rapport affectif dans la cure des psychonévroses*. But Le Bon, Marie's mentor, was not yet aware of psychoanalysis. At his suggestion, the princess, soon to be thirty, began to write an essay entitled *Les Murs* (The Walls), which she finished the following year. The walls are those of her father's house, which she had never left for a home of her own. Nothing had changed there, it was oppressively filled with memories. Only her relationship with her father seemed subject to change. She was no longer afraid of his paternal despotism. With him, she played to the hilt her role of married daughter, the calm and disciplined mother of a family. In her Journal, he was seldom mentioned. She simply listed his trips, his activities. No longer did she express the painful and always rejected wish to please him. She had also quickly recovered from trying to please George.

Her role as a Greek royal highness was soon to dominate a certain period of her life. It did not occur to her to complain about it.

Since 1910 the unrest in Macedonia had resumed. The Young Turks, who had not succeeded in setting up a government in accordance with the liberal façade of "Union and Progress," had fallen back into the Ottoman tradition. The following year, Turkey went to war with Italy, which had seized the Turkish province of Tripolitania. Incited secretly by Russia, the Balkan states finally decided to unite and launch an offensive against Turkey. A secret Serbo-Bulgarian treaty was signed on March 13, 1912, and a Greco-Bulgarian treaty on May 29. Both nations were preparing for an offensive war against the Turks.

George decided that they would leave for Athens on October 10, taking the children with them. He was to be appointed to the general staff at the Naval Ministry. "If things go wrong, we can always go to Corfu," Marie wrote to her father before leaving Paris. "And George does not foresee a revolution (except against Venizelos). Matters must be decided in Macedonia." Venizelos had been the prime minister of Greece since June 8, 1911, and actually had very few political enemies, most of them in circles influenced by the royal court. He had been the agent of important reforms. He was now ready to acquire new territories by a war in which victory over Turkey was assured.

Marie wrote to her father from Athens on October 17, 1912: "We have offered the army a few ambulances, there were only four for 120,000 men!" Turkey was then on the point of signing the peace treaty of Ouchy with Italy, thereby giving up Tripolitania. Serbia and Bulgaria declared war on her one day earlier than Greece. "The 'victory-bearing' armies, as the Greek newspapers write, are advancing into Turkish territory," Marie announced on October 22, 1912. "We must wait for the great shock of Adrianople. The queen and we women are trying to organize the care and transportation of the wounded and there is a lot to do. . . . As for me, I have an improvised hospital in the Military School and particularly the organization of one or two hospital ships, intended for the evacuation of the wounded from Volos to Athens." Like the other princesses, Marie opened a subscription in the newspapers for her hospital ships, giving 100,000 francs to her own subscription fund. The hospital ships increased the popularity of the royal family, and particularly Marie's, among the Greeks.

On November 10, 1912, she wrote from Volos that she was back from Elasson, "a picturesque village with five minarets." She had taken many photographs. George was general aide-de-camp to his father, the king. "We said goodbye to each other in Salonika." On her hospital ship *Albania*, she picked up the wounded, sometimes from as far as Salonika, and brought them back to Athens. In mid-November, she was in contact with Venizelos, who wished her to consult with one of the secretaries of the War Ministry in order to reapportion her time for other functions, since the hospital had ceased to receive any new wounded and the ship had stopped making its runs. On December 3, Turkey asked for an armistice.

At the time, Marie wrote from Athens: "We are afraid of Macedonian autonomy, with Salonika as a future prey for Bulgaria—we are afraid of having shed Greek blood for the benefit of the Slavs. If we do not keep Salonika, we cannot be sure of the people's attitude. The prime minister understands this. He is worried." She did not hide her sympathy for Venizelos and longed to be able to organize the evacuation from the battles in Epirus.

Christmas she spent in Athens, at home with the children. By the end of December she was busy again. She wrote to her father that now she was going to have three responsibilities: her Military School Hospital in Athens, her hospital ship and the hospital in Epirus. An article in the Athenian newspaper *Scrip* sang her praises. She charmed people by her naturalness and vivacity. In a letter of January 13, 1913, she told her father about a young surgeon from Geneva who was the delegate of the Swiss Red Cross in Philippias. "The nephew of the great Reverdin" [i.e., the inventor of the Reverdin needle, used in Europe by generations of surgeons] had come to welcome her in Preveza, at the time of her first trip to Epirus aboard the *Albania*.

Albert Reverdin became number six of the men she loved—"the

other lover," as she called him. "His arms were young, fresh, I consented to everything and to know nothing provided he would come back." Evoking him in a brief text, *The Events of the Heart,*[3] she writes: "The only events, for a woman, are those of the heart: a tear, a kiss." "What do I care if empires fall? He kissed my lips this evening."

She immediately organized herself: "December 28, I have a cold, the *Albania* sails without me." The cold seems to have been a "diplomatic illness," and she noted that in Ioannina people were killed the next day at "our observation post." She wanted to remain in Epirus. "My ship, now very well organized, will go on functioning by itself with the staff it has on board. It will regularly evacuate the eventual wounded to Athens." Marie tried often to rejoin the "other lover" without giving up what she considered to be her duty. But though the Ottoman government violated the truce on February 3, 1913, and the war was resumed for a few weeks, Marie was soon separated from Reverdin, without having broken off their affair. He was to reappear several times in Paris.

She returned in February from Epirus to Athens, and there to problems just as real as those of her hospital ship and the raising of money for the wounded, and closer to home. The nurse "asked to be relieved of her post after a scene with George," Marie noted. It was then that Violet Croisdale ("Croisy") appeared, who was long to play an important part in the lives of Prince Peter and Princess Eugénie. This did not keep Marie from immersion in Diderot's *Jacques le fataliste*. (She was to reread Diderot at the time of her death.)

On March 18, her father-in-law, King George I, was assassinated in Salonika. Marie, then in Athens, embarked on the *Amphitrite*, accompanied by Crown Prince Constantine and Venizelos. The ship was to bring back the king's body to Athens.

After the funeral, in which "eighty metropolites in gold" took part, George returned to Paris with Marie and the children. Then he left again for Greece, where the Greco-Bulgarian war now was in progress.

Marie had played her role as a royal highness with panache and had discovered that she could be effective in practical action. But she was still subject to self-doubts. "The folly of digging up the past, in order to see it as other than what it was, is my obsessive, painful folly. I dig in the past and say to myself: if on such and such a day, at such and such an hour, you had put such and such a stone here instead of there, the edifice of your present would be much grander and more shining. . . .

"Do not cry any longer over the impossible Palace. Stand up, O my Wisdom, to adorn with your charitable hands my house of the Present and the nakedness of its walls." She wrote this on board the *Amphitrite*, on March 28, 1913, during the funeral voyage from Salonika.

5

LOVE, WAR AND ANOTHER LOVE

*"After a few vain and unhappy attempts at love, I
experienced two great passions. Between the ages
of thirty and fifty, two men were my companions.
The first, by his age and authority, could have
been my father, and no one has loved me so much.
The second was an older brother, and it was he
whom I loved the most and the longest."*

MARIE BONAPARTE,
Notes diverses

A FEW DAYS AFTER THE ASSASSINATION OF HER FATHER-IN-
law, Marie Bonaparte wrote: *"My Husband.* He bores me,
he keeps me in chains, but he is the only man who will love
me until death. Thus my heart, when it suffers, needs a spouse's
broad and faithful breast. Others have come and gone, others come
and go, and our children along with them, whòm life will smilingly
take from us.

"We will remain, old and alone, and, life having passed, we will
then be all that remains for each other." And, still in Athens, she
adds: "12 April 1913, what I here write about my husband, plenty
of men write about their wives, whom they leave behind at home
but always come back to."

She was not at all times so sure of herself as it might seem from
this conclusion. Often she had the feeling of sharing the fate of
other women, and this is why she wrote about that time: *"The
Oppression of marriage:* Marriage [is] security but marriage [is
also] a sacrifice and an entombment of oneself.

"The free blossoming of oneself is blighted within the walls of
the conjugal home, and the soul and face take on that disheart-
ened tinge one sees in so many wives.

"The oppression of marriage is a universal, if necessary malady,
and I dare to believe there are more released widows than dis-
consolate ones."[1]

Such observations on the impact of marriage on women were
radical for the time. Most women in 1913 accepted their fate
without comment. But the "universal oppression" of which Marie

so bitterly complained, and with which she identified, applied much more to others than to herself. George was more absent—emotionally and physically—than tyrannical.

It was this indifference toward her—something she could not abide in any man—that fueled her anger. Although she was as yet unaware of it, her generalizations were, in part, determined by her resentment toward all men. Thus even the freedom which her wealth provided her, and of which she took full advantage, was no solace for her sense of oppression. Marie craved love and an equal give and take with a man, but she was so crippled by her neurotic conflicts that she could neither love fully nor wholly accept being loved.

That summer, while George went to Denmark to settle his father's estate, she remained in France with the children. They were growing up, and they were handsome and charming. Peter, four and a half, had everything in his favor. His father adored him, and Marie was proud of having given birth to a boy. Despite her principles of fairness in devoting equal time to the children in their games and education, she was unaware of the degree to which she favored the boy. But she was even more unaware that her love for Peter was more crippling than enabling for him.

To the world at large, Princess George of Greece was now a handsome, experienced and sophisticated society woman known for her generosity. Soon, however, her inner infirmity would dominate her personal life more clearly than ever before.

The war with Bulgaria was over. Marie took little interest in the new power relationships in the Balkans. All she saw was that now that her brother-in-law Constantine had become king, and Venizelos, George's archenemy, was still prime minister, she would no longer be obliged to spend part of the year in Athens, and could devote more time to her salon in Paris. She enjoyed the role of hostess and it enlivened her life.

When she gave a luncheon for Rudyard Kipling, the children were fascinated by the visitor, but their mother was no longer interested in a literary salon. Some as yet invisible changes had taken place. Despite his tender years, Peter was introduced as an admirer of the *Just So Stories* and even of the *Jungle Book*. Kipling handed the young prince a photograph, which he had inscribed to him. He had brought nothing for the little princess, who was never to forget the discrimination she suffered that day. But Princess

Marie noticed nothing. She had eyes only for another of the guests: that incredibly awkward-looking little man, with his rumpled suit, his untidy shock of hair, his thick mustache and his countless cigarettes. She called him "Monsieur le Président" and the children were seeing him for the first time.

Aristide Briand was then fifty-one years old and had already been prime minister four times. He was to hold this position eleven times in the course of his career, and to be a cabinet minister twenty times, a record that no one else ever matched, even during the Third Republic (1870–1940), when governments were often of short duration. Briand made a great name for himself in French political history. A controversial figure during his lifetime, he continued to be so after his death, but his admirers and detractors agreed in acknowledging the fascination of his voice and his keen intelligence.

Because of his beautiful hands and the lure of his voice, some people claimed that he was an aristocrat, but according to his biographer, Georges Suarez, this was not the case. However, Briand maintained a close friendship with the Lareinty family— grandchildren of Baron Clément de Lareinty, who may have been his father. Briand's official father, originally from La Vendée, was a café owner in Nantes, and his mother had been a linen maid in the Lareintys' château, in Brittany, before her marriage.

Starting out as a lawyer, and then becoming a journalist, Aristide Briand had entered politics and first been elected a deputy in 1902. He had been a member, and then secretary general, of the Socialist Party, from which he resigned in 1905. He was "the greatest impromptu speaker to be heard since the Revolution," said Paul Deschanel, who had been both president of the Chamber of Deputies and president of the Republic.[2] Marie Bonaparte, looking at Briand, his shoulders hunched, his right hand feverishly rolling a cigarette in the pocket of his coat, mounting the rostrum to deliver a speech in the Chamber of Deputies, said: "Look at him! He walks up like a pimp but he'll come down like a lord."

Briand's political career had a humanitarian side that appealed to Princess Marie. In 1906, when he was minister of education, fine arts and religion, he had drafted a plan to create a ministry of national education with a selective system for free education at all levels. The next year, he sponsored the law for the separation of church and state. Whatever he was engaged in, he demonstrated the kind of imagination that is so rare in politics, a capacity for perceiving and considering the opponent's point of view. He prided himself on being "flexible."

Briand had a reputation as a womanizer. As a leftist small-town lawyer in Saint-Nazaire, he had fallen desperately in love with a young married woman of the local upper crust. Caught making love in a meadow, they were brought to trial. The woman's husband and young Briand's political opponents had closed ranks to bring about this sensational outcome. In the late nineteenth century, in provincial France, a scandal of this kind might easily ruin one's career. Fortunately, the young woman was not lacking in courage; repudiated by her husband, banished by her family, she did her utmost to obtain justice for herself and her lover. After three successive trials, they were finally acquitted. It was following this perilous affair that Briand left for Paris, where his political career made rapid headway.

Marie had met him for the first time at a luncheon in Courances, at the home of the Marquise de Ganay, who invited them both again, less than a month later. They returned to Paris in the same limousine. Briand had immediately responded to Marie's attraction, and she was galvanized by this sudden passion. The first kiss was exchanged "in a dark car driving in the night toward Paris in November. The night streamed with dew and stars."[3]

At the time Briand was known to be having an affair with Berthe Cerny, an actress from the Comédie Française, who by an odd coincidence also lived in Saint-Cloud. She had found and furnished a three-room apartment at 52 avenue Kléber for her lover; Briand remained in this modest setting until his death. He was not a man attached to possessions. Marie, too richly endowed by fortune, could understand and even appreciate this. Simplicity suited her. As they soon realized, they had in common love of the countryside and the sea. Briand liked to hunt and fish; he escaped the city as often as possible to stay at a rented cottage in Cocherel in Normandy. The sea had been his great love, and he went sailing with friends whenever the opportunity arose. He also had a taste for poetry, and toward the end of his life appointed the great St.-John Perse as first secretary.

Marie soon took the measure of the man. Though he attracted her in many ways, she could not make up her mind to take the last step. She was indeed a strange person. A handsome woman, but so lacking in self-confidence that her beauty was not projected as strongly as it might have been. Briand's sensitivity and his long experience with women made him feel how exceptional she was. He was as much attracted by her intellect as by her body, and he certainly also loved the fact that she was a princess and that her true aristocracy was of the mind. Marie knew that Briand's feelings were genuine, but somehow she was reminded of Leandri's betrayal. She could cope with sexual adventures without love, especially if it was she who initiated them, but she felt it would be a long time before she could combine emotion and sex.

Shortly after meeting Briand, she began a new notebook with the promising heading *Le Bonheur d'être aimée* (The Happiness of Being Loved), in which she confessed that she loved the silence of this great orator but was afraid of his desire. For this reason in the early days she preferred not to be alone with him. They went to concerts, and in a screened box, cheek to cheek, listened to the music. They took walks. In the Trocadéro gardens they sat on secluded benches. But, quite soon, she was afraid of scandal, "which fails to take the measure of love and soils it." She thought of her children. Briand was possessed by a love so strong that he had a tendency to act imprudently, though more than anyone he ought to have been on his guard.

In *The Men I Have Loved*, Briand was the seventh and was called her "great love." Her physical attraction for Reverdin seemed debasing, but soon she hurried, heavily veiled, to clandestine meetings with this man, who was twenty years younger than Briand. She had no regrets since there was no emotional involvement.

By the spring of 1914, she had still not given herself to the man who was bringing her "the happiness of being loved." She found excuses: "You have been living for eight years under your ex-mistress's roof. I cannot put up with that and be yours at the same time. But I don't tell you to leave her. It is up to you to do that by yourself. I will be yours the day after."

This letter went unanswered; Briand was too experienced to act on it. He knew that it was best to let time slacken the ties that had to be broken. Much in love as he was with his intelligent, fanciful princess, he was not going to break up his agreeable equivalent of a home. Cerny did not hinder Briand's freedom. She had her career, her son, and the boy's father, a rich wine merchant, who kept them.

These were the last months of peace. Briand, though no longer part of the government, all the same was a man absorbed in political events. He was, however, willing to devote all his free time to Marie. They met in the country. They were lovers as chaste as adolescents of the period were said to be. They took walks in the woods around Paris. Marie was enchanted by these secret trysts with a man who adored her and whom she admired, a man who was her equal.

Unfortunately, they had to separate at the beginning of June 1914. Marie had to pay a family visit to Liebenstein, "this ugly village in Germany," from which she wrote to Briand that she was "sad and so cold besides, so cold. And it's not the logs in the fireplace that will warm my heart!" It was unusual for her to mention the cold. The previous winter, ice had been drifting on the Seine and she had enjoyed walking along the river with him, with no thought of complaining. This letter, which took three days to reach him, disturbed Briand. He wrote every day. His sensitivity and his experience allowed him to see that this separation was coming too soon. Marie was far from being sure of her feelings toward him. In *Le Bonheur d'être aimée*, she noted this dialogue dated from Liebenstein: *"The two friends:* V. asks me: Do you love him? don't you love him?—I wish I could say!—Have you been his, ever?—No.—Why not?—I want to wait. And if I should stop loving him, I'd regret my surrender. . . . I love thinking too much to be able to love as he would like me to: exclusively." Remote from the spell that he exercised over her, she reflected: "A great veil has just been rent. It's time to be frank with myself. I've deceived myself enough: I was bored, [Briand] came into my life bringing me his great love. It was a fine toy for my idle imagination, and so that the game would be more beautiful, I tried to believe that his great love was also my great love. . . ." And farther along on the same page: "I have to admit it, it's all the same to me to go on living away from him for long weeks, I can live without him, I can conceive of my life, tranquillity, happiness without him. . . . The veil is rent, here is my discovery: I don't love him any more; I never really loved him, with my heart."

But to the interested party himself, she did not betray her thoughts. She needed him to go on loving her, and far from discouraging him, she ends a letter written to him to announce her departure for Weimar and her imminent return with "I love you." In a previous letter, she had foreseen that in order to return to Paris as he wished her to, she would have to promise her husband to go north in early summer.

"Despairing" in her absence, Briand made Sunday pilgrimages to the places where they had been together. In his letters, he speaks only of her, of themselves, without sharing his fears for the peace of the world, or the political affairs that had become still more complicated since the last elections, after which he had kept his seat in the Chamber of Deputies but had not been given a portfolio in the new government. In the middle of June, he was invited through the intermediary of the Prince of Monaco to the imperial regattas in Kiel, where he would have the opportunity to talk to Kaiser Wilhelm. He consulted Poincaré, the president of the Republic, and refused. Franco-German incidents continued in Morocco. The situation between the Allies and the Central Powers was tense everywhere.

On Marie's return, Briand took care not to frighten her. He had other things to tell her in the little time they could spend together during the few days that she was to remain in Paris. He was moreover in poor physical shape and hoped to go to Cocherel to rest for a few weeks. It was during this stay that he bought, for 8,000 francs, the small farm called Les Hulottes, a country retreat where Berthe Cerny joined him.

Berthe had no illusions. Aware of her lover's new passion, she is said to have declared: "Men! you teach them how to comb their hair and to hold a fork, and then they deceive you with royal highnesses!"

The royal highness, even after the assassination, on June 28, of the Archduke Franz Ferdinand, the designated successor of the Emperor Franz Josef, did not seem to realize the gravity of the situation. She left, as planned, for Bernstorff, arriving there on July 2, 1914.

Briand again wrote his daily letter, speaking to her of his love, his solitude. Eight months had gone by since he had responded to her fascination. He evoked his memories of her—always the same ones, since there were not many to choose from! Later Marie Bonaparte noted: "He wrote on very large paper. I could not hide [his letters] in a time of political suspicion; I burned them. I kept ten and burned a hundred that were a hundred times the same thing."[4] In her correspondence, of which she kept copies, Marie was more reserved than he. She limited herself to reporting uneventful days in the northern castle.

But on July 27, while at sea on the royal yacht *Daneborg*, Marie, George and Waldemar heard on the radio the news of the mobilization in Russia. Thinking of what was to come, Marie wept.

The following days brought the declaration of war between Austria and Serbia. It was the beginning of World War I. By August 3, France was at war. Germany first invaded Belgium, then northern France. From August through October Marie remained isolated in neutral Denmark, writing Briand of her patriotic fury at the enemy and her frustration: "If I were in Paris, it seems to me I'd be able to do something." Briand, now minister of justice, preoccupied with the conduct of the war and French reverses, still wrote Marie only of his love for her. During October the princess was making unrealistic plans for returning to France. Soon she persuaded George to accompany her and the children through Germany and Switzerland since Greece was neutral. (But it took some arranging to get the Germans to allow Croisy, who was English, and the French chambermaid to accompany them.)

On November 11, Marie telegraphed Briand that her departure was definitely set for the following Monday, and that she would be living at Saint-Cloud. Finally, on November 14, "Arrived safely, please telephone Passy 91 77," her father's house on avenue d'Iéna.

Prince Roland was in Bordeaux, making maps for the army, and Briand was there with the government. The two men had become friends and Briand had kept Marie informed about her father, whom he called "*le paternel*" in his letters, just as she did. Briand rushed to Marie and persuaded her to remain in Saint-Cloud under his protection, promising her a military car should the Germans march on Paris. In a week she and the children took up residence in Saint-Cloud and George returned to his beloved Denmark.

Her position in France was entirely different from that in Greece during the Balkan wars. She was no longer French. She could donate and collect money, which she did, but she could not act in any direct way. This war, which had already caused so many deaths, was agonizing to her. She had soon lost her initial optimism. Paris had already been strongly affected by the war. The pace of life had slackened, the uproar of the city diminished. She noticed the sadness on the faces of the passersby, the lassitude of men in uniform, among them large numbers of wounded.

Briand, like the city, had changed. France's threatened position weighed on him. He spent his days at meetings that he was unwilling to discuss with a woman, even with the one he loved. She was the other side of his life, the dream side, luxury. She was meant to give him solace and restore his strength for the battle without sharing the details of the struggle. It is impossible to imagine her in this role, but this was his view, though he was surrounded only by superior women, superior by talent, mind or birth. The poet, Countess Anna de Noailles, the writer, Princess Marthe Bibesco, Princess Murat and Mme Bulteau had all been close to him. Furthermore, though she had not followed him to Bordeaux, Berthe Cerny had not disappeared from his life. But it seemed certain that Marie alone occupied his heart. In any case, she did not allow herself to be forgotten.

As soon as she returned, she seemed determined to keep his love, though she still refused to sleep with him. On November 24, she wrote to him of her regret at seeing him leave the day before for Bordeaux, and again on the 26th she voiced her sadness at the memory of his reproaches, which she found unjustified. Her tone was elegiac. On November 28, the anniversary of their meeting in Courances, Briand wrote her that she was the only woman he had *loved*. Now she wanted to believe him. Fascinated by his power, she felt now more attracted than at the beginning of their relationship and eagerly watched for newspaper accounts of him.

On December 6, Briand moved back to the small apartment on avenue Kléber, which she still had not seen. The government was returning to Paris and he had preceded it by two days. She was the reason for his haste. Without requiring anything from her, he wished to spend as much time as possible in her company. He never tired of telling her of his love. Talking of his love seemed to take the place of the act of consummation. Marie was content with this strange passion and pleased with the way he fitted in with the family. He made friends with the children. "M. Briand was so nice to us," Princess Eugénie of Greece recalls.

There were rumors that King Constantine would side with the Central Powers because of his wife, Queen Sophie, sister of Kaiser Wilhelm, while the head of the government might side with the Allies. Marie put her trust in Venizelos, but there was no point in mentioning this to her husband; he was deaf to anything concerning his old enemy and strove to convince himself and everybody that his brother Constantine was not pro-German.

Briand was willing to listen to him. He was curious by nature and Prince George's point of view corrected, in his eyes, the excessive pro-Slav bent of Delcassé, the foreign minister, whom he distrusted. George argued that what the Greeks wanted was to enter Constantinople with the Allies, and Allied protection from Bulgaria. Turkey was nominally on the side of the Central Powers, and the war in the trenches was stagnating. Briand was convinced that the decision could not come on the Western front. He pushed for a second front in support of Serbia and "to put an end to those tottering thrones, Turkey and Austria," according to his private secretary, Raymond Escholier.[5]

Briand has been blamed for the debâcle of the expedition against the Turks at Salonika. If Prince George had a role in convincing his wife's admirer to take this course of action, it was his most fateful moment in history. However, in his memoirs, Lloyd George attributes the idea for the Salonika expedition to General Gallieni.

During this period, Marie was preoccupied exclusively with her neurotic affair with Briand. They were seeing a great deal of each other. She had been visiting him on avenue Kléber since February 1915, and she had sufficient "trust" in him not to be afraid that he would force her. They lay together, and she let him embrace her in her clothes. She told him that she would give herself to him when a favorite tree bloomed in Saint-Cloud and immediately confided fresh doubts about her decision to her diary.

Briand was so involved in her neurosis that he seemed to share it, refusing in advance the "gift" of the woman he so much cherished. In one of his passionate letters he told her of his happiness. The fact that she offered herself makes her his. Their love was too vast to be bounded by four walls and the two sheets of a bed. He was as lyrical as she was and their love needed the immensity of the flowering earth and the changing infinity of the universe. At the same time he clearly made his point, reminding her of her duties toward her husband. He seemed to be afraid of her being ready to give up her marriage, pretending he would die if she did. He preferred to respect her forever. Of course this language, echoing her own mood, was only one phase of his strong passion, but Marie was exultant. This was the kind of love she had longed for. She wanted to remain in Saint-Cloud and with him forget the war; she would not leave him. On June 2, she noted: ". . . he took my hands and night fell, and the house around the closed drawing room where we both were was full of sounds, of the children already in bed who were chattering before falling asleep, of the servants turning down the beds, and of the footsteps of my husband along the corridor.

"My husband was walking along the corridor, his step echoed in my ear, his step echoed in my heart. And my beloved said to me: 'I feel remorse, a year ago I didn't. Then I didn't know your husband, he appeared to me to be somewhat simple and brutal, it seemed to me that I was avenging life, your life that he oppressed and offended, by making you love me. Now I know your husband: he is simple, he has confidence in you, and in me, he loves you in his way, he even admires you in certain respects. I feel guilty in taking advantage of the sympathy he now shows me, I feel as though I am playing a low, unworthy role toward him.'

" '—My husband is a brother to me.'

" '—A brother who is the father of your children.' "

On June 8, 1915, Marie left for Athens with George. King Constantine had been seriously ill, and it was hoped that he would now be well enough to receive them. The month-long stay was "suffocating" for Marie. The heat was oppressive and the political situation worse. On June 17 she wrote: "The Greeks believe in a German victory, and so they have no wish to emerge from their neutrality." Not only was the court pro-German, but the government as well. Marie hoped for the return of Venizelos, "who at least is more intelligent than they are." She also reported that the queen was less pro-German than "the rest." She found "her psychology rather interesting." A week later, she sent a telegram: "King better, convalescence progresses." On July 8 she wrote that their visit had made him so happy that he was asking for them morning and night. "I want to go home, go home, I'm sick of it!

"Weather more and more tropical. Only the night is bearable, it's the only time I go out, or else at seven in the evening to swim. At night I go for a drive. The stars are of all colors, the sky is so clear." She was to leave on July 14 and arrive in Paris on the 20th. George, as always in the summer, would go to Denmark.

In George's absence, Marie and Briand could not resist the happiness of spending more time together. They even went so far as to commit "imprudences," as she noted in her Journal: "Thus our great love got dragged into the streets of Paris. We have not been prudent, perhaps it was inevitable." She suffered from it more than he did, she thought. But Briand said he was jealous of her husband's rights when, on September 4, George was to return from Denmark. Ten days later, she wrote: "Our love is causing a scandal in the city, I hear about it from all sides." And the evening of the same day: "My husband has been wondering about our intimacy. He said so to a friend who repeated it to me. My husband

said to him last evening: 'What do you think of [Briand]'s intimacy with us? Why does he come to our home so often? What
pleasure does it give him?' And the friend answered: 'The pleasure
of conversing, of coming into a lively, hospitable house, since
[Briand] lives sadly alone.' But my husband remains melancholy
all evening. I look at him, and I'm afraid." She also noted that she
would only see Aristide Briand in her own home, since there she
was protected by the presence of her children and everything else
around her. The word "protect" implies that she still dreaded
Briand's love. In September, however, considering her past and
her sad solitude with George, she discovered for herself the right
to return his love.

In late October, Briand was again named prime minister, and
also kept for himself, as in his previous cabinets, the ministry of
foreign affairs. He was thus very busy. The Allied landing at
Salonika had just taken place, under the command of General Sar-
rail, and Russia had declared war on Bulgaria, which had
launched an attack on Serbia. George, more than ever before, felt
ready to play the mediator. Without further explanation, Marie
noted in her diary: "11 November. Establishment of my hospital in
Salonika"—a hospital for the soldiers of the expeditionary force. It
was her way of taking a stand and participating in the war on the
Allied side, despite Greece's continued neutrality.

Briand's new accession to power did not make it easier for them
to meet. Marie again had to go to avenue Kléber. During the night
of November 11–12, she wrote: "If I had not yielded—tomorrow
it will be eight years—to the prejudices of others, father, aunt,
friends, and relatives, by getting married, on the day I met you I
would have had a more slender and upright body, I would have
been a virgin." It was a curious fantasy, since Briand, even more
than George, was a father figure. But little by little she got used to
the idea of having a complete love affair with him. On January 16,
1916, she announced: "I have made the decision to surrender myself in your arms." On January 24, he made her take off her
clothes. Forgetting her promises, she resented this. Still he did not
penetrate her, "only held [me] naked in his naked arms. My resentment in several respects was stronger than any pity. You were
suffering to see me shiver and I liked that. Something akin to a
desire for vengeance wrenched my heart. . . . We cried, I wanted
you to cry, and I wanted to cry, and above all I wanted to leave."

Few women, even today, would be capable of such admissions. But her honesty was with herself. Her lover was never to know anything about it. Moreover, the powerful statesman had no idea that his dazzling and idealized princess wanted to see him reduced to tears or that, "above all," she wanted to leave. He was simple— as he said of George. He believed he was going to triumph, and he rejoiced—to the extent that his government duties left him time to do so. The Salonika expedition was being debated by both civilians and the military, the Battle of Verdun was about to begin.

It was probably about this time that Marie noted: "He dozed off beside me, I had almost given myself to him. I confided my distress to the Doctor [Le Bon] who told me I would have to make myself desired again."

Her "distress" at a common failing in a busy man in love betrays a selfish, narcissistic interest in this man whom she found pleasure in frustrating. But there were other grounds for Marie's anxiety that seem more reasonable: "The fuss around our names—a friend has come to say, 'Wouldn't it be more honest of you to leave your husband than to make him the butt of common scandal?' There is a lot of talk going on about our three names."

She finally yielded. On April 27, 1916, Briand spoke to her of his "unbearable" solitude and she compared his isolated life on avenue Kléber or in Cocherel with her "peopled solitude," her own source of unhappiness. They experienced the customary difficulties of lovers separated by society, and, like others, suffered from it. But their shared joys were intensified by being secret and forbidden. To contemplate apple trees in bloom brought them a happiness enhanced by the fact that they could so rarely be together in an apple orchard.

George was jealous, and on May 15, "he makes a scene: 'You don't always have to go with him, as though he were God knows what.' Several times already in my presence he has belittled your looks, your behavior, your mind's fantasy. It's not that he's jealous of my flesh, of my heart. Love of woman is alien to him. Abnormal and chaste, he goes through life deprived of both the instinct of life and that of beauty." Soon he left on a trip. His jealousy was forgotten, but she found it increasingly difficult to bear this divided existence. "My house, jail of my life! Houses enclose within their prison walls the antagonistic souls of masters, servants, wives, husbands. And one must pretend to be attached to houses."

On June 12, she was ill and stayed in bed. "13 June. It seems to be rumored that people have met me with my husband, my children, and my lover."

"1 July—George is back. He exclaims that France is vile because it is humiliating his country. A painful dizziness makes my eyes flutter. For France is my country and yours. . . . Outside, I die."

Marie went to Compiègne, where her friend Geneviève was serving with the Women's Emergency Canteens for Soldiers, and where Jean Troisier, her husband, was mobilized as a doctor. Once, she forgot her bag in the bachelor quarters where she was now meeting Briand. She was frantic because the concierge, who cleaned the place for them, would thus come to know her name, which public rumor was already coupling with that of her lover.

On September 25, she noted that Venizelos had set up the government of northern Greece in Salonika, and on December 1, that some French sailors were killed in Athens. These sailors had been sent to obtain by force war supplies promised by King Constantine two months earlier. Following this battle, which had been provoked by discharged Greek reservists, the French fleet bombarded Athens. After this "felonious attack," Briand proposed to the Allied governments the deposition of the king and the recognition of Venizelos. Suarez pointed out in a note[6] that "in French political circles and the press, Briand, by deposing Constantine, was suspected of trying to promote the accession to the throne of Prince George of Greece." The possible, if improbable, queen notes in her diary: "December 11, 1916, Constantine, George's brother, rises up against France. It is a crime for you to love me, and, says the crowd, a piece of bravado for me to remain near you." She felt the hostility of others. "There are not ten people who would dare to come to see me at Saint-Cloud," she noted next day. And on December 14, 1916, "You have not felt, you will probably never feel, what I have seen, the great defect of your mind, the hapless illusionism that makes one believe, in the worst moments, that what one hopes for or desires, is happening or will happen.

"Thus, over there, in the East, out of generous pity for a small butchered nation, you have, despite all my objections, launched a French army, though I foresaw that we would not have enough cannons to arm it nor men to reinforce it.

"Thus you have left at their posts the generals, the admirals, the diplomats, those subordinates of yours who were incapable—I could see it at a glance. But you acted timidly because of too much tact and of your hope—humoring your indolence—that time always takes care of everything.

"You did not touch these men until it was too late, when, after the misfortunes created by our heedlessness, the grumbling of the crowd forced you to.

"If I, your beloved, tried to bring down your illusion, you were ready to declare that I was acting like an enemy, disturbing your charmed placidity, your calm.

"And believing that each day of happiness is a day gained, you awaited, in your dream, the moment you did not anticipate, when Reality, whose face I watched approaching, would come and seize you by the collar.

"You did not understand the reason for my objections!

"My life is ruled by the horror of being a dupe. I would not have wanted you to be duped."

In the evening she wrote again: "My mind is equal to yours, it is even better sometimes, owing to its realism."

"20 December. The crowd would like 'that female evil genie to be expelled.' George did not understand the crowd's hostility and wanted to stay. It is said he is complaisant out of political treason, in order to make your passion for his wife useful to his distant country, against yours.

"It is said that you are my blind prey and I am said to be baleful for my native country."

All "those distorted images," as she called them, she was aware of and they made her suffer. Next day, December 21: "My name belonging to an enemy country coupled to yours besmirches your name as head of state, which should be shining. . . . And the unjust crowd is right when it accuses me of your mistakes."

Briand did not suspect her capacity for criticism. "Your misfortune is to speak too well. . . . Lover, poet and farmer, that should have been your life, so as to live—the only happiness—in accordance with your deepest inner rhythm."

Relations between the lovers became uneasy. She noted that they could no longer go out freely together and that they were reproaching each other. In January: "My name hurts me, theirs (that of my children), when I see it dragged through the streets of Paris."

On February 25, she left for Nice, with George and the children, since Mimau had moved there. During her stay at the Hôtel Ruhl, she addressed several love letters to the Presidency of the Council,

Quai d'Orsay; on Monday morning one of them reports that she was getting ready to spend the whole afternoon with Mimau, who was "weak, pale, wasting away . . . the doctor says that Mimau will not live another winter."

She returned to Paris and renewed the torments. On March 14, Briand resigned. Momentous events outside France led to his fall. On March 10, the revolution began in Moscow, and on the 15th Nicholas II abdicated. On March 25, Marie intercepted an anonymous letter addressed to her husband, but might there not have been others? Would they have to see less of each other now that the good weather was coming and they would have more time?

Her love affair was not her only cause for concern. She still wanted to realize her potentialities as best she could, and her children were part of this self-realization. The fact that their father insisted on giving them strict religious instruction upset her. "12 April, first confession by my children. A black-robed priest came and the children trembled and wept with fear. An idea of their father's, since tomorrow they take communion. And I, the mother, I am banished. George was watching on the staircase so that I wasn't able to approach."

Between 1916 and 1919, she wrote some sixty pages entitled *Le Livre de l'enfant et des bêtes* (The Book of the Child and the Animals), "to the memory of my son as a child." These tales evoke the events of everyday life and illusions of innocence. But all of them have a melancholic undercurrent. Death and cruelty are frequent themes and so is love, particularly her love for her son.

In May, the family went to spend the day in Cocherel. After lunch, George took a nap and the children played in the garden. She went off with Briand and suddenly was seized with anxiety: the children might drown, "and I cannot stay seated beside my love. I ran back to them. Then I was sorry, with the same pang as a moment ago, to have left him." This was symptomatic of her obsessional neurosis.

On June 12, 1917, King Constantine had to leave Greece and surrender the throne to his second son, Alexander. Next day, George expressed his rage against France, in front of Briand and Marie. She felt that she would have to go with him if he left the country. It was obviously France and the Allies that had supported Venizelos, allowing him to return to Athens and take over the government. Briand understood George's anger. All he wanted was not to be separated from Marie. He hoped to calm her by assuring her that wherever she went he was ready to follow her. But she had no illusions, and in the Journal he was never to read she wrote: "The love I have for you . . . is rather that of a child in need of a confidant, a support, it is the love of a child-woman."

The emotional outburst over, George left France alone, as had become his habit. Before going back to Waldemar, he spent three days in Sankt Moritz, Switzerland, where his brother had taken refuge. He was to go there again on his return. "Pity is my supreme chain, stronger than my love," wrote Marie as she watched him leave. In many ways, Prince George became a tragic figure during these years. The war was destructive to monarchy in general and to his family in particular. His brother had lost his throne and the Bolsheviks had forced his cousin "Nicky" from the throne (they were later to condemn to death Nicholas and his family, including George's brothers-in-law the Grand Dukes Paul and George of Russia); closer to home, his wife, Marie, had eyes only for a leftist politician of the new order.

This summer of 1917, Marie and Briand still spent much time together, and they seem to have achieved a certain form of intimacy more real than the lyrical effusions that had stretched over so many months. Ary, as she called him, introduced her to his friend, air force Commandant Jules de Lareinty-Tholozan, who invited her to visit his château, Pont-Piétin. Within a year she had decided to buy the historic Lareinty castle of Blain, living at Pont-Piétin until the old castle was sufficiently restored. For Aristide Briand it was a childhood dream come true. The castle and the land he loved, as a boy, with an obscure feeling of belonging, was now owned, thanks to him, by his beloved princess.

In September George returned. He spent his days in his study. "In the morning, he reads the Bible and the newspaper, then all day long he smokes and scribbles his indignation at the injustice of the world, in which dishonesty triumphs and ability combined with honesty, as in himself, are left in the shadows. . . . After dinner, he lights all the chandeliers, and tells us of his resentment and if I yawn he gets angry." On the 24th: "The grapes in the arbor have finished ripening in the sun. George pinches my leg in front of A.B., while I am up on a ladder in the garden, but for five or six years he has been relieved of his conjugal burden."

Life assumed a regular pace among the three of them, made tolerable by the good breeding of the married couple, the love and kindness of the lover. Marie, however, suffered from "the frightful void of Sunday evenings. Once again you left too early. . . ." In her solitude, she played the piano. Schumann, "who spoke to [her] heart."

Events in Greece brought all kinds of repercussions that they had to face. Thus Lembessis, the aide-de-camp, was not allowed to re-enter France with George because he had made some idle remarks expressing hope for the defeat of the Allies out of sympathy for his deposed and humiliated king. Briand did his utmost to have him readmitted, as George desired.

It was only then that Marie learned of the rumors circulating in Paris at the time of Constantine's deposition the previous year. "It seems that I could have become queen and some people thought that I was tempted by it," she wrote in November 1917. "Crowns should be left to the poor, the poor in heart and mind. . . . I am more queen of the world, by my outlook and thought, than by all the crowns, external to myself, that I could have worn." George took little interest in his title to the throne. Marie had always known him disillusioned. Only her father would have been perfectly satisfied, and it might have consoled him for the huge loss he suffered with the collapse of the Russian loan. Marie remarked that it cost him half his fortune.

In the early days of 1918 the political scene became greatly agitated. Though the high command had finally been entrusted to one man only, General Foch, all kinds of rivalries persisted. There were also many peace feelers. Prime Minister Clemenceau was an old opponent whom Briand observed unsparingly but usually from a distance. On March 10, 1918, Marie wrote: "Enemy airplanes bombed Paris yesterday and A.B. announced that he was leaving for the country to hire a tenant farmer. Will he really leave when last year he criticized my husband who, knowing that Paris was being bombarded, did not return from abroad? You sacrifice me for your farm and the stables full of warm, solemn cows and the chickens pecking in the yard."

She went with the children to see Mimau in Nice. Briand wrote to her from Cocherel. He was living far from the parliamentary world. In Paris there was cannon fire by day and bombs at night. Despite his wish to see her again, he advised her to stay away because of the children. The Germans were again at Noyon, where they had been repulsed a year before. They were making a desperate effort to break through the British lines, threaten Paris, and dictate peace. But Briand didn't think they would succeed. They failed at Verdun and now the Allied artillery was more powerful.

Despite Briand's advice, Marie came back. She was lonely and sad. Her visit to Mimau she felt to have been her last. Briand did not see her. In May she wrote in her Journal: "Last year, would you have let three months go by, the months of spring, without giving me a single evening?"

She resented being abandoned once more without explanation. It was during this period that she wrote *The Men I Have Loved*. At the end of the section on Briand, she notes that she has discovered an anomaly: she missed his letters more than his love. She was with the children in Pont-Piétin. Briand visited her only once that summer and the return to Paris that fall was delayed because of the Spanish flu epidemic there. As she pondered on Briand's love, she remarks that it was his glory to have "redeemed me; to have lifted me above the slope down which I was sliding." She also noted that she was suffering. "But you could not understand, and not being able to speak to you of it, I am dedicating to you this book in which I reveal myself, though you will never read it." "This book" is undoubtedly *Le Bonheur d'être aimée*, which she began, as we have seen, shortly after they met.

War was going on, still very bloody and close. At last, on All Saints Day, a letter arrived expressing Briand's hopes. Peace had been made with Turkey; the Dardanelles and Constantinople were opened. Kaiser Wilhelm II's dream had turned to the Allies' advantage.

On November 10, the field was silvered with hoarfrost and the canal bordered with ice. The retaking of Sedan had had an immense repercussion in Paris. Marie was making a little progress in Virgil, but above all she was reading the newspapers. On November 11, she was awakened by the three cannon shots for the Armistice and all the bells. "In the evening the children, allowed to stay up, sang the *Marseillaise* and *Sambre et Meuse* with me all evening, with the household staff lined up around us and singing in chorus. I want to see you again and also see Paris on the day that French troops enter Strasbourg."

On November 15, she arrived back in Paris by train. On the same day, he wrote her a letter addressed to Pont-Piétin. It is among the most moving he sent her. She seems to have apologized to him for having harmed his career. In reply, he calls her simply "my friend," for the first time. He begs her to expel all thoughts of harmfulness from her mind—quite the reverse: she had been his precious, invaluable comfort in the most stressful of times. He recalls to her his indifference to easy popularity and official honors. His country knew him and had shown its appreciation in many forms.

Among the daily entries in her calendar, Marie notes: "I did not want to be awakened from my four-year-long dream"—a comment which could apply only to this letter. After this, she hardly wrote at all. No notes in her diary, no entries in her Journal. She was leading the life that others expected of her. Still, on December 2, 1918, she signed a contract with the publishing house of Flammarion for a work entitled *La grande guerre: Méditations*, to appear in the collection *Bibliothèque de Philosophie scientifique*, edited by Dr. Gustave Le Bon. This was something unheard of at the time in her family milieu.

On December 30, the first warbler was singing at Saint-Cloud, the sort of event that she never failed to note.

At the beginning of 1919, the Allies met in Paris to prepare the peace treaty. Sir Harold Nicolson has written: "We were journeying to Paris, not merely to liquidate the war, but to found a new order in Europe. We were preparing not peace only but Eternal Peace. There was about us the halo of some divine mission. . . ."[7] Briand, being out of the government, did not participate in the proceedings of the Conference.

On April 23, Mimau died in Nice. On that day, Marie wrote: "I realize that he no longer loves me in the same way. There is no longer the ardor that he promised me even for the day when my hair would be white."

On April 28, the League of Nations pact, Wilson's idea, became a reality. Marie noted it in capital letters in her diary, thinking of the importance attached to it by Briand. On May 6, Mimau's funeral was held at Versailles; she had wished to be buried in the same cemetery as Prince and Princess Pierre Bonaparte and Marie's mother. Two days later, Marie, who had been much affected by the loss of Mimau, wrote her lover: "You are there with me to witness the rebirth of the cherry and apple blossoms, the flight of the bees and the warbler. . . . Those who are dead in the tomb, I no longer wish to mourn them or pity them . . . I do not have the right . . . to avert my eyes and mind from the great duty of breathing Love with the sun." A few days later she adds, more down to earth: "You come to see me as one keeping a nice old habit."

On May 18, she went to see him in Cocherel; they sat at the edge of the woods, under the laburnums on the hillside, but she was to go back to Paris alone; he was staying in the country to rest. She wept. "Next day I spent the whole day in his arms and all was forgotten."

And then, on the next page: *"Epilogue:* I've learned that for the past year he has loved another woman. *End."* Marie might have made a scene, but she was mature enough to handle the situation with style. So the lovers whose passion had been greatest before consummation became friends again without either confrontation or recrimination. They were both experienced enough now to let time take care of the inevitable.

On the date of the signing of the Treaty of Versailles, June 28, 1919, Marie noted: "I must increase the servants' wages." Life went on, Marie took the children to Verdun to show them the scene of the terrible battles. On their way to Blain they stopped at Bonnétable to visit the duchess of Doudeauville. That summer she wrote Briand of her progress in correcting the proofs of her book, *Guerres militaires et guerres sociales.* Briand advised her to listen to Le Bon's suggestions but not to let him encroach too much on the boldness of her conceptions and the flight of her imagination— a quality in which the doctor was notably deficient. It was possible, he told her, to ally originality with philosophy. A touch of fantasy and art would not be amiss in a book published in the red bindings of Le Bon's collection. He had not read her manuscript but his confidence in her powers was justified. This first book of hers is anything but trite and reflects the individuality of its author's mind.

That fall Paris was shaken by strikes and Marie was attending political gatherings with her friends, the Troisiers. She was reading Trotsky, Lenin and, as she wrote Briand, "also a little Bolshevik catechism sold by the Socialist Party in which your name is mentioned as one of the Fathers of the New Church." Then came the account of the meeting to which she had gone the day before with the Troisiers, as planned. "This evening, I go to the 'pure' Leninists." On November 13, she wrote him a jesting letter. "Yesterday Hedwige [Princess of Bourbon-Parme, "cousin Lise" 's daughter] got married. The wedding was superb and scarcely suitable for the new times! Much velvet and pearls. No one would have recognized in myself someone who attends political meetings."

Her venture into political life was for the purpose of gathering information for her book. She did her best to become absorbed in her work and not to complain, but the fervent love of the man who had been her companion for over five years was sorely lacking. Now it was Briand's turn to write of the cold, of frost, of his extinguished stove, etc. Years later, she described this letter, received December 1, 1919, in which he "expressed himself to me symbolically, probably without himself fully understanding what he was writing, since shortly thereafter he was to desert me," to Freud, according to her Journal of Analysis. "His ardor found me too frigid, from every standpoint—'And he wasn't wrong!' " Freud answered. Briand was not a man to be easily forgotten. She missed his quickness, his intelligence, his conversation and his wit. But she had changed, during the Briand years, to her advantage. She was no longer the woman he had met at their first luncheon at Courances. He had given her enough reassurance so that she knew herself as desirable in other men's eyes. Yet she still wanted to depend only on herself.

Music did not mean as much to Briand as to her. She decided to make up for what she had missed because of him and also to begin a new book, very different from the first, which had just appeared, to be entitled *Printemps sur mon jardin* (Spring in My Garden).

During the summer, Marie divided her time between the château in Blain, which she always liked though it was uncomfortable—one had to climb ninety-one steps to reach it—and the Hôtel du Rivage in Pornic, where the children and Croisy stayed at the seashore. Briand went sailing with friends and stopped in Pornic, visiting and taking her to Beg-Meil.

Except for this meeting in Brittany, she was hardly to see him that year. George asked no questions about the absence of their familiar guest. Events in Greece demanded his full attention. His nephew, the young King Alexander, died in October from a monkey's bite. The Greeks were tired of the war, represented in their eyes by Venizelos, and which had resumed after the signing of the Treaty of Sèvres against the Turkey of Mustafa Kemal. In November, the Cretan was defeated in the elections, and on December 5 a plebiscite in favor of King Constantine took place. On

December 13, George left for Athens to rejoin his brother. Marie did not accompany him.

It was at this time that she had her portrait painted by Laszlo. It shows her in the fullness of her beauty, with the melancholy, gentle expression of earlier years. With Briand's love withdrawn, her main preoccupation, solitude, reasserted itself. *Solitudes* was the title she chose for a work she planned to write.

In January 1921, Briand again combined in his person the functions of prime minister (for the seventh time) and minister of foreign affairs. The following month, he went to London to participate in the conference called to settle the border question between Poland and Germany in Upper Silesia, and also that of war debts. He kept Marie informed about developments on the political stage, finding the Germans much more difficult to deal with than the Turks and the Greeks. He was terribly bored, and the prospect of spending another week in London terrified him. On March 5, he wrote again, telling Marie that he was not coming back empty-handed, and described a luncheon party with only him, the king and queen, to whom he had talked a lot about her and "the giant" (his sobriquet for George). She no longer kept copies of her letters to him. We have only Briand's letters to throw light on their changed relations. He wrote readily of government matters, but occasionally there is a more personal note. In a letter she received in Beig-Meil in September, he wrote that he would like to be with her and spend a night at sea fishing for sardines.

In November he described New York to her as a gigantic jumble of disparate buildings, miniature versions of French castles cheek by jowl with high-rise department stores, all this curious rather than beautiful.

Marie was trying to divert her interests into other channels. With her brother-in-law Christopher she attended the trial of Landru, the lady killer who incinerated his victims in his cooking stove and from whom Chaplin was to draw his inspiration for his film *Monsieur Verdoux*. With her friends, the Troisiers, she attended performances of Gluck's *Orpheus*, Stravinsky's *Sacre du Printemps*, Ravel's *Shéhérazade*, and Handel's *Messiah*. She read voraciously as always. She read Zola on the beach at Beg-Meil, and it was there that she wrote *Dialogue avec la mer*, which remained unpublished. She redecorated the house in Saint-Cloud and "expelled" the pictures that crowded George's walls.

In Greece, meanwhile, Constantine's return had not led to peace with Turkey as the Greek people had hoped. The war continued in Asia on Turkish soil, leading to the Sakarya defeat of the Greeks, in August 1922. The Allies had not supported Constantine, and England and France continued their economic blockade of Greece. Officers of the Venizelos faction blamed the king for the military defeat and forced Constantine to abdicate in favor of his eldest son, who succeeded him on September 26 under the name of George II. The Venizelos party resumed power, while the war ended with the relinquishment of Asia Minor and the burning of Smyrna, occupied by the Turks on October 11. Constantine and the royal family went into exile.

In a house close to her own in Saint-Cloud, which she owned, Marie gave hospitality to Prince Andrew—sentenced to death in Greece—along with Princess Alice and their five children, the youngest of whom, Philip, was then one year old and was later to become the Duke of Edinburgh.

Briand's seventh government had lasted only until December 1921. He wrote to Marie again while she was visiting the Troisiers in February 1922, at the La Moutte estate she had dreamed about as an adolescent.

Since the break with Briand, Marie had sought the friendship and company of the Troisiers, both of whom were freer in mind and manners than the people of her own world. Geneviève was her age, and her three children, Annette, Solange and Olivier, called Marie godmother, though only the eldest was actually her goddaughter. Marie was very fond of them but they were too young to be playmates for Peter and Eugénie. In spite of this Marie decided to spend July 1922 with the children, in Saint-Gervais in the French Alps, because the Trosiers had a chalet in the vicinity. Briand was still writing to her, complaining that he slept badly, that he was exhausted and was going to Cocherel for a rest.

In August, Peter and Eugénie went to Beg-Meil with Croisy, while their mother remained in Saint-Cloud. Several letters between Marie and Croisy reflect their cordial relationship and Marie's efficiency. She addresses Croisy as "darling," she discusses the rooms to be repainted, the curtains to be changed. No mention of Prince George, who had left for Denmark at the beginning of July, the same day Marie had left for Saint-Gervais.

Ever since spring, Marie's diary records otherwise unexplained excursions to the outskirts of Paris. And then, on December 22, 1922, a new notebook begins, entitled X *Mémoires**: "One evening, leaving my father alone in his suffering [Prince Roland had had a prostate operation on August 28], I ran away at the call of what remained of my youth, for a whole day with X." They reached the woods of Chaville by train, and there they made love. "The woods are bare. It is cold. No one else around! Only the far echo of a jay. On the carpet of damp dead leaves . . . Then we walked toward the reddening horizon to the spot where the valley begins, with the pond at the bottom and the first lights of the village. We had tea at an inn. Our eyes kissed (he has flecks of gold in his eyes)."

Thus secretly, but far more simply than with Briand, the second "great passion" began. The affair with "the older brother" whom she loved "the most and the longest."

---

* In her diaries Marie called X. by his name, his first initial, or nickname, and makes no attempt to disguise him. Although he has been dead for many years, his children apparently still do not know of his relationship with Marie. For this reason he is referred to as "X."

THE END OF A LIFE

"Alas, I cannot keep my eyes fixed on only one face, one pain, one feeling. . . . The immobility of eyes and heart is forbidden to those who survive."

MARIE BONAPARTE,
Monologues devant la vie et la mort, pp. 62–63

"Our mourning and our grief are often based on remorse."

MARIE BONAPARTE,
The Life and Works of Edgar Allan Poe, p. 52

WHEN ASKED TO CHARACTERIZE MARIE BONAPARTE IN A SIN-gle word, Anna Freud replied without hesitation: "Straight-forwardness." However, for many years, because of her love affair with X., Marie Bonaparte's private life unfolded not only in secrecy but also in falsehood.

She had known X. for a long time. He was married to one of her few women friends. He had no difficulty persuading her that his wife would suffer a breakdown if she knew of their affair. Having spent her childhood in a closely knit family, she was not prepared to accept a solution that to her would mean the ultimate failure in her life. Divorce, at the time and in their circumstances, was un-thinkable, if only because of the children, for whom Marie felt much tenderness and who considered her a sort of fairy godmother.

Handsome, elegant, and a renowned physician, X. had not been a scrupulously loyal husband, but his wife was unaware of this. His was the classical behavior of the distinguished seducer. When it was already too late, since he had taken the trouble to please, he advised Marie: "Leave me!" When he felt like talking about his private life, he admitted having "tormented" his mistresses and "made them unhappy." Marie, however, believed him when he assured her that he loved her more than any woman before her, and she in turn hoped that he would not torment her.

He had, of course, been aware of her affair with Briand, and knew that no one had replaced the brilliant statesman. After the break, he had maneuvered to draw Marie closer into the circle of his family, and little by little he persuaded her that they had much in common. Like her, he was a musician and an accomplished piano player. Furthermore, his profession impressed Marie. She still had dreams of studying medicine. Certainly she was more interested than his wife in what he was doing. She wanted him to succeed in an already distinguished career. She asked him all sorts of medical questions, which he answered gladly and in detail.

Thanks to him, Marie came to learn a great deal. After Briand's rejection, she again doubted her physical charm. X.'s unexpected appreciation meant so much to her that Marie, for a time, lost her common sense. Her great-great-uncle Napoleon, no feminist as everyone knows, is said to have stated that "the intelligence of women is measured by the size of their follies." It is certain that, from Marie's point of view, it was "folly" to become attached to X., even though, thanks to him, she experienced the elation and the anguish of a woman deeply in love.

Blinded by passion, she did not draw the parallel with the secretiveness of her love for Leandri. There was no more embarrassment toward X.'s wife, her friend, than she had felt toward Angèle Leandri, of whom she had been equally fond. Suffering and jealousy came later, when X. felt the need to inform her of the frequency of his marital intercourse, adding that he did not find it repulsive, since he found in his wife a response that Marie only rarely succeeded in giving him. It is certain, however, that despite his mistress's frigidity, which was openly discussed between them, X. was caught up in his own game and that he loved Marie. At the same time, in details the quantity of which shows their importance, he could not relinquish his role as a capricious tyrant: he kept her waiting for hours for trysts at which he finally did not appear, or he stated that he never gave flowers and immediately afterwards sent her a primrose, for which Marie thanked him with disproportionate joy. Despite their mutual behavior, childish in many respects, he was surely impressed with her intelligence and fascinated by this woman who opposed him with arguments superior to his own. Nor was he insensitive to the fact that she was a princess.

Their affair began at a time when Marie, much disturbed by Prince Roland's illness, gave in without reflection to her lover. No one, not even X., who knew, had yet informed her of the exact nature of the disease, but she realized that her father, who had been strong enough to go "rambling in the high mountains" each summer in the Swiss Alps, was rapidly declining.

Instead of recovering after the first operation, the patient only worsened, and there was now talk of a second surgical intervention. Marie was frightened, and yet her secret intimacy with X. gave her new strength in the presence of the sick man. She no longer felt dependent as she had before. It was now she who provided protection, made the decisions. She went back to live on avenue d'Iéna, but having caught measles from her daughter, she was isolated from her sick father and from X. for several weeks.

She came out of her seclusion just after her father's second operation. It was then, in April 1923, that the doctors finally told her the truth. Afflicted with cancer of the prostate, Prince Roland was to fight for a year against the disease.

In a short volume entitled *Monologues devant la vie et la mort* (Monologues in the Face of Life and Death), published in 1951, Marie expressed her love for her father, and her pleasure of possession: "Because of his illness, he will remain mine for a long time, forever, unable to go away, to escape, to make me cry, as when I was a little child and he was going out to dinner or leaving on a trip. . . ."[1]

In order to protect them both, she soon re-created in the sickroom a sheltered world where, despite the dangers, they felt at ease. During the day, Prince Roland lay on a chaise longue. The herbaria were arranged around him, and every day the prince spent hours examining fern specimens. He is credited with describing over 50,000 specimens and he was using what little strength he had left to keep up the illusion of working. She talked to him about the coming year and kept saying that they would search together for additional ferns. Sometimes, when the weather was fine, she took him outside to walk a few steps leaning on her arm. At last she could express her tenderness to him. She enjoyed their new intimacy and their daily life together. Now it was she who ordered the meals, and they had lunch and dinner by themselves.

During the long hours spent at Prince Roland's bedside she often tried to imagine the reality of his death, but was unable to accept the idea. It seemed to her that as long as she was present in this room, nothing dire could happen.

In this barred situation X. soon became a great help to her. As a physician, he measured her grief and her distress. He knew professionally how to soothe, advise, console. During the long months of her father's agony, X.'s arms were an immense comfort to Marie. They became more and more attached to each other. He was closer to her than any man had ever been—"her lover and her brother." George was unfitted for either role.

The news from Greece was bad. Her brother-in-law Constantine, former king of the Hellenes, died in exile in Palermo. George II, who had succeeded his father on the shaky throne, was in trouble. He was finally exiled and Admiral Koundouriotes became regent. In July 1923, by the Treaty of Lausanne, Greece, which had signed an armistice with Turkey the previous fall, gave up Asia Minor altogether, while the Dodecanese Islands went to Italy and northern Epirus to Albania.

For Marie, the Greek chapter had long been closed. She had her own ideas about the royal family's handling of their affairs, but she kept them to herself.

As she wrote in her introduction to the *Five Copy-Books*,[2] it was at her father's bedside that she read at Le Bon's urging Sigmund Freud's *Introductory Lectures on Psycho-Analysis* in Jankelevich's French translation that had just appeared, and began to rethink the problems of her life.

Her friendship with Gustave Le Bon had cooled. The author of *La Psychologie des foules* was aging and Marie had gradually outgrown him intellectually. X. and Dr. Talamon, her family physician for many years, were more subtle in their tastes and judgments. It was with them that she now could exchange ideas. Later she was to tell Freud: "Le Bon and Briand are now dead for me. I withdrew from them like a snail, which goes back into its shell after having expanded."[3]

Aristide Briand had almost vanished from her life. During 1923, he came to Saint-Cloud for lunch only once. What she saw was a disappointed, troubled man. The postwar period was not going well. He had been unable to impose his views on the need for an Anglo-French *entente*, the only way, he thought, to preserve future peace. By now Marie had moved completely away from him and his concerns, and felt herself incapable of listening. Whenever she was away from her father, she was in anguish.

At that time, a new name, Dr. René Laforgue, makes its first appearance in her diary.

A young Alsatian practitioner who had studied medicine in Berlin, Paris and Strasbourg, Laforgue had discovered psychoanalysis and Freud in 1913 through *The Interpretation of Dreams*, and had defended his thesis in 1922 on *L'Affectivité des schizophrènes du point de vue psychanalytique*. He first practiced as a psychiatrist at the asylum in Hoerdt (in his native Alsace), and then in 1923 returned to Paris, where Professor Claude named him assistant and psychoanalytic consultant at the psychiatric clinic of Sainte-Anne. This was the first official Freudian influence of its kind in France, and in October 1923 Laforgue began corresponding with Freud.[4] He was a man of practical enthusiasm. As an Alsatian he was bilingual and hence a natural link between the French and Freud. Laforgue had been analyzed by Mme Sokolnicka, a disciple of Freud's who had been analyzed by Jung, Freud and Ferenczi, but could not practice at the psychiatric hospital of Sainte-Anne since she had no medical degree.

Marie Bonaparte was not aware of these difficulties. Her interest was in psychoanalysis, not in the rare practitioners of analysis in France. She had no wish to meet Mme Sokolnicka, who, though rejected by psychiatric circles, had been adopted by literary ones. Gide, in *The Counterfeiters*, was soon to describe her in the guise of Mme Sophroniska. Her career and her past, which showed her to be a woman of intelligent tenacity, ought to have attracted Marie, but she was not in search of new friends. She was trying to save herself. Her first reading of Freud had left her with the intuitive knowledge that in psychoanalysis she would find the profession she had been seeking and that would allow her to accomplish something of her own.

Marie continued to write. In 1924, she published *Le Printemps sur mon jardin*, but that year she could not enjoy either springtime or garden. The book, dedicated to her children, is as strange as the tales that she never got into print. Based mainly on impressions of nature related to Saint-Cloud, it also contains four stories which have suffering and death as unrelieved themes. It was marked by the familiar despair; death still seemed to her the only refuge.

Her main preoccupation was to overcome her frigidity, if necessary by surgical means. She had heard of the work of Professor Halban of Vienna, "biologist as well as surgeon," and soon she became his enthusiastic propagandist. Under the pseudonym A. E. Narjani, she published, in the journal *Bruxelles médical* of April 1924, an article entitled *Considerations on the Anatomical Causes of Frigidity in Women*.

"There are three attitudes toward the problem of female frigidity," she writes. "Men are not really interested; ardent women despise frigid women; frigid women console themselves for their misery by attributing their affliction to the whole feminine sex." She goes on to describe a type of frigidity due to psychic inhibition, subject to cure by psychotherapy. Finally she describes a type of frigidity which she attributes to too great a distance between the clitoris and the opening of the vagina. Her description of such women speaks for itself: "At the beginning of their sexual life they often blame this deficiency on the partner, accusing him of being too hasty and not knowing how. But these women may change lovers time and again, they may even meet one with whom the act lasts for an hour, to no avail. They end up by understanding that the deficiency is in themselves, and they console themselves with the idea that all women are alike and that shared pleasure between lovers exists only in novels. They do not reject men and are glad to give pleasure, contenting themselves with the lover's caresses before and after. But when they happen to love an egotist, who has no thought for the woman, their situation becomes dramatic. They are reduced either to chronic deception, which leads to nervous disorders, or to masturbation which is always psychically unsatisfactory, or to the search for a more attentive new lover."

She championed Halban's operation, which consisted in moving the clitoris closer to the urethral passage. "Narjani" claimed that five women had been operated on, with positive results. Later, her personal experiences led her to admit that the operation was not always successful. Since then, the work of Masters and Johnson has proved "the false basis of surgery for frigidity."[5] Marie Bonaparte never repudiated the pages signed Narjani, and included them in the bibliography of her works that she herself prepared.

In addition to the concerns that her immediate family caused Marie, there were regal weddings and funerals in the four corners of Europe, which she had to attend. These functions, as she complained, interfered with her keeping up with her main interests, which were seldom political. Nowhere in her notes does she mention the occupation of the Ruhr or Hitler's putsch in Munich, nor even the rise to power in France of the left coalition, which provoked social upheavals of which she could hardly have been unaware. The proclamation of the first Greek Republic she noted only as a point to be remembered for her future autobiography.

When it came to France, she remained an ardent republican, believing this to be the best form of government for her native country. "I am by no means a Bonapartist."[6]

The period was one of intellectual turmoil and growth. Berlin, Paris and the United States were well into the "Roaring Twenties." Though it was a thriving time for all the arts, for Marie it was again a period of introspection and retreat behind her father's walls. She seldom left the house on avenue d'Iéna. An evening at the theater to see Jules Romains's *Knock ou le triomphe de la médecine*, the theatrical event of the Paris season, was memorable for her only because she had gone in the company of X., and even more so because it coincided with the rapid deterioration of Prince Roland's condition.

Her father's approaching death aroused in her all kinds of contradictory feelings. She protected herself as best she could, filling the hours with trifling occupations: "My diaries resemble the Journal of Louis XVI (on July 14, 1789): visit to doctors, to couturiers, ordering furniture, plants for the garden, etc.," she wrote.

Prince Roland died on April 14. His funeral, held two days later, was everything he might have wished. There was a maximum of pomp, a good number of royal highnesses and ambassadors, and many eulogies in the name of the Académie des Sciences, the Société de Géographie, the Fédération Aéronautique, the Aéro Club, the Club Alpin, and the Société d'Anthropologie. In addition to Roland's own many publications, the scientific world took note of his financial support for the marine laboratories at Banyuls-sur-Mer, and Roscoff, the physiological research station at Parc des Princes in Paris, the observatory on Mont-Blanc, and the measurement of the meridian line at the equator. Summing up, Jules Louis Breton paid the prince this tribute: "Thanks to his liberal generosity, the Bonaparte Fund was set up in 1908; its purpose is to aid discoveries by supporting the research of scientists who have already proven their worth in original work but lack sufficient means to undertake and follow through their investigations."[7]

The prince was buried at Versailles, in the family chapel. Though Marie was proud of the tributes to her father, she was now more than ever preparing to deserve such recognition for herself and determined to surpass her father's fame.

She came back from the funeral with a high fever. Her illness

Princess Marie-Félix Bonaparte, née Blanc

Prince Roland Bonaparte

Marie Bonaparte, age seven.
PHOTO ROLAND BONAPARTE

Princess Pierre Bonaparte

Christian de Villeneuve

Jeanne de Villeneuve

Marie Bonaparte with her family of dolls.

PHOTO ROLAND BONAPARTE

Marie Bonaparte, dressed for her first reception, at seventeen

Marie Bonaparte, age sixteen

Marie Bonaparte at the Villa Giramonte, Nice-Cimiez

Marie Bonaparte, age twenty-three

Above: *Princess Pierre Bonaparte with her Villeneuve grandchildren and Marie*

Right: *Prince George of Greece with his uncle Prince Waldemar of Denmark*

Left: *Princess Pierre Bonaparte, Prince Roland and Marie in the "grand salon," Avenue d'Iéna, Paris*

Marie Bonaparte with her fiancé, Prince George of Greece

Prince and Princess George of Greece at their wedding, Athens, December 12, 1907

was attributed to the ordeal of the day, but it was in fact an attack of salpingitis. She was to be in poor physical condition for months. Nevertheless she had to keep active. An estate as sizable as Prince Roland's was fraught with problems. Despite his wartime losses, her father's fortune still amounted to sixty million francs. There was the big house, where she had no desire to live, which would have to be emptied and sold. There was also the huge library, a great quantity of furniture and objects—Marie, who detested the Empire style, was now submerged in it—manuscripts, herbaria and papers to sort out and dispose of. To dismantle a house filled with too many memories was a very painful experience.

Fortunately spring was not over. Marie moved back to Saint-Cloud and X. once more visited her there. They resumed their habit of making love in the garden under the stars, after the children were asleep and George and the servants had retired for the night. She was happy but apprehensive that some day their love would end, that X.'s wife would find out, that she would become old and ugly.

In July, the children left for Beg-Meil and George for Denmark. She stayed on in Saint-Cloud and wrote what was to become *Les glauques Aventures de Flyda des mers*, published only in 1950. Despite the clumsiness of the narrative, one is gripped by the depth of Marie's despair. The symbols are transparent. Marie is the protagonist, an astonishing character for a forty-two-year-old woman. Every aspect of the heroine's life corresponded to some aspect of Marie's, as she saw it. Submission to the father, the trunkful of dresses of gold and silver cloth to attract the suitor whom the father wanted, the marriage-prison, the call of love, the desertion by the beloved, the degradation of sex without love, with multiple partners. But she escaped from "the void of cold lust," and shared the happiness of a family whose servant she became. Apart from the children, however, whose fleeting attention shifted constantly, a passionate heart was "desperately alone and essentially alien."[8] Yet when a man appears ready to love her, and she is willing to follow him, she is again abandoned when he discovers the "errant love"[9] of her past, and this at the very moment when she envisages a shared life of harmonious bliss. Flyda in desperation drowns herself with a stone around her neck.

It was a summer in which she slid back into her periodical depressions, though she did everything to conceal them from others. X. remained the means by which she kept her troubles in check.

In August, she went to Brittany, and X. managed to join her briefly. They spent a night together, a whole night, stolen from their married lives; Marie was so elated that while he slept beside her, she stayed awake to savor his presence and their happiness.

The children remained in Brittany while Marie returned to Paris. Eugénie wrote her mother of her studies of Chinese, under the direction of Soulié de Morant, a distinguished sinologist. Marie, in spite of her inner turmoil, kept aware of intellectual quality and never hesitated to approach people of distinction. On that score she was a realist, using without qualms her social position, which opened all doors to her. Several times she noted that she had been well received because she was rich.

Since childhood she had known that one can be a prisoner of one's wealth. She also claimed to hate philanthropy: "It is a condescending paternalism to relieve the conscience of the rich."[10]

In her relations with her children Marie Bonaparte forcefully tried to impart her values to them. She found it natural to send her nephews and nieces, the children of Princess Alice and Prince Andrew, to private schools providing the kind of education they would have received as royal princes and princesses had they not been in exile; she sent her own children to public schools. She approved of the quality of teaching in the state-supported *lycées* and wanted her children to come in contact with other social classes.

"No one in the family thought of questioning my mother about it, and nobody except my parents knew what a *lycée* was," her daughter Princess Eugénie said later.

Indeed, there was already a discrepancy between the life Marie meant to live and in which she wished her children to participate, and her role as a royal highness. The conflict was to be heightened in the future, but Marie tried to avoid an atmosphere of confrontation. She always showed much good will, understanding and respectful benevolence to those who, being different from herself, could not imagine her interests and true tastes. Knowing that in most cases it would be futile, she made no effort to explain herself. Her life was split in two, and she managed to make each part look coherent to those who were involved in it.

Only her husband might have realized this fully, but his nature as well as his upbringing kept him from becoming drawn into Marie's intellectual life and achievements. His world was limited to traveling and hunting, to sports that he shared with his uncle

Waldemar, and to the family. Having insisted that his children receive religious instruction in accordance with his faith, he left the rest of their education to their mother. He was a rather benevolent paternal figure, especially to his son, but without any great strength. From their early years, the children had become used to seeing him most of the time with his uncle Waldemar, whom they called "Papa Two." Later, when they were at an age of more advanced understanding, their mother told them about X. While they were proud of being privy to her life in its dual aspect, they were also jealous of the rivals for her affection and concern. They resented being excluded from their grandfather's illness and death, and from their mother's mourning. Marie preferred not to involve them in her past. Croisy, their governess, was a staunch ally on this matter. As the years went by, she proved her devotion and intelligence, but she had none of the imagination and intellectual stimulus that Marie sought to introduce into her children's way of life. Croisy was conventional and tried surreptitiously but firmly to impose her point of view on Peter and Eugénie, who were only confused by two sets of values. Their belated rebellion against Croisy was harsh; it even made them reproach their mother for exposing them to her influence.

Marie took her task as an educator very seriously, though it did not come easy to her. She loved her son and daughter passionately, but she lacked patience, and she felt always "essentially apart." She was intent, tense, too present or too absent, always a little off center. Even before she became absorbed in her profession, her children did not get all the attention that they would have needed.

Soon Marie was seeing Dr. Laforgue often and regularly. She was not having an analysis, but they had what she called "chats" (*causeries*) that were of great importance to her. When one or the other was away from Paris, letters went back and forth.

On February 21, 1925, Laforgue came to dinner for the first time. Marie had invited him with Otto Rank, and dinner was served at her bedside.

Rank was ten years older than Laforgue. Born in Vienna, he was introduced to Freud at the early age of twenty-two. Freud quickly took him up. Six years later, Rank, along with Hanns Sachs, became cofounder of *Imago*, a journal for applied psychoanalysis. He was also the leading editor of the *Zeitschrift*, the major publication for psychoanalytic literature. His book *The Trauma of*

Birth, published in 1923, had created tensions with Freud. A year later, Rank went to the United States, and afterward traveled often between New York, Vienna and Paris, where he was to settle temporarily in 1926. It was the year in which he resigned from the Vienna Society, shortly after Freud's seventieth birthday. In Paris, he had made friends with Henry Miller and Anaïs Nin. At a time when he was still a transient visitor, a dinner at the house of Princess George of Greece was for him a diversion not to be missed.

Marie Bonaparte was receiving the two psychoanalysts in bed because she had undergone a series of operations. First an ovarian cyst had been removed. After having been confined to her bed for three months, she summoned Gilliès, a plastic surgeon from London whom she had met through King George V the previous summer during a visit to the British capital. Gilliès came to Paris to "correct" her breasts, which he did on December 31, 1924, and next he retouched, for the third time, the scar at the base of her nose. She herself was perfectly aware that all these operations were a sign of her shaken psychological state, and she asked Dr. Laforgue to write to Freud. He did so on April 9, 1925:

"I do not know if Rank has told you that we spent an evening at the house of Princess George of Greece. The lady in question suffers from a rather pronounced obsessional neurosis, which, though it has not impaired her intelligence, has nevertheless somewhat disturbed the general equilibrium of her psyche. Rank already has various ideas about her case.

"This lady intends to go to see you in Vienna, and she asks me to inquire if you could possibly undertake a psychoanalytic treatment of her."[11]

Freud answered, on April 14:

"Dr. Rank has told me nothing that could give me any idea about Princess George. I am quite ready to receive this lady if she wants to come to Vienna before July 1, and I will also be able to take her in analysis if you can guarantee the seriousness of her intentions and her personal worth. In any event, the analysis could not begin before October 1, because I am busy until then. Another condition would be that the princess speak either German or English. I have not trusted my French for a long time. In other respects, this analysand must accept the same conditions as any other patient."[12]

Meanwhile Marie had succeeded in getting herself out of bed

and had gone to Salies-de-Béarn for a cure, from where she wrote to Dr. Laforgue: ". . . Life seems to me dreadfully crowded. I do not feel up to facing it, and the furniture in the rooms and the fences between the fields are very heavy to move. I am tired, tired. . . . I pity the whole world and would let myself be devoured by it. I wish I could be just a little barbarous. But I am only so inside: it doesn't come out."[13]

The man she considered as the principal exponent of psychoanalysis in France had now become her confidant. Later she mentioned to Freud how good Laforgue had been to her during this period. He introduced her to Strindberg's works. She also started reading the works of Freud that had not yet been translated.

On April 27, 1925, still in Salies-de-Béarn, she writes: "I'm afraid that the walls around my soul, in spite of you, in spite of Freud whom I hope to see in the fall, will crumble only very late! Joshua of the walls of Jericho is often only the Horseman with the hollow eye sockets! While waiting for that liberating evening, let us live as we can and envy the boatmen on their barges! Would you try to become a boatman? You would get bored very soon. Though I am worried, I am not bored here—I am susceptible to suffering but not to boredom."

In her letters she also mentions *Vaga*, the novel on which she had been working since the fall with great regularity and application, and whose heroine, Vaga, once again resembles her, a fact she is fully aware of.

On May 1, Laforgue again wrote of her to Freud:

"About the patient, I consider her a very sensible and conscientious person. At the moment she is taking a cure in the South of France for persistent pains in the lower abdomen, whose psychological origin we have already pinpointed. The analysand firmly believes—as do the doctors—that in the fall she will be able to risk the stay in Vienna. She will be back here in a week and will then make final decisions. Of course, she will have to accept the general conditions. This is not where the resistances are, they lie entirely in the intellectual realm, where the patient, because of the superiority of her mind, tries to challenge everyone's superiority.[14]

"It is essentially for *didactic reasons** that this lady would like to go to see you. She has, in my opinion, a marked virility complex, and also many difficulties in her life, so that analysis would be

---

* Underlined in text.

indicated anyway. I have been charged to ask you if you could take her in analysis for between six weeks and two months, as often as possible *twice a day*.* I did not want to give any precise answer before asking you. I have, however, made the lady understand that she should submit strictly to your conditions, on which by the way she agrees. Nevertheless, the question of time also brings some difficulties on the family side. But it is not excluded that, if necessary, the analysis, after a brief interruption, could be resumed for another two months."[15]

To which Freud, doubtless uneasy that she wished to learn rather than be cured, and that seemingly only on her own terms, replied on June 16, 1925:

"With the princess, it looks as if nothing can be done. Since I take only very few cases, an analysis of six to eight weeks, forcing me to give up another one and extending over a season, cannot tempt me.

"For the same reason, it is impossible for me to devote two hours a day to one case, something I have accepted to do only on very rare occasions. Besides, given the limited number of my working hours, I do not think I have the right to squander anything on an analysis without a serious goal (either didactic or therapeutic)."[16]

The earliest analysts had themselves had no analysis or only a few weeks of casual contact with Freud. The second generation of analysts now being trained had at least several months of analysis. On June 27, Marie finally wrote directly to Freud, to let him know what it was she wanted. She wrote a first draft in French, then prepared her text in German. Freud replied on July 1 from Villa Schüler, on the Semmering, that he was expecting her in Vienna on the afternoon of September 30. "Formal, typewritten letter," she notes in her "black notebook," the record of her correspondence with Freud.

Though no letter has been found among Marie Bonaparte's correspondence with Laforgue informing him of her direct approach to Freud and of Freud's answer, Laforgue must have known of it, since as early as July 25 he writes to Freud: "The princess is very grateful to you for agreeing to take her in analysis."[17]

That summer Marie remained alone in Saint-Cloud, where she had returned in May from her cure in Salies-de-Béarn to observe

---

* Underlined in text.

that there were no more nightingales in her garden. She was busy emptying the house on avenue d'Iéna, "moving the past from the basement," she writes to Laforgue, and a few days later: "The moving in which I live every afternoon is a frightening thing. I move dust and the past in armfuls. The other day I found the bills for my baby linen, my first vaccination, my mother's funeral. I've been able to make some macabre observations." (This, undoubtedly, refers to Roland and Princess Pierre's preoccupation, to the exclusion of all else, with money.)

As a distraction, she took driving lessons with Auguste, one of the chauffeurs of her household. They went preferably to the Bois, and Auguste, when interviewed, said that she was not a very good driver. "She'd forget to hold the wheel, she'd start talking and not keep her eyes on the road." The children were in Guéthary in the Pays Basque. Peter had passed his baccalauréat in June. He and his sister were alone because Croisy had rushed to England to be with her sick brother.

George came back fairly early from Denmark, to join the children with Marie. He stopped in Saint-Cloud, and Marie notes that they had dinner with X. Later Marie and X. went into the garden. "A warm fog made the black air heavy. The half-moon was veiled by fog. He wept," because she was leaving him for a long time. She had announced to him that after this stay with the children and George, she would leave for Vienna.

"He loved me then," she writes again, "despite his divided commitment. . . . I promised to come back if he called me, but I had to see [Freud]. The call of the mind, the urge to find the father again, were too strong. And he had hurt me too much. . . . I wept too, because I had loved him more than any other lover. I loved him despite his partial love, his lies, and despite the fact that his mind was not the equal of mine, and despite his aridity and inadequacies. I loved him because like him I felt there was nothing like the enchantment of the nights, the expectation of the sunrise, the perfume of the leaves and grass, because before him nothing had been poetic to the same degree."

In the notebook devoted to X. she entitled this passage *"L'Appel du père"*—the call of the father.

George too was opposed to her departure. He could not understand what she was going to do in Vienna. Ordinarily he did not question her travels. She came, she went; he was used to it. But this time he wondered if she was not going through a mystical crisis.[18] Why was she already saying that she would probably be gone for a long time? The children needed her, as did the whole house. He knew that it was useless to complain, but this time he could not help himself.

Husband and lover did not know exactly what they were afraid of, but they both felt threatened, abandoned. They were right, and Marie was aware of it. But for her this departure was essential. The closed door against which she had been beating her fists as far back as she could remember, was going to be opened. Her real life was going to begin.

A brief sentence, in a letter to Dr. Laforgue dated September 30, 1925, from the Hotel Bristol in Vienna, represented the beginning of Marie's real life: "This afternoon I saw Freud."

· 7 ·

THERE IS NO SUCH THING
AS CHANCE

*"Ghosts fade in the light of day. But one must
first have the courage to summon them in broad
daylight."*

MARIE BONAPARTE,
Psychanalyse et anthropologie, p. 107

MARIE HAD LEARNED FROM LAFORGUE THAT FREUD HAD
been operated on in the spring of 1923 for a malignant
tumor on the right side of his palate and jaw. The operation was the first of thirty-three. She also knew that Freud was
married, the father of six children, and a grandfather. Preparations
had already begun among his followers for the celebration of his
seventieth birthday, in 1926. He was revered, but the years of
solitude had been long. A few friendships with male colleagues had
given him support and hope, but by and large they had ended in
distress. The most emotional tie had been with Wilhelm Fliess, the
alter ego who had made sexuality the center of their interest. The
lacerating rupture dragged on for years, until there was nothing
left between them but bitterness and resentment. Adler, Jung and
Rank were at first disciples. When, later on, one after another
preached dissent, Freud broke with them. He was also torn by the
rivalries among his followers. Still, as Anna Freud told Ernest
Jones, the British disciple and author of the major Freud biography,
the quality that best characterized her father was simplicity.[1]

Fame had not changed him. Freud still needed the approval of
those around him. Essentially he remained the man who in 1902
had created the "Psychological Wednesday Society," which met at
his office and home on Berggasse 19, a small group of colleagues
and friends ready to participate in his experience and apply his
methods. In 1908, this society, which had grown and set up a
library, became the Vienna Psychoanalytic Society. In that year,
the first International Congress of Psycho-Analysis had met in
Salzburg and in 1910 the International Association was founded.

New societies were formed. The American Psychoanalytic Association goes back to 1911. Two years earlier, Freud had made his famous trip to Clark University in Worcester, Massachusetts. The invitation had been the proof of his growing reputation. By 1914, Freud's fame had spread to Russia. There were psychoanalytic societies in Moscow, Petrograd, Odessa and Kiev.

In France, with its entrenched hierarchy and strongly established tradition, psychoanalysis had not been able to find a place in psychiatric training. The French milieu was a fortress not easily breached, and efforts to penetrate it had so far been in vain. Freud attributed this failure to "the perpetual reference to the Latin genius, which [owed it to itself] to clarify psychoanalysis."[2] There were less honorable reasons: xenophobia was not unusual at the time, nor was anti-Semitism. The psychiatric milieu—the medical milieu in general—was conservative; it displayed considerable coolness toward this new, foreign and, moreover, Jewish "science."

When Marie Bonaparte first saw Freud, there was still no psychoanalytic society in Paris, and Laforgue, who was trying to promote one, had declared his candidacy for the Vienna Psychoanalytic Society, where it was unanimously accepted at the end of the year (1925).[3] In intellectual circles, the group behind the *Nouvelle Revue Française* had been introduced to psychoanalysis by André Gide, who had been analyzed by Mme Sokolnicka. As early as 1922, Jules Romains had published in the *Revue* a general presentation of psychoanalysis and its therapeutic importance, though not without voicing his skepticism toward some ideas of its founder. André Breton and the Surrealists had laid claim to Freud, who in 1924 had also been visited by the exiled Romain Rolland, accompanied by Stefan Zweig.

Freud was by now so famous that Hollywood asked him to cooperate in writing scripts based on world-famous love stories, starting with Antony and Cleopatra. He also received proposals (an "incalculable number of dollars," his daughter Mathilde later told Marie Bonaparte)[4] from Hearst and the *Chicago Tribune* to follow the trial of Leopold and Loeb and give diagnoses of them. In the following year, the Danish literary critic Georg Brandes made the trip to Vienna to see him, and Freud met the Indian philosopher-poet Rabindranath Tagore. Philosophers and psychiatrists, as well as writers and poets, were interested in his work. Now he only received those who had come from far away. The suffering caused by his prosthesis—which was changed often, always in the hope of improving it—increasingly prevented him from conversing with visitors.

Marie had already shown signs of her interest in psychoanalysis before her trip to Vienna. In a letter to Freud of November 1925, Laforgue wrote: "Loewenstein will be able to come here from Berlin. He owes his entrance permit to the intercession of the princess."[5] He had no conception that Marie's activities would one day go beyond this kind of help. At the time, Marie's support was not negligible, however; the French group, in order to develop, urgently needed qualified people from the outside.

Rudolph Loewenstein, a physician born in Poland in 1898, had studied in Zurich and Berlin. He was among the first formally trained analysts and had been an assistant at the Berlin Policlinic. Loewenstein's invitation to settle in Paris to teach and train psychoanalysts was urged on Laforgue by the International Association. Marie knew that Freud was aware of the help she had been able to provide.

"I was very depressed last evening on my arrival, at the end of that superb but endless corridor of the Vorarlberg and Tyrol, which separates one from the rest of the world," Marie wrote to Laforgue in her first letter from Vienna. With her chambermaid Solange, she had taken up residence at the Hotel Bristol, on Kärntnerring. She did not yet know how long she would stay in this huge building, which like all the others in the city had witnessed past glories. She found her suite "gloomy," but the hotel had the advantage of being near the Opera.

Vienna, once the heart of a far-flung empire encompassing forty nations, was now the capital of a small republic, but its citizens had kept their taste for grandeur and knew how to recognize true class. Her Royal Highness, Princess Marie of Greece and Denmark, could not pass unnoticed. She was an immediate success.

Unlike many visitors who have left us detailed descriptions of the place made familiar by so many photographs, the first time she climbed the few stone steps at Berggasse 19 leading to the Herr Professor's consulting room, she paid no attention to the house. "But the impression he made on me surpasses everything I expected. First his great kindness, combined with so much power. One feels him in 'sympathy' with all humanity, which he has been able to understand and of which one is only an imperceptible fragment."[6]

Still, she wasted no time, and the schedule of the weeks to come was established on the first visit. "He will see me every day at eleven. He told me that I myself will judge when the analysis should end." And he was willing to grant her a few days of absence if she needed them. She thought that he did not look to be in poor health. He looked only "a little tired."

Mutual trust was immediate between them. They felt at ease with each other, as if their relationship had been of long standing, something neither of them had foreseen. Very soon, Freud spoke to her of his cancer and added: "I am seventy. I was in good health, but there are a few little things that don't work any more. . . . That is why I warn you: You mustn't attach yourself too much to me." In response, Marie started to cry and told him she loved him. "To hear that when you're seventy!" he exclaimed, rather pleased. Another time he observed: "Look, I've known you for only three weeks and I'm telling you more than to other people after two years. . . . I must also add that *I am not a connoisseur of human beings.*"

" 'No, that's not possible,' I said, forgetting Jung, Adler, Rank, etc.

"Fr. 'No, I'm not an expert. I offer my trust and later I'm disappointed. You may disappoint me too . . .'

"I extended my hand behind the cushions and he took it.

"M. 'My dear friend,' I dared to say, with tears in my eyes. 'No, I will not disappoint you.'

"Fr. 'I think that with you I am not mistaken.' "[7]

To discover a princess who corresponded to a youthful dream touched Freud. He had given the nickname "princess" to the woman who had become Frau Sigmund Freud. "Princess," for Marie, was a familiar appellation. Everyone called her that, with more affection than deference, since she was accustomed to treat everyone with equal warmth. Freud had not imagined that H.R.H. Princess George of Greece would behave with the naturalness that he liked so much. But "Prinzessin" was a word he rather relished saying, and he continued to use this form of address, even after she had asked him to call her Marie or Mimi.

Shortly after the start of the analysis he granted her request for two hours of his time a day. A few months after their first meeting he told her, "just between us," that at the period of her arrival he had given up all expectations from life. His daughter Sophie had died of Spanish flu four years earlier, and his grandson Heinerle, Sophie's son, whom he adored, had also died, on June 19, 1923, of tubercular meningitis, three months after Freud's first cancer operation. The death of this little boy was the greatest sorrow of his life and after this trial all joy seemed impossible to him. He was old. His beloved daughter Anna was not getting married. Marie had brought him the unexpected: a renewal of interest and hope. He expected something from her. Thanks to her, he was thinking once more of propagating his teaching, of developing it in France.[8] He had found a new disciple, on whose unwavering devotion he could count. Marie had finally found the ideal father, the one surpassing her hopes. "What a marvelous, unique being, such as the world has not seen in a long time and will not see again! . . . The quality of his character equals that of his thought, and daily contact with such a mind is the greatest event in my life."[9]

Enthusiasm is contagious, and Marie's compliments, though not the most discreet, sounded sincere. They were accompanied by all sorts of questions to which Freud was not accustomed: Had he read Einstein? Did he know that before meeting him she had compared him to Einstein? While Laforgue preferred to compare him to Pasteur.

"I find his comparison completely accurate, but something needs to be added: You are a combination of the two."*

"Fr. 'Do you really think so? I'm very flattered. But I can't share your opinion. Not that I'm modest, no. I have a high opinion of what I have discovered, not of myself. The great discoverers are not necessarily great minds. Who has changed the world more than Christopher Columbus? Now who was he? An adventurer.' "[10]

As was her custom, Marie took numerous notes. Freud allowed her to do so. To her writings of this period we owe some information used by Jones in his Freud biography.

Freud found her "bisexual," which, he said, must allow her to understand men, having a man in herself. The new analysand liked this idea. He also made other pronouncements that she enjoyed hearing: "Lou Andreas-Salomé is a mirror—she has neither your virility, nor your sincerity, nor your style."[11] He recognized that Marie had "no prudishness whatsoever." And he added: "Nobody understands you better than I. But in my private life I am a petit bourgeois . . . I would not like one of my sons to get a divorce or one of my daughters to have a liaison."[12] After such a confession,

---

* In German in the text.

Marie would not leave him in peace. She had shown him her breast, and she demanded intimate confidences that he denied her. "I dare to say to Freud that he must have had a supernormal sexual development. *'Davon,'* he says, *'werden Sie nichts erfahren. Vielleicht nicht so sehr!'* (Of this, you will not learn anything; perhaps not so super.)"[13]

He was more talkative about money, confiding to her that in 1918 he had lost his life savings, 150,000 crowns invested in Austrian state bonds, and the 100,000 crowns of life insurance in favor of his wife. Following the collapse of the Austro-Hungarian empire, the economic state of the country was most precarious. In her notebook recording these figures, she added in the margin: "He too little, I too much." And also: "Would he keep me [as patient] if I were ruined?"[14] She was too rich for this fact ever to be forgotten. Money was part of her, and she still had trouble admitting it. She lived a life different from that of most people, she had to acknowledge and to accept it. Freud made her aware of both her exceptional position and her need to be understood, approved by others. He compared himself to her and thought that he had over her "the great advantage of total intellectual independence." Marie listened and wrote everything down.

Laforgue had told her that the combination of her marriage to a latent homosexual and her frigidity with men meant that she herself was homosexual. She became obsessed with this idea and regretted not having pursued homosexual experience when the opportunity had presented itself with a cousin and when Pelléas's wife had attempted to seduce her.

The Viennese experience was a great adventure. She had not known such solitude since her childhood years. Except for the hours spent in Berggasse, she did not want to see anyone. She explored the city, which she found to be of "a pleasing immensity."[15] Music filled her evenings. She went to hear the *Ring*, conducted by Weingartner. "It is quite splendid."[16]

She had left Paris at an unfortunate moment. Croisy, whom she counted on to replace her, was in London, where her brother was dying. Returning after the funeral, Croisy complained about her absence as loudly as George and X. She threatened to leave. She did not get along with Prince George. Their mother's absence was bad for the children. Once again they were being sacrificed for a reason that escaped them. Eugénie was entering adolescence. She needed her mother's presence. Her relationship with her father had not improved, and she felt that he loved her little, if at all. They had in common only their anger against Marie's stay in Vienna. After more than a month of silence, Peter wrote a letter to his mother "to remind [her] of [his] existence." He showed his jealousy more clearly than his sister, but his appeals, like those of Croisy, were fruitless. Nothing would have made Marie return. She even decided against returning when called to the bedside of her uncle Christian, partially paralyzed by a stroke and asking to see her.[17]

"The analysis is the most 'gripping' thing I have ever done. *Ich bin*, as they say in German, *gepackt! aber vollständig*," she wrote to Laforgue in October 1925, but she gave him no details. Before the end of October, she handed over to Freud the five copybooks from her childhood, for him to decipher and reconstruct their lost meaning. Once she had come to know the nature of her unconscious conflicts, she would be freed to act, and to learn a profession that would allow her to realize her potentialities. She also hoped to be cured of her failures in love. She had come to her teacher in search of "the penis and orgastic normality."[18]

She had started to talk about her marriage. Over the years she had built up a strong hostility toward George. Freud pointed out that George in no way threatened her intellectual development. He spoke up often during the sessions, interpreting the material she supplied. Marie resisted only one of Freud's interpretations: in the third week he told her, following her report of a dream, that she had witnessed adults in the act of intercourse as a young child. She objected violently, but Freud assured her that several of her associations were confirmatory as the analysis proceeded.

"The princess is doing a very fine analysis, and she is, I think, quite pleased with her stay here," Freud wrote to Laforgue. "I am glad now to have yielded to your wish, as well as to the impression produced on me by her letter, and to have accepted her. She is considering going back to Paris in mid-December, but she allows me to hope that she will return soon. An analysis interrupted after so short a time would leave nothing but a great regret."[19]

The return to Paris was difficult, as Marie had foreseen. She felt the separation deeply, as a depressing loss of something now essential to her. In a fine example of a Freudian slip, she found that she had forgotten her wedding ring at the hotel. Having left Vienna on December 17, she wrote Freud a melancholy letter as early as the 19th, and another, "hypermelancholy" one on the 21st. "Boredom is worse than anxiety." On Christmas Eve, she complained of breathing difficulties, but this letter she did not send.

She had come home to universal complaints and all of a sudden she realized the problem of establishing a real dialogue with her children. The analysis, as well as the long absence, had given her a certain detachment. Eugénie would have liked to accompany her to Vienna, and imagined she would do so when her brother was at Cambridge. But Cambridge was a dream that Peter was never to realize—of that Marie was already certain. George would not allow their son to go to England to study. It was not right to let Peter go on hoping, as they had let her believe in the past that she would take her elementary diploma. She did not want to repeat the same mistakes. But "my children are half me, half my chains." As for Eugénie, she was not so much tempted by Vienna as by the idea of escaping her father. "Everybody is bored with George." Croisy suffered because in the evening, and not only on Sunday, she was banished to the small dining room. Marie also discovered that in her absence George had not paid a single visit to Uncle Christian, which infuriated her.

When she saw X., after the longest separation since they had become lovers, she realized that she had not stopped loving him. However, her persistent frigidity made her want even more to be free of him. He was opposed to her becoming an analyst. He had written to tell her: "It would be ridiculous for you, who are not a doctor but a society woman, to get involved in psychoanalysis." The day she recopied in her notebook the passage from her lover's letter, she added: "I will acquire the analytic technique."[20] He no longer had the power to discourage her, but neither was she able to win him over on the matter. This disagreement and her lack of sexual satisfaction intensified her wish to return to Vienna. She was not yet able to modify her behavior, and so her presence in Paris was of no use to anyone around her, whatever others might think.

On January 5, 1926, she was back in Vienna. After the New Year celebrations, never a favorite time of hers, the Hotel Bristol was a haven. Marie now felt completely at home there. She was working hard. She had been given permission by Professor Wagner-Jauregg, a former schoolmate of Freud's who occupied the most prestigious chair of psychiatry at the university, to follow his rounds at the psychiatric clinic of the general hospital. And she began the translation of *Leonardo da Vinci*, a book published by Freud in 1910, which she had wanted to translate as soon as she had read it. As Ernest Jones wrote: "Leonardo was torn by two impulses: the passion for scientific knowledge and the passion for creating works of art."[21] Freud had certainly identified with his subject. The same kind of identification took hold of Marie Bonaparte. It was from affinities such as these that the friendship and trust between Marie and her teacher developed and deepened.

Marie also wanted to further herself professionally. She was eager to be invited to meetings of the Society, eager to meet those colleagues and disciples whose names had become familiar to her: Paul Federn, Max Eitingon, Wilhelm Reich, Helene Deutsch, Heinz Hartmann and his wife, Dora, the Bibrings and Ernst and Marianne Kris, two couples who shared the profession of psychoanalysis.

She met two young women who were her rivals.

Ruth Mack was an American, fifteen years younger than Marie. Elegant and cultured, she had both charm and intelligence, combined with a moral courage that Freud found attractive. Her name had been Ruth Blumbart when she first went to Vienna at the age of twenty-five. Her father, Judge Julian Mack, was a well-known Jewish philanthropist. After graduating from Radcliffe, she had studied medicine at Tufts, interned in a psychiatric hospital, and she wanted to become an analyst. In fact, her first analysis had ended during Marie's brief return to Paris. In Vienna, Ruth separated from her first husband, Blumbart, a cardiologist. Ruth Mack was deeply attached to Freud, and Marie Bonaparte's arrival seemed to her a threat. Later, as Freud had hoped, they became good friends.

Anna, the youngest of Freud's children, was thirteen years younger than Marie and her father's favorite. She had been an elementary-school teacher for five years. Later, after faithfully attending the lectures given by Freud at the university, she worked for her father, at first as his secretary. From 1918 on, without being a member of the Society, she attended its lectures. In June 1922, she gave a talk that impressed the audience; like her father, she spoke without notes. She became an analyst in 1923, just before Freud, who had been analyzing her for some time, became ill. When Marie met her, Anna was specializing in child analysis.

Anna Freud was dark, short and slender, with a youthful appearance both lively and serious, which she has kept all her life. Marie found her pretty, young and charming, but this did not prevent her from feeling jealous. This jealousy, however, was short-lived. Before Marie went back to Paris for Christmas, the two women had accepted each other. Freud had told the princess that Anna thought she would make an excellent analyst.

After her return to Vienna, the analysis again progressed rapidly, helped by the five copybooks, which were divulging their secrets. The copybooks perfectly illustrated Freud's theories, and added further confirmation of his reconstruction concerning Marie's early witnessing of the "primal scene." The protagonists could only have been her nursemaid and Pascal. Marie discovered suddenly that at a very tender age she had known the details of the male anatomy and that she had observed the sexual act performed in varying positions. The child Mimi had enjoyed her situation as *voyeuse*; when it was denied to her, this provoked a strong resentment shown by her ambivalence toward her beautiful wet-nurse. Her hatred expressed itself in Mimi's first memory at the age of four, which was obviously a screen memory in which Nounou's appearance did not correspond to reality.* From the detail of the horsey face, Freud deduced that the lover had been Pascal, the groom. The child had recorded the sexual activity simultaneously as a desirable experience and as an act of aggression against the woman. All her ensuing fantasies proved it, and she had deduced that Papa had killed Petite-Maman by doing to her what Pascal was doing to Nounou.

Mimi had repressed the memories even more forcefully than would have been the norm, because of Mimau, who had kept a stern eye on her childish sexual activities and had made her feel so guilty that Marie had not succeeded in recovering the slightest trace of them. But her stories in the copybooks contained elements of the repressed observations. Freud pointed out that her use of "mouth-pencil" must be some reference to fellatio, and that there were all sorts of other references to specifics of various sexual acts. Flon syrup and poisoning occurred in the stories and Freud postulated that she had been drugged to sleep with this opiate, which was widely available in Princess Pierre's house, when she became old enough to interfere with the lovers. This, too, he thought explained her childhood fear of being poisoned by Mimau.

---

* See chapter 2, p. 26.

While analyzing these traumatic events of her childhood, Marie became obsessed with sex and all sorts of impulses. She and Ruth had become intimate friends and sexual confidantes. Ruth gave her advice on techniques of masturbation and told Marie that she was "prouder of her masturbation than [she would be] of 10 doctoral degrees. She *thinks* [Marie's italics] she is independent from Mack and from Freud!"[22] This kind of conversation between two friends was rare and difficult to imagine in those days. Not all women were prudes, but the Judeo-Christian tradition forbade transgressing moral rules, in words at least. These two women were acting frankly, unaware of the audacity of their talks. Busy trying to achieve their total liberation and to find sexual happiness, they did not care if they acted in a very unorthodox way.

When, after five months of analysis, she went back to Paris, Marie did not rest until she had obtained from Pascal, then eighty-two years old, the confirmation of Freud's interpretations and constructions. She questioned him at length.[23] After much reticence, the old man finally confirmed Freud's deductions in great detail. He had indeed been the lover of the beautiful wet-nurse. Their affair, which began when the baby was about six months old, had lasted until Nounou's departure when Mimi was three and a half. At first, they paid the baby no mind and made love in broad daylight, then resorted to Flon syrup, etc.

"Then, like peoples glorifying in epics the humble beginnings of their history, I had used some universal symbols of mankind to celebrate my first observations and my first emotions."[24] But the symbols she had spontaneously reinvented had become so buried that she had been unable to rediscover their meaning by herself. The little girl who had written such a surprising number of stories had taken care to write them in English in order to protect herself from her grandmother and Mimau, neither of whom knew that language.

Her return home was dictated as much by the imminent founding of the Paris Psychoanalytic Society as the end of the first period of analysis. "The princess will surely become a zealous collaborator," Freud wrote to Laforgue on February 5, 1925.[25] At the first meeting of the Society on March 9, at the home of Dr. Laforgue, she was the person closest to Freud, the delegate of the founder of psychoanalysis. He was relying on her. He had told her so and the others were aware of it.

Dr. Laforgue had succeeded in gathering around himself and

Mme Sokolnicka a few friends and psychiatrists, among them Ange Hesnard, a navy doctor who had studied medicine in Angers and Bordeaux, where he was assistant to Régis, professor of psychiatry at the university. Jointly with him, he had published the first articles in French on Freudian theory, and as early as 1914, *La Psychanalyse des névroses et des psychoses,* a work written in collaboration. In 1923, Laforgue and Hesnard had founded the Evolution Psychiatrique group, with the first periodical that was open to French psychoanalysts. Nevertheless, in 1926, Hesnard had still not been analyzed. Dr. René Allendy, analyzed in 1924 by Laforgue, had published with him *La Psychanalyse et les névroses,* with a preface by Professor Henri Claude expressing his doubts about the new science. Dr. Edouard Pichon, in analysis with Mme Sokolnicka, was the son-in-law of Pierre Janet, who had spread the rumor that Freud had appropriated ideas from him, although at the time when Freud was taking Charcot's courses at the Salpêtrière, they had never met. Pichon was also a linguist and a chauvinist (his political sympathies were with the Action Française, which meant that he was a royalist and possibly an anti-Semite). Also participating in this meeting were Dr. Adrien Borel, Dr. Georges Parcheminey and Loewenstein.

Next day, Marie made her report to Freud. She gave him her impressions of those who were to become her working companions. The question of translating the terms used by Freud had been discussed at length. Pichon wanted to preserve the French analytic vocabulary from "barbarous" imports, urging the replacement of "libido" with the term *"aimance."* This translation problem worried Freud. The complete translation of his works into English had been done by a dozen people but supervised by only one, Mrs. Joan Riviere, and this had guaranteed a unified terminology. Freud wished to see Marie Bonaparte take similar charge of the French edition. He had some illusions in thinking that there would be a French translation of his complete works. It has not been done to this day.

Marie had not given up her wish to study medicine, though Dr. Talamon was trying to dissuade her. She had meanwhile established social relations with Professor Claude; when he told her that he ought to prosecute Mme Sokolnicka for practicing medicine illegally, she kept her intention to become an analyst to herself. Throughout that spring she was very busy with the establishment of the Society and the preparation of the review that her new colleagues and she hoped soon to publish.

George and X. were, of course, excluded from her new activities. George was jealous and made no effort to hide it. When his mother, Queen Olga, to whom he was very devoted, lay dying, Marie left with him for Rome on June 29. He took the opportunity solemnly to ask her to give up her activities, and to be what he had hoped she would be all along: a wife and mother.

The queen's funeral was held in Rome. It was the vacation period. The Paris group had dispersed, and Marie had planned to take her children to join Freud, who was spending the summer at the Semmering. While George went to Tuscany, where his mother was to be buried, and then, as every year, to Denmark to spend the summer with Waldemar, she returned to Paris on July 10, in order to attend the oral part of Peter's second "baccalauréat" examination, and that same evening she left for Vienna with the children and Croisy.

The children were to stay in Austria only a little over two weeks. Marie exerted herself to make their visit successful. Croisy immediately found that Professor Freud was "a dear." The Freud family intrigued them. Peter liked Martin Freud, the eldest son, and Eugénie was asking herself whether Dr. and Mme Freud got along well. Every evening was spent with the Freuds. Once they all went to see Dorothy Burlingham, an American friend of Anna Freud's who was at the Semmering with her children. But another time Freud refused to play cards with Marie: "It's too intimate." She was again in analysis. At the Semmering, Freud worked much less than in Vienna, receiving only a few privileged patients, whom he charged forty dollars a session, twice his usual fee.

During Peter's and Eugénie's brief stay, Marie tried to elucidate with her teacher certain terrors of her childhood which she could not imagine her own children to have had. The fear of ghosts from which Marie had suffered for so long revealed itself to be still active when she reread the tales of Edgar Allan Poe, in particular *Ligeia*, which had frightened her when she was Eugénie's age. She had feared the return of "that mother whom I had killed by being born, and who would come back, an Oedipal ogress, to take revenge."[26] For it was her fantasy that her birth had made her an accomplice in the murder committed by her father. The *Ser-*

quintué was to divulge its secret only on the last day of this visit. Freud again had helped her. This monster threatening to crush Mimi if she did not hide completely under the blankets when it entered her room at night, was the railroad locomotive and also the male in coitus. It had killed her mother and would also kill the "little *voyeuse*" to punish her for having caught it in the act. These revelations drove her to self-expression by way of a book. Her choice went to an analytic study of the life and works of Poe.

After putting the children and Croisy on the train back to France on July 29, she had her first consultation with Halban, the surgeon known for the operation described in the article in *Bruxelles médical* that she had signed "Narjani." Then she returned to the Semmering.

She remained in Austria while on August 1, 1926, the first conference of French-speaking analysts took place in Geneva. It had been scheduled to precede the August 2 to 7 congress of alienists and neurologists from France and French-speaking countries, to be held in Geneva, so that members of that congress could participate. Dr. René Laforgue and his wife, Paulette, Dr. Hesnard, Dr. Edouard Pichon, Dr. Gilbert Robin, Dr. Raymond de Saussure, his wife, Ariane de Saussure, and Dr. Borel were attending.

Paulette Laforgue and Ariane de Saussure were both lay analysts. Freud, at that very moment, wrote the pamphlet *The Question of Lay Analysis*, following a suit alleging quackery that had been filed against Theodor Reik, one of his disciples, by a patient. Reik was not a medical doctor, but a doctor of philosophy (in Vienna he had defended a thesis on Flaubert from an analytic point of view).[27] In the course of two evenings Freud read his article aloud to Anna and Marie,[28] both of whom were directly interested in the question of analysis by persons not medically trained. Freud, according to Jones, was even in favor of dissuading intending candidates from studying medicine.[29]

Freud was firm in his belief that *"no one should practice analysis who has not acquired the right to do so by a particular training* [Freud's italics] so whether such a person is a doctor or not seems to me immaterial." For him, a "quack" should be defined as anyone practicing analysis without this training, and he asserted: "Not only in European countries doctors form a preponderating contingent of quacks in analysis. They very frequently practise analytic treatment without having learnt it and without understanding it."[30] He thought lay analysts would be a force to prevent psycho-analysis from being "swallowed up by medicine" and thus destroyed. Furthermore, he pointed out that lay analysts working with children filled a void that neither pediatrics nor general medicine could fill. Consultations by their patients with medical doctors for purposes of diagnosis would by no means undermine the work of lay analysts.

In the autumn of that year, 1926, in New York State, a law passed allegedly at A. A. Brill's instigation declared lay analysis illegal,[31] while in England at the same time forty percent of the analysts were not medical doctors. Freud addressed a further brief reply on the issue to the Americans. He found their actions "more or less equivalent to an attempt at repression."[32]

Theodor Reik won his case because his patient was too unbalanced to testify. The question of lay analysis became one of the major subjects at the Congress of the International Association in Innsbruck the following year. Its defense was to occupy Marie for the rest of her life, though she never lost her interest in medicine. It was one of the main reasons for her attachment to X., whom she often called the Friend. She questioned him ceaselessly, kept up with his work, read medical publications, asking for his comments. She learned much, thanks to him, and she stimulated him by keeping him abreast of work and research being done elsewhere.

As Marie was leaving Vienna, she had another preoccupation: her period was a week overdue. She was tormented by the fear of pregnancy. Peter would not stand having a brother and she was also thinking of the "moral and social" scandal that would ensue. At the same time, she began dreaming of the Friend's child, a love-child. She liked the idea even better once her period had come.

Marie spent the rest of the month of August in Saint-Cloud, which allowed her freely to devote more time to the Friend, whose wife and children had left on vacation. Eugénie and Peter were in Guéthary, where she was to join them at the end of the month. She escaped for one more night with X. Where? When she came to enter it in her notebook, she had forgotten the place, but she remembered that it was near a river—the Oise or perhaps the Seine—close to Paris. They never had time to go farther.

When she finally joined her children in the Pays Basque, they made it clear to her that they had missed her and were full of reproaches. She understood and accepted their complaints, but her career and her private life came first. Again she prepared to leave for Vienna to pursue her analysis. Peter wanted to take the entrance examination for a school of applied chemistry in mid-October. Should she return for the examination? Freud persuaded her not to and she agreed. During this stay, which lasted two months, he asked her to stop writing about the analysis. He had not done so before, contrary to his general practice, since he understood the exceptional importance for her of the act of writing. The five copybooks were the proof of it, but now she must stop recording everything in writing, for this would prevent her from reaching the deeper layers of herself.

Marie returned to Paris for the official founding of the Paris Psychoanalytic Society on November 4, 1926. Laforgue was the president—it was always in his home that the meetings took place —while Mme Sokolnicka was vice-president and Loewenstein secretary-treasurer. Allendy and Pichon were in charge of drafting the by-laws. Besides them, there were four other members: Marie Bonaparte, Hesnard, Borel and Parcheminey. Only Marie and Mme Sokolnicka were not physicians, but Mme Sokolnicka was her superior in experience. Marie was totally new and professionally unproven; her training analysis was still uncompleted. The Society was soon to include some other founding members: Henri Codet and two Swiss colleagues—Charles Odier, analyzed in Berlin by Franz Alexander, and Raymond de Saussure, analyzed by Freud.

During this meeting of November 4, the foundations were laid for a review that would be published by Denoël and whose editorial committee included, for the medical works, Laforgue, Hesnard, Odier and Saussure; for the non-medical works, Marie Bonaparte; the secretary-general would be Pichon.[33]

As soon as she was back in Vienna, on November 9, she wrote to Laforgue: "I have told Freud about our meeting and it occurred to me later that before drawing up the by-laws, you should ask Eitingon to let you know of the various by-laws of the different psychoanalytic societies—it could help us.

"I already know, for example, that Freud does not like those *annual* board elections which hamper the stability of the work of the president, secretary, etc. . . . I heard this not from him but from Mme Mack. I will talk to him about it myself. Of course, there could be variations depending on the country, but it would be interesting, before making any final decisions, to compare the various by-laws."

It was not only a matter of by-laws; there was also the thorny question of the names to be put on the cover. They now had the support of Professor Claude, who represented the "Establishment." To avoid offending him, it had been decided not to put Freud's name on the cover of the review. On November 12, Marie wrote to Laforgue: "But *I* know that we are cowards, triple cowards, if we do not dare to put the name of the founder of the science we represent on the first review in France devoted to his work. It is for *us* that I say it. Claude's name must not appear, *he* has nothing to do with it. He is not a psychoanalyst, and I even wonder if he would accept if it were offered to him."

Marie also discussed the title of the review, which at first was to be called "An International Review." But there was no reason to adopt such a title, since the editing would be done by French-speaking psychoanalysts. There would be few translations. She insisted that the phrase "under the high patronage of Professor Sigm. Freud" be on the cover. She wanted the French names to be on the second page and wished to avoid Claude's name altogether. It was she who, to a great extent, financed the review. "No more than you by yourself can I go against the majority, but since I happen—as you do, by the way—to have funds, we could have a voice in the matter—the money depending on us." She also told him that Claude would not close Sainte-Anne (his hospital) to them and that it was in his interest to remain on good terms, "for his youthful glory and for the profit for his hospital that his friendship with me—to be frank about it—can bring him." Once more she was willing to pay in order to assure herself of power. She also told Laforgue that it would be difficult to dissuade certain persons from using Claude's name, because they would fear losing their positions with him. She was thinking in particular of Borel. It was certainly not an easy game for the psychiatrists. If they became analysts, they were obviously seen in a bad light. As for the lay analysts, in spite of Freud's text, translated by Marie Bonaparte, they had difficulty in getting themselves recognized and taken seriously.

The foundation of the Society and of the French review of psychoanalysis did not take up all the time that Marie spent in Paris during the fall of 1926.

Loewenstein had written her some enthusiastic letters about a talk on Leonardo da Vinci that she had given to the members of the new Society, putting more emphasis, however, on her beauty than on the substance of her talk. He had just passed his French baccalauréat examination, the first step in a series of examinations required for practicing medicine in France. Marie felt attracted by this new admirer, sixteen years her junior, and with the reputation of a Don Juan. She was to call him "the Lion," and she did not keep him on a string for long. Their first rendezvous was on November 2. It was the beginning of an affair that brought her distraction rather than satisfaction. She felt esteem for the Lion, but never got passionately involved with him. He did not have the power to make her suffer, which was her criterion of love. The Friend sensed a rival but suspected the wrong person, accusing her of deceiving him with "little Laforgue." X., though their relationship left her stinted, was still the man with whom she was deeply in love.

As a result of her analysis, Marie had decided to purchase a town house in Paris at 6 rue Adolphe Yvon, near the Porte de la Muette, for the sum of 6.5 million francs. Although George kept living quarters at Saint-Cloud, rue Adolphe Yvon was to become his principal residence. It was a move toward their further separation, allowing George and Waldemar to be in the city itself and giving Marie more freedom for her career.

George was not in the best of spirits that fall. Peter had failed the entrance examination for the study of chemistry, and was now preparing to switch to law; Eugénie exuded unhappiness. George's grumblings about Marie's analysis and its effects on the children failed to touch her, for she was sure that everything would improve once they were living in separate houses and she was completely settled in her profession.

Back in Vienna, she resumed the daily analysis. She noted that following the advice of Ruth Mack and Mark Brunswick (a cousin of Ruth's mother's whom the young woman would soon marry), Freud had raised his fee from twenty to twenty-five dollars a session, in order to maintain his income while reducing his work load. Her life in Vienna was well employed. Working in her suite at the Hotel Bristol, Marie finished the translation of Freud's text on *Laienanalyse*, lay analysis, and she also translated his text on Moses for the review. She collected articles for the review, which had not yet appeared. Soulié de Morant, "my half-Chinese friend," as she called him, sent her a "very interesting translation of an old Chinese dream book." She also thought about her book on Poe, which she hoped would be her masterpiece. She talked about this book to Freud during her analytic sessions.

Soon, for the first time, she attended an evening meeting at Freud's home. These small gatherings, held twice a month, had just begun. Ten or twelve analysts would sit in the waiting room around an oval table. Six of them were regular participants, the others were chosen from the Vienna group. The procedure was the same as at meetings of the Society: presentation of a report, a break, discussion. At the beginning of the discussion period, there was silence while waiting for the master's remarks. Freud always concluded with: "Now let me hear what you have to say!" On the evening when Marie was present, Wilhelm Reich enlarged on his theory of character analysis. The next day, Ruth made a jealous scene, reproaching Marie for not having told her about the meeting.

Two days later, on November 25, the first bad news about Eugénie's health arrived. Telegrams from Croisy and Dr. Talamon announced that Eugénie had jaundice. By December 7, she was found to be suffering from pleurisy, and Marie left immediately for Paris, where, on her arrival, Talamon warned her that her daughter probably had tuberculosis. George, likewise informed, remarked that doctors were pessimists and went on to state that he was glad it was not Peter.

Because of Eugénie's condition there were no preparations for the approaching holidays. Marie buried herself at Saint-Cloud. She had caught the flu and busied herself with some research for her first contribution to the *Revue française de psychanalyse*. She was planning an article on Mme Lefèbvre, central figure in a crime that she had followed with great interest. This upper-middle-class woman from the north of France had premeditatedly killed her pregnant daughter-in-law, shooting her in cold blood, while out for a drive with the young couple on August 26, 1925. Mme Lefèbvre was tried in October 1926 while Marie was in Vienna, and she was sentenced to death by the court in Douai. The newspapers were full of the case. Marie, by questioning Mme Lefèbvre, hoped to discover "how completely differently the universe is painted in this head than in other human heads," as Schiller, whom she quotes, had written.[34] At the prison in Lille, she had obtained permission to talk with the murderess for four hours. Freud had recommended that she confine herself to writing about herself, but here she had found a subject that inspired her, and she did not treat it like a beginner. Marie discovered that Mme Lefèbvre's thinking, intelligence and personality were normal. She had been driven to kill by an isolated delusion that her victim was persecuting her. The murderess thus suffered from a rare form of paranoia without other stigmata of psychosis. Her life would now be spent in the obscurity of prison because in France death sentences of women were always commuted. Executions, Marie observed, were socially sanctioned expressions of the wish to kill. Her second article, which came out the same year, 1927, in the *Revue*, "Du Symbolisme des trophées de tête" (Symbolism of the Head Trophy), though revealing her interest in anthropology, is less original and consists to a large extent of quotations.

She was launched on her new career at a time when her daughter was fighting a terrible battle against disease. From December 10 on, it was clear that Eugénie's pleurisy was of tubercular origin, proved by examination of the chest fluid. But she was brave and kept up her spirits. She enjoyed watching the birds pecking a coconut and liked the *Krampers* that her mother had brought her from Vienna. She was going on seventeen, the age of her mother's imaginary tuberculosis. Marie decided to take her to Pallanza, on Lago Maggiore. Since Peter looked exhausted, she took him too. On January 27, 1927, they were in Pallanza with Croisy. After making sure that the young patient was comfortable at the Hotel Metropole, Marie left for Vienna to continue her analysis for two months. Freud told her one day (February 15, 1927) that she was a realist with an admixture of *wilde Phantasie*.

It was this side of her character that led her to seek an easy answer to her sexual problems in surgery. After a week's vacation in Pallanza, she let Halban sever her external clitoris from its position and move it closer to the opening of the vagina. She always referred to the procedure by the code name "Narjani," her pseudonym. The operation, performed in the presence of Ruth Mack under local anesthesia, took only twenty-two minutes. Freud sarcastically congratulated Marie on her "heroism," adding that he would have no time to see her at the Loew clinic. She remained there until May 2 and Freud recanted and visited her.

When she returned to the Hotel Bristol, she was depressed. Her operation marked the "end of the honeymoon with analysis."

Freud scolded Marie for having had it done. From Paris, where she returned on May 7, she wrote him that she was in despair over her stupidity. She asked him, a little tardily, for advice: how to behave with Halban, who counted on her as a collaborator? On May 14, Freud, from Vienna, wrote her a "noble letter," in which he no longer spoke of her "stupidity" but of Eugénie, who would have to spend a year in a sanatorium. The young princess had had three hemoptyses, and Marie had decided to take her to the Swiss health resort, Leysin. In the same letter, Freud told her that she had long been in a position to afford herself great freedom of action, but that being an analyst called for greater restraint. He reminded her of the two goals of analysis: analysis frees the instincts, and analysis allows one to master them.

Marie was for a time completely absorbed by Eugénie's illness. She went to Leysin to arrange for her daughter's care. Eugénie's suffering, and "her hunger for love," overwhelmed her. She realized that she had hurt her daughter. "One cannot live without doing harm around one." Her young lover, Loewenstein, professed his passion, complained and suffered. She was unmoved. A correspondence began in which Freud continued in the tenor of his "noble letter" and reproached his princess, who took it badly. She noted that he was becoming annoyed with her narcissism: she had not realized how tired he was when she had kept him for five hours and fifteen minutes one evening during a visit. Each time she rebelled against this "Father," who always ended by speaking his mind to her, she came back to the idea of studying medicine and giving up psychoanalysis. "I don't want to be a nun," she wrote on June 1, back in Saint-Cloud. She spent a day with the Friend; though again he displayed his jealousy, she kept returning to him. This was part of the pattern. Loewenstein was not fooled, and told her that her feelings for him were prompted by revenge.

Their affair was not over, but Marie had other things on her mind. She had written to Laforgue on April 1, 1927: "Having to go back and forth between her [Eugénie] and my son I can't yet undertake analytic treatments. . . . How wonderful analysis is! One cannot embrace another profession after savoring this one. But when will I be able to analyze [*analyser*, in French]—I was about to write murder [*assassiner*]—living beings?" Perhaps her slip of the pen reveals her identification with the male "murderers" of her childhood, her father and Pascal. Achievement for her was the province of the male.

On June 3, she met Charles Lindbergh, whose solo flight across the North Atlantic in his *Spirit of St. Louis* had thrilled all France. Observing the young hero, Marie wondered if he was still a virgin. She remained in Paris because the first issue of the review was about to appear, on June 24, 1927, carrying the bannerline: "This review is published under the high patronage of Professor S. Freud."

Marie soon left to join Eugénie in Leysin. Her analytic upheaval was calming down. On August 15, Freud sent her back the jacket design and copy for the *Leonardo* translation to be published by Gallimard, pointing out to her that he too had begun with translations (of Charcot).

After her stay with Eugénie and three months of analysis, more fruitful than the two previous years, she returned to Paris on December 17. Echoes of a scandal had reached her in letters received in Vienna, but she had no idea of the outcry produced by *Un Souvenir d'enfance de Léonard de Vinci*.

Hitherto, in her circles, psychoanalysis and even Freud's name were most often unknown. But Leonardo's name was familiar to all, and the "revelations" of his homosexuality in Freud's text seemed an intolerable defamation. "Society people are in revolt against me, the artists against Freud," she wrote to Laforgue on December 18, 1927. One of her cousins threw the book in the fire. George complained. Nothing good could come of her career, he had been sure of that from the beginning, but now she must promise him to stop writing, to cease mixing her name, his and that of their children, with such trash. For him it was a horror and degrading. Marie was not at all impressed. Her son, at least, took the scandal calmly. He read *Leonardo* and commented that though he had not understood everything, he was far from shocked.

Marie spent Christmas in Leysin, from where she wrote Freud that only Eugénie understood her, a sentence she was often to repeat. Eugénie, still doubting her mother's interest in her, nonetheless was pleased with the new attention she was receiving. "Analysis isolates," Marie also wrote for the first time, "and so does intelligence." Her relations with the Friend were at a low ebb. He had not dared to express his reservations over the Leonardo translation, but she knew what he thought of the text. In defiance she decided to finance the expedition planned by Géza Róheim, the Hungarian anthropologist and psychoanalyst for whom a chair had been created at the University of Budapest during the Béla Kun regime. Born in 1891, he had been analyzed by Ferenczi in 1915–1916. Freud had suggested that he do field work on sexual freedom, latency, the Oedipus complex, the virility complex in women. He was to go to Somaliland, Central Australia, Melanesia (Normanby Island), and among the Yuma Indians in Arizona.

Freud congratulated Marie on the progress she had made in indifference to public opinion. In the year 1928, she did other translations, in particular Freud's *The Ego and the Id*. She took analysands; six had applied, but she kept only three. Freud supervised her by mail and Loewenstein was nearby for advice. A French writer, Alice Jahier, who was one of the princess's first patients, said that the analysis revolutionized her life and remained a powerful influence more than fifty years later.

From the beginning and throughout her career, her patients were analyzed in rather unorthodox fashion. She sent her chauffeurs and splendid cars to bring them to Saint-Cloud for their sessions. Weather permitting, she conducted the hour in the garden and herself lay on a chaise longue behind the couch. Indoors or out, she crocheted while she listened. In later years, she would take along as many patients as possible when she left Paris for Saint-Tropez and Athens, thus becoming both hostess and analyst.

Two anecdotes about Marie Bonaparte the analyst still have currency: In a discussion with Professor Claude, at Sainte-Anne, the princess tried to convince him that a young girl's phobia of touching a bar of soap in her bath was related to the girl's wish to massage her father's testicles. Claude, apoplectic, asserted that his daughters would never harbor any such thoughts, and fled the room in horror, with Marie pursuing him down the corridor, calling out to him, "But you *cannot* behave this way."

The other story has the Bois de Boulogne as setting, where Marie, as a child, had been frightened by men exhibiting themselves. As an analyst, she walked up to an exhibitionist, told him, "Put that away, I'm not interested! But please come to see me tomorrow, I would like to talk to you," and gave him her address.

It was now her habit to spend part of the summer in Saint-Cloud, and she did so again in 1928. X. was then alone in Paris for two or three weeks, and they took advantage of it. Ruth Mack, now married to Mark Brunswick, was also staying in Paris. Marie saw little of her, which earned her some reproaches from Freud, but she insisted on devoting all her time to X. She even took him along to Deauville together with Peter and an Englishman, for the Fourteenth of July celebrations. On the 22nd, she left for Leysin by car with the Friend, stopping at Auxerre to spend the night. But she was translating *The Case of Dora* with Loewenstein, who came to join her and Eugénie in Leysin. They spent much time together, both of them working.

In September, Marie left for Berlin to join Freud, who was there to have a new prosthesis made by Schroeder, "a famous oral surgeon."[35] She stayed at the Tegel sanatorium in order to be near him. Loewenstein was there too, as well as Peter, who at this time discovered a letter written by Loewenstein to his mother which left no doubt about the nature of their relationship.

Again, unforeseen events were interfering with Marie's professional plans. Eugénie was not improving, and though she accepted her illness with good grace and much consideration toward others, she remained a great concern. She was now settled in a house, La Pyrole, with a staff of servants supervised by Croisy: Jules the chauffeur, Mme Jules the cook, Sabine the chambermaid, and a kitchen maid. Eugénie was reading Dickens, Croisy Thomas Hardy. Eugénie asked for two dogs to keep her company. Her father followed her example, and the first chow-chow, Tatoun, entered the Paris household, where he was to occupy an important place.

In mid-October, Aunt Minny, the former czarina of Russia and mother of Nicholas II, died. While previously Marie would not have failed to attend a family funeral, this time she remained in Vienna to pursue her analysis. But on November 20, she fell ill with cystitis caused by coli bacilli. Dr. Max Schur, who was in analysis with Ruth Mack-Brunswick, treated her and had her readmitted to the Loew clinic. She asked Freud to analyze her at the clinic, so that no time would be wasted, offering to pay double the usual fee. Freud refused, but as soon as his own health permitted, he came to pay her a visit. On this occasion Freud met Schur, who became his doctor and remained so until the end. Her illness forced Marie to spend New Year's in Vienna, while Eugénie remained alone with Croisy.

It was then that Marie obtained, without overly insisting, the impressions of the wife of her revered master: "Mme Freud told me how much her husband's work had surprised and shocked her, in that it treated sexuality so freely. It was almost *on purpose* that she did not take cognizance of it."

" '*Meine Frau ist sehr bürgerlich* [My wife is very bourgeois],' Freud said when I told him. She would never, he said, have expressed herself so straightforwardly to him."[36]

Marie returned to Paris on January 12, 1929, and for the first time stayed at 6 rue Adolphe Yvon. "Pretty new house, adorned by Tatoun." She no longer ran a temperature, but X. was afraid that she still harbored bacteria. Two days later, however, they resumed making love. X. was "impatient and reproachful." This did not keep him from making vague plans to go with her to America to join Róheim. She observed at this time that "work is easy and sexual pleasure difficult." "Psychoanalysis can at the most bring resignation and I am forty-six years old," she wrote in one of her notebooks. "The analysis has brought me peace of mind, of heart, and the possibility of working, but from the physiological point of view nothing. I am thinking of a second operation. Must I give up sex? Work, write, analyze? But absolute chastity frightens me."

She was still locked in the same problems, but another unforeseen event produced new reactions.

On January 29, 1929, Albert Reverdin, the handsome young lover from the Balkan wars, who had pursued her in Briand's time, died in Geneva. She had never loved him, but she mourned him deeply, since, as she wrote to Freud, it was the death of her youth. Through Dr. Flournoy, a psychoanalyst from Geneva, she asked to have her letters back and learned that they had been burned. This news shook her to the point that she could neither sleep nor work. Salvation might lie in making a short story out of this grief: "Like the Rajahs of India, [Reverdin] had the women he loved burned with him in the form of their letters . . . including me. All I can do is write the story. I will see the Friend again."[37]

She left for Leysin in March. Eugénie had lost four pounds and had pains in her leg. With her, Marie recovered her balance. Revenge is a defense mechanism that she had practiced a lot, as her analysis had proved to her. Once again she would take revenge by burning Reverdin's letters. "Freud is right, I was killing him by burning his letters," she wrote, back in Paris on April 25. She had reached this point, finally aware of her strength and her means of action. She no longer believed in chance. "There is no such thing as chance to the psychoanalyst, even in the psyche's utmost depths."[38]

·8·

AN ANALYST AND A FRIEND

"*More important than what one does is what one is.*"

    SIGMUND FREUD, QUOTED BY MARIE BONAPARTE
    in Journal d'analyse, February 18, 1926

"*All my life I was to attach a value to nothing but the opinion, the approval, the love of a few fathers chosen higher and higher, and the last of whom was to be my great master Freud.*"

    MARIE BONAPARTE,
    Derrière les vitres closes, p. 113

IN 1929, HER ANALYSIS WAS OVER, BUT FROM TIME TO TIME Marie returned for a few sessions, in order to increase her knowledge and improve her technique. As expected, her profession allowed her to assert herself intellectually. She would be able to do research, to lecture, to present papers at congresses, to publish articles on psychoanalysis. Her intention was to become one of the best among Freud's disciples. She still needed experience, but she did not doubt her success, for she had kept intact the pride and hopes of her youth. Ever since her experiences in the Balkan wars, she had known that she had the gift of understanding and helping people.

Freud's trusting support put her on an equal footing with the closest of his followers. She was aware of all that had happened before and since the existence of the Committee. This Committee, founded secretly in 1913—but with Freud's approval—to further and protect psychoanalysis and to ensure that the disciples remained united, consisted of five members: Abraham, Ferenczi, Ernest Jones, Rank and Sachs. Marie soon had the opportunity to meet them all except Abraham, who had died in December 1925. In October 1919, Freud had suggested including a sixth member, Max Eitingon, whom he trusted and who was ready to provide important financial help.

Max Eitingon, a Russian doctor, had been analyzed by Freud for a few weeks during nightly walks through the streets of Vienna. He had an independent income until 1930, when its source, an American fur business, went bankrupt. The Berlin Policlinic, opened in February 1920, had been financed by him. In 1921, he had become one of the directors of the publishing house founded by Freud in 1918, the Internationale Psychoanalytische Verlag. He was completely devoted to his analyst, and it was he whom Freud had sent to Paris in 1924 to check on the French movement in the process of formation. Eitingon had suggested the addition of Loewenstein to the group.

The Verlag was of great significance to Freud. Disagreements with his publisher, Heller, had led him to want his own publishing house, in order to be free to publish without argument whatever seemed important to him. It was not an easy operation to organize in a Vienna in the throes of defeat and economic chaos, where both paper and qualified manpower were in short supply. Anton von Freund, a Hungarian who had been in treatment with Freud, had decided "to devote [his vast fortune] to the furtherance of psychoanalysis"[1]; with the help of Ferenczi and Rank he set himself the goal of establishing the enterprise. He thought first of setting it up in Hungary, but Freud insisted on Vienna. Since it was impossible to have the books printed there, they were manufactured in Czechoslovakia. Each printer's bill was a serious threat to the survival of the Verlag, since the Austrian crown was decreasing in value while the new Czechoslovakian currency strengthened. As early as 1920, Brill, "the leader of Orthodox psychoanalysis" in the United States,[2] sent $10,000 that he had collected for the Verlag, and Rank packed the books for shipment himself, buying the string at his own expense, since the smallest economies were not to be overlooked. There was, however, a public eager to follow these publications, and Freud refused to take any royalties. He turned them over entirely to the Verlag, which in July 1921 had bought back from Heller, for the sum of $15,470, the rights in all of Freud's books.[3] After 1927, business was doing so badly that Storfer, the managing director, wanted to withdraw. When she heard about it, in January 1929, Marie saved the Verlag from bankruptcy. It was the first time she intervened but it was not to be the last. From then on, each time the Verlag was in trouble, she refloated it.

In England, where an Institute of Psycho-Analysis had been established in 1925, things were going better. In 1921, Ernest Jones organized the International Psycho-Analytical Press, in Vienna, to publish Freud's work in English. In 1924 he concluded an agreement with Leonard and Virginia Woolf, which made the

Hogarth Press the publishers of British analysts and of translations of analytic works from German.

Marie Bonaparte took a lively interest in these matters, drawing from them a lesson for Paris, although she had no intention of founding a publishing house since the public was too small. She was eager to know what others were doing to spread Freudian doctrine, and was always ready to travel to a meeting or a congress. Thus, although ill, she went to Oxford with her son, Peter, for the International Congress in July 1929. She was very active within the Paris Society and observed with lucidity the growing internal conflicts there as well as those among the editors of the review.

Two controversies threatened disruption of the Society: medical analysts were afraid of losing their position in the hospitals and medical schools because of the acceptance of lay analysts in the Society. The second controversy was more complicated. There was, as has been mentioned, legitimate concern and confusion about how best to translate Freud's terms into French. Marie sat on the committee created to resolve the many questions. The chauvinists pushed for a "typically French" terminology which would have changed Freud's work in its basic aspects. Freud had been thinking of them when he alluded ironically to the "Latin genius."

Her friendship with Freud allowed Marie Bonaparte to be an arbiter, or at least an adviser. She also took very seriously her editing of the review, and there she published some texts that concerned her directly: "The Identification of a Young Girl with Her Dead Mother"[4] and "A Small Attack of Masked Kleptomania."[5] These articles eventually found their place in a volume entitled *Psychanalyse et Anthropologie*.

In the first paper, in which she went back to her childhood experiences, she had settled her problems, taken some distance, and analyzed with detachment all the ways in which she unconsciously identified with her mother. Now she lived in greater harmony with herself, understanding her drives and controlling her actions. She owed this new state to Freud's analysis and their continuing relationship. She asked his advice on all aspects of her life, keeping him informed of what was happening in her family, of her love affairs, of her sexual life, and discussed with him what course she should follow.

The year 1929 did not bring Eugénie the hoped-for recovery. Though rid of her pulmonary tuberculosis, the young princess still had a leg ailment and had to remain in Leysin. Freud rented a house for the summer in Berchtesgaden, "Schneewinkel" (Snow Corner), "in the middle of the fields in a little corner of forest belonging to it."[6] He was enthusiastic over the beauty of the site and invited Marie to come. It was by now a habit: each year, she spent several weeks with the Freud family. In August 1929, she took Eugénie with her, in the hope that this new experience would help her recuperate from the trauma of countless medical examinations. The cyst in her leg, which was not healing, had finally been diagnosed as tubercular, but the doctors were not yet sure whether to operate. Marie set out to distract Eugénie. Once a week she took her to the festival in nearby Salzburg, to hear *Fidelio* and Mozart's *Requiem* and to see Hofmannsthal's *Everyman* on the steps of the cathedral. After her analysis, Marie had lost her fear of meeting Frifri again, the German governess whom thirty years before she had betrayed under the influence of the Leandris. She invited her for a visit, which turned into the beginning of a new friendship. At the same time as Frifri, Peter arrived with his father, and Marie reports their rowing together on the Königssee. But then the family dispersed—Peter to travel in Rumania, Eugénie returning to Leysin with Croisy, and Marie following Freud to Berlin, where he again stayed at Tegelsee sanatorium to have his prosthesis modified.

That summer, Freud was working on a new book, *Civilization and Its Discontents*, published early in the next year. In November 1929, Freud gave Marie a ring, an intaglio, as he was in the habit of doing with his close disciples. He had begun giving away these stones, which he had had mounted as rings, before the 1914 war. According to Jones, these rings were the distinctive signs of the six members of the Committee, and it was believed that only Anna, Lou Andreas-Salomé, Mrs. Jones and Marie Bonaparte were the other recipients. However, there were many more, among them Princess Eugénie of Greece, who felt deeply honored by this gift.

Back in Leysin, Eugénie was again restricted to bed and permitted a drive only once a week. It was a frustrating existence for a girl about to turn twenty. Moreover, she lost one of her dogs. Freud, who late in life had become a dog lover, wrote her a very kind letter of condolence.

Marie continued to be deeply worried about Eugénie's health, but apart from that the year 1930 had begun well for her, sustained as she was by her two friends X. and Loewenstein. Predictably, her relations with the Friend were soon complicated by her frigidity, and she decided to have a second operation. But Peter came down with the mumps and she had to take care of him. During this period, a pause in their always diverging lives, he had time to confide in her and she to listen. He was in love with a young American woman, O., whom he wanted to follow to the United States. He had lost his virginity with her. When she sailed, he accompanied her to Le Havre and cried on his way back to Paris. He wanted to be analyzed after his law examinations in June, as his mother suggested.

Peter chose his analyst for an unusual reason. He knew Loewenstein to be his mother's lover and was jealous of him. Marie assured Peter of her wish to continue their conversations, but he already knew that she was going to disappear again. Indeed, on April 12 she left for Vienna, to consult Halban. The sensitivity in the place from which the clitoris had been moved persisted. This time Halban recommended combining further surgery on the clitoris with a hysterectomy because of her chronic salpingitis. He was willing to come to Paris and operate on her at the American Hospital. Ruth Mack insisted on being present.

Before entering the hospital, Marie deliberately linked up with her past. She attended a luncheon at Marnes-la-Coquette, at the home of her old friend Le Bon. At six o'clock on the same day, she received Briand in her home. She had neglected him in recent years. Her notebooks mention him only rarely. Although he had not ceased to be in the public eye, he had departed from her life, and when they met she no longer showed interest in his plans and activities. Age had not diminished his missionary zeal; he remained the clairvoyant Breton stubbornly fighting for a lasting peace. At the time, he was prime minister for the eleventh time and, since July 1929, also minister of foreign affairs. On May 1, 1930, he offered a "memorandum on the organization of a system of European federal union" to the League of Nations. The proposal had been drafted by Alexis Léger, the Nobel Laureate in poetry, St.-John Perse.[7] This memorandum laid the foundations for what later became the Common Market and the European Parliament.

Marie, liberal and cosmopolitan, could not fail to see the importance of a United Europe, which would have forestalled the Hitlerian adventure and its fatal consequences, consequences that she was to follow very closely. But when Briand saw her, on May 6, 1930, a few days after submitting the memorandum, he did not even get a chance to mention it, since Marie had only one thing in mind: to recover the letters that she had once written him. Not having succeeded she wrote to him three days later:

"My friend, as I told you the other day, I am to be operated on next Wednesday at the American Hospital in Neuilly. Would you, when you return from Geneva, then from Cocherel, bring me there the letters I asked you for? I hope at that time to be able to see you for a moment myself—that would give me great joy—otherwise, if I am too ill just then, you can give the sealed bundle to the lady who is going to stay at the hospital with me, and who is a true and devoted friend of mine and will lock it in the iron chest that I am taking with me to the hospital in expectation of my recovery. This lady is an American doctor, Mrs. Mack-Brunswick, like myself a pupil of Freud, and to whom I have been very close for some years. She is coming moreover from Vienna expressly to stay with me at the American Hospital until I am back on my feet, which is a true expression of friendship on her part. She has a heart and a very high intelligence besides. . . .

"These are my wishes, which I ask you, in memory of our attachment, to carry out. Thank you. And I hope besides that it is to myself that you will be able to hand those letters, and that my eyes will have the joy of rereading them.

"I tell you adieu, my friend, and that my heart remains attached to you."

She had already written him a letter in the same vein, even more pressing, from Vienna, when she was thinking of having the operation there, but she had not sent it. Despite this insistence, she received nothing. The operation took place on May 14, and on the 17th Halban and Dr. Schur, who had also made the trip, returned to Vienna.

On the 28th, Marie got up for the first time. George and X. were at her bedside. She confessed that she had thought of dying of an embolism in X.'s arms, as her mother had died in her father's. On May 31, she went home, without her letters to Briand.

She recovered rapidly from the operation, even though it resulted in a mild menopause. She was forty-eight years old on July 2, spent Bastille Day at Hardelot, situated in a fertile, hilly countryside of alternating woods and meadows, extending to the jade-green North Sea, pastureland for the horses of the Boulonnais. But the beauty of the spot became secondary. X. and his wife accompanied Marie, who writes of the trip: "I am crazy about the Friend. Three nights in which I didn't bear their lovemaking. Blazing return [to Paris]." Her sexual jealousy of the Friend's wife persisted.

In 1930, Marie published her translations of Freud's *Autobiographical Study* and *Jokes and Their Relation to the Unconscious*. This was the year in which she bought land with vineyards and a pine grove on the shore in Saint-Tropez. She loved the scented air of the Mediterranean coast, and the white sand where wild flowers bloomed whose name—*lys de mer*—would be that of her house. She swam, she worked in the sunshine facing the sea, or in the shade of the tall umbrella pines, and she became the neighbor of her childhood friend Geneviève Troisier, who welcomed her to La Moutte, the family residence that she had heard so much about when she was an adolescent.

Eugénie continued to be the object of serious concern; she was not improving. In November they were again to try a new treatment. After two months in bed, Eugénie got up again, and on February 20, 1931, along with Croisy and the two dogs, joined her mother, who had been in Vienna since the end of January. She stayed at the Cottage clinic, where she underwent a series of X-ray treatments. Marie had had herself operated on for a third time by Halban. At the end of March, mother and daughter left Vienna for Cannes. X. visited them in April, "accompanied, unfortunately."

For Freud's seventy-fifth birthday, Marie gave a lecture at the Sorbonne. It was the first time she addressed an audience of five hundred. She sent her teacher a Greek urn, of which he became especially fond. But she was worried about him and at Schur's suggestion consulted Professor G. V. Rigaud, director of the Curie Institute, inquiring whether radium treatment might help; Rigaud was against it. Freud was later operated on again.[8] Marie was also actively concerned with her daughter's health. On May 26, Eugénie's leg was operated on. Marie tried to comfort Eugénie, who was in great pain physically, and whose relations with her father were not improving. As soon as she had recovered, Eugénie was to begin analysis in Lausanne with Mme Odier, the wife of one of

Marie's colleagues, while Peter, as planned, was in analysis with Loewenstein.

Marie spent July as usual in Paris alone with the Friend; then they left together to join Eugénie in Switzerland. From there, Marie was to go to Freud. During the automobile trip with the Friend, Marie's mind was entirely absorbed by Kürten, "the vampire of Düsseldorf," a criminal who had committed some thirty sadistic crimes against women, and had been executed at the beginning of August. Once again she was obsessed by murder and fascinated by the murderer. In the fall she was to go to Düsseldorf to gather information. She planned to travel with Raymond de Saussure, the handsome Swiss founding member of the Paris Society, expecting to have an affair with him. The act of love was still painful for her. She wanted to revenge herself for her suffering by asserting her superiority through infidelity.

After the holidays, which ended in Saint-Tropez, she noted a recurrence of sadism in X. It occurred to her that he was sadistic with her while behaving masochistically toward his wife. She decided to find another lover. "At the age of fifty!" she noted in parentheses, astonished at her own dynamism. Then once again the relationship improved. X. had been suffering from a sinus condition and he had also been absorbed by all the proceedings connected with his appointment as professor in the faculty of medicine. She spent two peaceful days with him in Fontainebleau at the end of October. On her return, she noted that there were two kinds of men: enemies and friends of the phallic woman. X. and Freud fell in the first category, Loewenstein in the second. She also noted: "The Friend and I, we have to accept each other as we are." For twelve years now it had been the same: "His wife twice a week, me three times."

She continued to be active in the work of the Paris Society, pleased with the growing official recognition of psychoanalysis. Thanks to Henri Claude, a post of *chef de laboratoire* was created in 1931 and assigned to Dr. Sacha Nacht. Psychotherapy and consultations were provided by Nacht, Laforgue and Loewenstein. At the Children's Hospital, Professor Georges Heuyer had, as early as 1927, accepted psychoanalysis in his neuropsychiatric division, where Mme Morgenstern practiced child analysis. Marie still had four patients in analysis, one of them Loewenstein's sister Lydia, and she was finishing her book on Poe. She had submitted her manuscript in installments to Freud, who was impressed by the end of the work. "It seems to me that it is the best part of this good book and the best thing you have ever written. These are not only applications of psychoanalysis but truly enrichments of it. Even the subtle paragraph on the theory of drives is very well done. . . . The spirit with which these last chapters on Poe are written is probably the result of your enthusiasm for K. [Kürten] and reconciles me with that enthusiasm. . . ."⁹

In that year and the previous one, Marie had given the *Revue* extracts from her book. Her name appeared frequently in the table of contents and her articles were translated for both the *Internationale Zeitschrift für Psychoanalyse* and *Imago*.

In the fall, Gustave Le Bon died of pneumonia. Freud wrote that on reading this news he understood why he had not had a letter from Marie for a long time. "You were expecting me to die too. That is still quite possible but is not more likely now than usual, although my temperature is very low and I display corresponding symptoms."¹⁰ He always spoke of himself with detachment, well aware that Marie trembled for his life.

At the end of the year she went to the Little Scheidegg with her children. She traveled with Peter, who had dislocated a shoulder, and in the train she confessed to him her affair with X. Later she told this to Loewenstein, who approved of her action. During his analysis, Peter had been "working on" this for months, Loewenstein said. Peter had suspected X., then Briand, and had come back to X. Afterwards he was more courteous to X., as Marie noticed, although she did not mention it to the latter. Freud also congratulated her on her decision. At this time, Marie's relations with X. were improving. "My libido is all in my head," she wrote, but did not take this into account in her actions.

She was unable to determine precisely when the tension between Peter and herself had begun. They both discovered, however, that they were tempted by incest. "If I were to spend a night with you, it might cure me," Peter told his mother in April 1932. The very next day, she noted that her "own temptation was extinguished in the arms of the Friend." Freud, whom she immediately consulted, wrote her on April 30, 1932, a letter (reprinted in full in the Jones biography)¹¹ whose conclusion must have given her pause, if her desire for incest had not already passed: "It might be possible for someone who has escaped the influence of the phylogenetic repressions to allow himself incest without any harm, but one could never be sure of that. These inheritances are often stronger than we are prone to estimate; then the trespass is followed by feelings of guilt against which one is quite helpless." A prudent warning!

Peter, in the wake of these rather uncommon preoccupations, and the likewise uncommon discussions with his mother, failed his law examinations and decided to enlist in the guard in Denmark. Marie accompanied him to help him get settled. They left on May 3, and she stayed with him at Bernstorff from the 6th to the 10th. She returned via Amsterdam, in order to see the tulips in bloom. Back at Saint-Cloud, she noted: "Joy of getting away from people. Rest." But soon she was at work on translations: Freud's *The Future of an Illusion*, and "Psycho-Analytic Notes on an Auto-biographical Account of a Case of Paranoia." To translate "*das Es*" (the id), she chose "*le ça*" although Freud preferred "*le soi.*"

She was eager for the arrival of summer. The spring had been painful. On March 6, Briand died in his sleep, exhausted by overwork and mercifully unaware that what he had tried to set in motion in Geneva was already doomed. Freud sent a letter of condolence. Marie paid a visit to the dead man's house, which had not changed since the time when she had been a frequent visitor there. On March 12, the state funeral was held. Marie, accompanied by Eugénie, followed the procession on foot.

X. and Marie again had their month of July together. From the 23rd, Marie spent a week in Vienna, and Freud told her that she ought to content herself with the Friend. "I would if he satisfied me sexually," she wrote in a letter of "virile protest." Freud wrote her a conciliatory letter, reproaching her for seeing in him only the transference of the father. Her masculinity pleases him, the fact that she loves sexually and intellectually makes it all the better! Thus teacher and disciple were not always in agreement. In Marie's developing theory it was a woman's "masculinity" which procured her sexual pleasure.

She returned to Bernstorff from Vienna, in order to attend the tenth Congress of Psychology in Copenhagen. There she met the Russian physiologist Pavlov, who had read Freud and respected him, but did not think that sexuality was of such prime importance.

From Bernstorff, she went to the International Congress in Wiesbaden. This congress, scheduled to have been held the previous year, had been postponed for two reasons: the international economic crisis and the rise of Nazism. German and Austrian psychiatrists feared reprisals for participating in such a congress. The Nazis had already taken a position against this "Jewish pseudo-science" and emigration to the United States had begun. In Wiesbaden, an international committee, of which Marie Bonaparte was a member, was set up to oversee the administration of the Verlag;[12] Ferenczi took the occasion to distance himself officially from Freudian theories and techniques, refusing the presidency of the Association, which was offered to him, for this reason.

In Wiesbaden, Marie Bonaparte read her first paper before the International Association, *La Fonction érotique chez la femme*. "Women who have not renounced their masculinity . . . most often preserve the phallic organization with regard to the erogenous zones; in short, they become heterosexuals in whom the clitoral zone nevertheless stubbornly remains the dominant one."

Two days after, she left for Saint-Tropez. There, she stayed at the Bungalow Hotel, where the anthropologist Bronislaw Malinowski joined her for two days. They had first met in Toulon. Malinowski would have liked to take her to America. The Friend was also present, and one evening all three took a walk in the moonlight. "Malino" immediately guessed the situation and remarked that after a liaison that had lasted twelve years X. would never be able to leave her. The day after his departure, Marie spent a magnificent evening at the Bungalow with the Friend, "without jealousy or reproaches over Malino." It was then that she first thought of having another year of analysis with Loewenstein.

Marie had to go to Denmark, where Peter had an appendectomy on October 6. Her son now wished to be an ethnologist. He wanted to study in Berlin and then in London. She doubted that he would succeed in persuading his father, who remained traditionally dominant in such matters. After having been in analysis, Eugénie and Peter could no longer stand Croisy's presence; they accused her of having suffocated them. Marie had to resolve this problem, no simple matter since Eugénie was again ill and Croisy insisted on taking care of her, as she had done for so long. But Eugénie was in full rebellion, and so was her brother. Croisy was given a pension and Marie bought a house for her in England, where, after all the years spent with Peter and Eugénie, she had to accept her new condition of solitude.

In that year, 1932, Marie Bonaparte published her translations of *The Future of an Illusion* and, in collaboration with Mme Edouard Marty, the *Essays on Applied Psychoanalysis.** Although she immediately confessed her "analytic infidelity with Loewenstein" to Freud, who gave his permission, she felt guilty, so guilty that she vomited and was physically ill. All the same she began the analysis, and the weeks following her return to Paris were very crowded. Malinowski was there, George arrived, she escaped for a day to Fontainebleau with the Friend, and on November 15, reread her paper on female eroticism to psychoanalysts who had not been at the Wiesbaden Congress.

A celebration on the occasion of her silver wedding anniversary was planned in Denmark for December 12, 1932. Marie did not comment on the event, which took place, in conformity with usage, with a certain grandeur. George's royal family was more than well represented, but the state of Eugénie's health disturbed and saddened Marie. The young princess remained in Denmark while her mother, on the following day, the 13th, left for Sweden, where she was to meet Selma Lagerlöf, the author of *Gösta Berling*.

In 1933, Eugénie was operated on twice for the tubercular cyst that had developed in the muscle of her right thigh; both operations were performed at the Finsen Institute in Copenhagen. The second, necessitated by a relapse, required a three-month stay in the hospital. She was visited daily by her uncle Waldemar; Peter also came to see her but had a tendency to fall asleep. Her father, in her opinion, came "too often." The second operation took place on June 25, and as always he was in Denmark for the summer. When she left the hospital, Eugénie stayed at her cousin Axel's house. For nine months she was unable to walk; altogether she spent three years in Denmark, where she felt at ease.

On January 30, 1933, Hitler became chancellor of the German Reich; the dollar was devalued on April 12 of the same year. The two events touched Freud closely. As early as March 16, he wrote to Marie concerning the coming persecutions:

"How fortunate you are to be immersed in your work without having to take notice of all the horrible things around. In our

---

* Five papers which appear in English in vol. IV of Freud's *Collected Papers*, and *Psychoanalysis and the Establishment of Facts in Legal Proceeding* from vol. II of the *Collected Papers*. *The Complete Collected Papers*, as they are known to English readers, never appeared as such in French.

circles, there is already a great deal of trepidation. People fear that the nationalistic extravagances in Germany may extend to our little country. I have already been advised to flee to Switzerland or France. That is nonsense; I don't believe there is any danger here. . . . If they kill me—good. It is one kind of death like another. But probably that is only cheap boasting. . . ."[13]

And ten days later: ". . . The brutalities in Germany seem to be diminishing. The way France and America have reacted to them has not failed to make an impression, but the torments, small but none the less painful on that account, will not cease, and the systematic suppression of the Jews, depriving them of all positions, has as yet scarcely begun. One cannot avoid seeing that persecution of the Jews and restriction of intellectual freedom are the only features of Hitler's program that can be carried out. All the rest is weakness and utopianism. In Austria, that should not go very far. But the cowardice of the dear Jews has already been brilliantly demonstrated."

On May 11, in Berlin, a solemn public burning of all books by Jewish writers and many non-Jewish anti-Nazi writers took place, an event reported on in detail by the Viennese press. Freud made the famous comment: "What progress we are making! In the Middle Ages they would have burned me; nowadays they are content to burn my books." In his anxiety over the situation, Freud was unable to concentrate on writing. "The world is turning into an enormous prison. Germany is the worst cell. What will happen in the Austrian cell is quite uncertain . . . I am happy to think that you still dwell as on an island of the blessed."[14]

The dialogue with Freud was continuous and wide-ranging. Marie followed the events in Germany and Austria with anxious suspense. In February, she had been in Denmark for Eugénie's operation. In this atmosphere, the publication in two large volumes of her work on Poe did not give her the pleasure she had hoped for. The German translation was published early the following year, by the Verlag. In that spring of 1933, she had the opportunity of traveling to Corsica. She invited Freud to accompany her, but such a journey was for him out of the question. He was suffering from bouts of dizziness, resulting from a disturbance in the inner ear, and from depression.

In the company of a Corsican, Marie visited the "family island" for two weeks. In Ajaccio, she received an enthusiastic welcome, which greatly moved her. The month of July was spent as always in Saint-Cloud, because of the Friend, and on the 26th she left for Bernstorff to see Eugénie. From there she went to Saint-Tropez, where for the first time she was able to move into Le Lys de Mer, the house she had built. Stark and modern, the low white house rose from the sand as close as possible to the Mediterranean on a then deserted beach. The windows of her bedroom and study were the closest to the sea. From now on, Le Lys de Mer would be her place of work and her refuge. She began writing *De la Sexualité de la femme*.

In October, Eugénie finally left the hospital and went back to her cousin's house, while her mother returned to Paris, devoting herself completely to the organization of the Institute of Psychoanalysis, for which she had found space at 137 Boulevard Saint-Germain, near the School of Medicine. It was thanks to her generosity that this Institute was founded.

The Institute was urgently needed as a training ground. Marie Bonaparte, Borel, Laforgue, Loewenstein, Odier, Parcheminey and Pichon formed the training Commission, which, at the Wiesbaden Congress in 1932, had recommended three years of training, two of them devoted to theory, the third to supervised work on two cases. The training analysis was to last not more than a year, or eighteen months at the utmost. On January 25, Marie wrote to Anna Freud that there were 150 pupils at the Institute, and she had begun her first course there ten days earlier.

At this time, X. became a full professor of medicine, which pleased them both. Together they experienced a period of calm. They played music or listened to it in their rare leisure hours. Thanks to their professional success, they had recaptured their former relationship. But the times were troubled. On February 6, 1934, there were bloody riots in Paris. The Right was hoping to seize power. At the same time (February 1–16) there were disturbances in Vienna as well. And on February 19, in response to a letter from Marie offering him hospitality, Freud wrote: ". . . Only one thing seems clear to me: there is no need for an urgent decision; in any case, we can wait for weeks, probably months.

"If the Nazis come here, and bring injustice as in Germany, then of course one would have to leave. I think instead that we will get a fascism of the Austrian kind, which, deplorable though it would be, would still be much easier to bear, so that one could remain. What danger threatens me personally? I cannot believe that it would be all that Ruth and Mark [Ruth's second husband, Mark

Brunswick] keep telling me all day long. I am relatively unknown in Austria; people who are better informed know only that the fact of my being mistreated would have a great repercussion abroad. The atmosphere of civil war this week was and still is frightful. The immediate consequences did not last long: one day without electricity. Work was not interrupted."[15]

But one day H. D., the American poet Hilda Doolittle, was the only patient to come to his office. She was jealous of Marie Bonaparte, whom Freud called "our princess," and she had heard that "the envoys of the princess . . . were waiting on the door-steps of various legations" to protect Freud.[16] She braved the revolution to prove to Freud that she too loved him.

It was the year in which everything tottered. In June, Hitler and Mussolini met in Venice; on the 30th of that month there was "the night of the long knives," during which Röhm, Hitler's onetime friend and head of the S.A., was murdered, arousing false hopes for the collapse of the regime; a month later the Austrian Chancellor Dollfuss was assassinated in Vienna. Hindenburg died shortly thereafter, and on October 9 the king of Yugoslavia was assassinated in Marseilles along with Louis Barthou, the French minister of foreign affairs.

Marie's profession and friendships determined her travels that summer. She attended the London Anthropological Congress (taking advantage of the opportunity to go to Cambridge and Oxford), and then went to the International Congress in Lucerne, where she spoke on *Passivity, Masochism and Femininity.* Her divergence from Freud in this paper now seems small but was significant: she spoke of the pleasure women receive from caresses of "the whole body" or from some "particular zone" and the "harmonious collaboration" of the clitoris and the vagina. She also differed with Helene Deutsch in arguing against the centrality of female masochism, and for orgasm.

From September 28 to October 8, she visited Freud in Vienna. Then she went to Le Lys de Mer, which she loved more and more, taking Ruth Mack-Brunswick there for the first time. George and Waldemar, Peter and Malinowski came to join them.

In November, she went to London for the wedding of her niece Marina, daughter of Prince Nicholas of Greece, to the Duke of Kent. While there she gave a lecture on women to the British Psycho-Analytical Society. "Jones took my theme as a challenge since for me the fear of penetration is biological, not moral." What she was doing seemed so natural to her that she did not realize that her lecture itself was another kind of challenge. None of the guests at Buckingham Palace suspected that Aunt Marie, H.R.H. Princess George of Greece and Denmark, was going to speak on female sexuality before an audience of psychiatrists and psychoanalysts. The royal family was certainly not on the invitation list of the British Psycho-Analytical Society.

Marie became interested at that time in the work of the ethnologist Marcel Griaule. She spent the end of the year at Le Lys de Mer and returned to Paris on January 7, 1935, to be present for the departure of her new friend and his expedition to study the Dogon, an African tribe, in their territory. She intended to join Griaule later and had herself inoculated against yellow fever, which gave her a high temperature and a rash. X. nursed her with a devotion that she found "touching." She recognized that her "longing for Africa" and her sadness on the day of Griaule's departure were repetitions of her father's departure by sleigh, without her, that snowy day in Paris. She would have taken Mme Griaule along with her, to silence gossip, but could not have stayed more than three weeks, too short a time to make it worthwhile; she also feared the curiosity of the wives of the members of the expedition, and the rumors that might reach the ears of the Friend.

X. was going through a period of crisis, suddenly and unexpectedly. At the age of fifty-four, he seemed to suffer from a kind of male menopause. Four times he had been impotent with her. She complained to Freud, but she soon learned from his wife's confidences that he had proved to be quite "reserved" in the conjugal bed as well. This was a comfort, and she felt "more courage, joy, understanding, love." She knew that she was still competing with X.'s wife, despite his proofs of attachment and their shared interests in medicine and biology. More and more she had become the Friend's alter ego. She had even thought of participating part-time in his research work, always with the goal of enriching her scientific knowledge and widening her horizons.

Malinowski was still on the scene. He visited her in Paris on March 1, and urged her to invite one of his graduate students at the London School of Economics, a Kikuyu tribesman from Kenya, to Paris as her guest. Marie invited Malino's protégé and paid for his trip. Jomo Kenyatta arrived on April 4. The princess was intrigued by her black guest who had left Kenya for the first time three years before, visited Moscow, and who had "Bolshevik tendencies." Kenyatta spoke Russian, English and the languages of East Africa. He taught his hostess some Kikuyu.

Marie took Kenyatta to Versailles on April 9 and noted that he liked the gardens and Marie Antoinette's *hameau* at le Petit Trianon best. Over tea that afternoon he enlightened her on the puberty rites of his tribe. She was most interested in how the girls were treated and he subsequently sent her a twenty-page, detailed description of the girls' initiation rites, including the excision of the clitoris.

Jomo Kenyatta later became first the most notorious leader of African rebellion against colonial rule and eventually prime minister and president of Kenya. Marie prolonged her Easter holidays in Saint-Tropez to write up Kenyatta's comments on the future of Africa and everything he had told her of his and other tribes. She also found time to further her commentaries for the *Five Copy-Books*.

On her return to Paris, Marie noticed that her dog Topsy, daughter of Tatoun and her mate, Cheekee, had a tumor of the lip that proved to be a lymphosarcoma. She, who had already donated vast sums to the Curie Institute to save human lives, decided to order X-ray treatments for the chow-chow. She took the dog there every other day and began writing a book that is a curious and touching hymn to life and love.

In July, Marie went again to Vienna for a week. On her return she found Topsy improved, and settled down at Le Lys de Mer to continue working on the *Five Copy-Books*; Freud approved. Peter came to lunch with a young Russian woman named Irène Outchinikova, who had recently appeared in his life. Marie scented danger. Irène was only separated from her second husband. Marie found her good-looking and intelligent, but too old for Peter. "The Russian woman" (as Marie usually called her in letters) claimed to be thirty, but was actually thirty-four; Peter was twenty-seven. If she were to obtain a divorce and Peter were to marry her, he would be left a royal prince cut off from the royal family. Neither Peter nor Marie seemed to have perceived the parallel with Princes Lucien and Pierre Napoleon Bonaparte which was beginning to develop. On September 19, Marie described herself as "literally disgusted with humanity, children included, and I no longer love anything except animals and nature and work that one does all alone." Peter, who had written Eugénie from Gibraltar a letter hostile to both his mother and sister, had provoked this mood.

The letter from Gibraltar was the first manifestation of the hostility between mother and son that continued over the years. Marie at first did her best to keep George from knowing "the danger." She knew beforehand that her husband would not accept the marriage and busied herself in an attempt to have the affair broken off. Loewenstein, in the beginning, advised her not to attempt to forbid Peter's seeing Irène. He told her, without explaining why, that Peter had interrupted his analysis before there had been much benefit. Peter reproached his mother for having let him travel with Irène, for having had them both to lunch, for having let him play with fire. Now it was too late. He attacked his mother's way of life. "You pursue leftist ideas (psychoanalysis) and you keep your fortune (all this dictated by the Russian woman)," Marie wrote to Freud on December 13, 1935. "The Russian woman has got him. Loew. will speak to him. But it is too late."

King George II had been recalled to Greece and offered Peter a position. Prince George, who never had anything but "Venizelos on his mind," did not urge him to accept the king's offer and Irène threatened to commit suicide. She was "impulsive, an Anna Karenina."[17] Nevertheless she agreed to be analyzed, provided Marie paid for the analysis. Irène was becoming very expensive. Marie wrote that Peter "tells everything about our private lives to the Russian woman." She had no doubt that it would be used against them.

In October she went with Peter and Eugénie to London to visit her nephew the king before his return to Greece. Eugénie was courageously getting over a hazardous romance that would have had no future. Despite her worries, Marie went to hear, "with Peter, the discussion of Melanie Klein's Congress paper, 'The Genetic Relation Between the Paranoid, Depressive and Manic Position in the Infant'—we got an earful of it!"[18] She did not approve of the theories of the British school and was on the main subjects an orthodox Freudian. As usual, she published articles in the *Revue*, and the translation of Freud's case histories, *Five Psychoanalyses*, done in collaboration with Rudolph Loewenstein, appeared that year. She had not yet finished writing the commentaries on the *Five Copy-Books*. Christmas and New Year's were spent with Eugénie and Topsy in Saint-Tropez.

In 1936 the fires of fascism were smoldering in Europe, despite the successes at the polls of the Frente Popular in Spain in February and of the Front Populaire in France in May. March brought Hitler's reoccupation of the Rhineland, while Mussolini's armies held sway in Ethiopia and seized Addis Ababa.

Marie, who had always kept aloof from politics, conducted her fight on another plane. She wanted the Nobel Prize for Freud, and against his wishes she wrote to Thomas Mann and Romain Rolland. Neither of them gave her any hope. At the beginning of the year, the Friend had been detained outside of Paris by his wife, whom Marie called "*the Crampon*." On his return, their reunion was a celebration. She and the Friend saw each other two or three times a week, and he became "a young man" again. But this did not last, and his impotence once again became a problem. They decided to see each other only three or four times a month, and "he fled from love into his work. Resignation. To live again in his children." She too worked; at the *Revue* they were busy preparing a special issue in homage to Freud for his eightieth birthday; the date was approaching. Once again she was suffering from cystitis. On May 6, the ceremony in honor of Freud was again held at the Sorbonne under the chairmanship of Professor Claude, with Marie making a speech.

George, Eugénie and Peter sent telegrams to Vienna for the birthday. With time, George had come to accept Freud, whom he respected and esteemed as a man, while preferring to ignore his work. A month later George returned from Denmark, very sick with chicken pox. Marie caught it too, but her case was less severe. Then her daily life resumed its pace: the four patients, Saint-Cloud, the beauty of the garden, less frequent trysts with the Friend that summer.

In July 1936, civil war broke out in Spain. Hitler and the fascists were supporting Franco. The Western powers opted for non-intervention. The Soviet Union's support was tempered by Moscow's political strategy, of which those who idealistically joined the "Red" side in order to save endangered freedom were unaware.

From August 2 to 5, the Marienbad Congress was held. Lacan gave his first paper on *Le Stade du miroir* there.[19] Marie was elected vice-president of the Congress with Anna Freud, which gave her great pleasure, but Marie's paper, "Vues paléobio-logiques et biophysiques,"[20] came under critical discussion by Helene Deutsch and Jeanne Lampl, who were also disciples of Freud. Their friendships with him were of longer standing and jealousy doubtless played a part, which upset Marie.

As soon as the Congress was over, Marie sailed for the Amazon with Eugénie. Leaving on August 7, they arrived at Belém in Brazil on the 22nd. "Palm trees, huge insects, exhausting heat." They sailed up the Amazon River. On August 29, from Manaos, Marie wrote that she had a horror of the tropics and was longing for the sea, despite the alligator hunt. Eugénie loved the tropics, flirted on the boat, enjoyed the parrots and was perfectly happy. On September 28, they were back in Paris.

The purpose of the voyage had primarily been to distract Eugénie, who after eight years of illness and her romantic misadventure needed a lift to her spirits. The return was melancholy. Marie was still hoping for a rewarding personal life. The Friend's impotence did not abate. She again regretted not having had a child by him, to ease her sense of loneliness. Peter and Eugénie now had their own lives to lead. From October 26 to 31, she went to Vienna to have six hours of analysis, which helped her achieve the resignation she was in need of. The Friend was apparently turning into an ascetic. "If I try to kiss him, he recoils. 'No, I'm afraid,' he claims, and states that with his wife he acts the same." "He is afraid for his work, for his life. Courage takes the place of happiness." Marie turned to her animal friends.

On November 14, she left for Athens with Eugénie and Peter, for the return of the ashes of her brother-in-law Constantine and of the queens, her mother-in-law and her sister-in-law Sophie. She hoped to go to Mycenae and Delphi. Peter was enraptured; he had not seen Greece since he was four years old. They had rain and snow in Delphi.

An attack of flu that immobilized her for several days gave Marie ample time to think and elucidate her relationship with X. "His father-fixation explains the Friend: as an adolescent, he had a religious crisis. He doesn't smoke, doesn't drink, came late to women—now he's becoming a vegetarian. The father is taboo."[21] She could not change his attitude and had to accept it. X. tried to extend his "father taboo" to her by forbidding her to mention her father's cancer of the prostate in *Topsy*. She refused.

On December 23, Peter returned from Greece torn between his

love for Irène and his duty as a prince. "He is reluctant to cut as poor a figure as 'the King' who has just given up his throne for Mrs. Simpson."[22] But he soon joined Irène, who had broken off her analysis and got her divorce. George, still ignorant of his son's predicament, left for Athens where he had not been for sixteen years.

On December 30, Marie received an unexpected visitor: Reinhold Stahl, introduced as writer and art dealer, who offered to sell her Freud's letters and papers belonging to Fliess, who had died in 1928. The handwriting was certainly Freud's; Marie had no trouble recognizing it from the specimen that Stahl showed her. Frau Fliess had thought of giving these papers to the Berlin National Library, but since the Nazis were burning Freud's works, she sold them to Stahl instead. He had received offers from America, but before resigning himself to seeing these documents leave Europe, he brought them to Marie. He wanted 12,000 francs for the lot (250 letters, including some from Breuer, and some theoretical outlines). Marie recognized the importance of this correspondence, which extended from 1887 to 1902. Wilhelm Fliess, otolaryngologist and biologist, had been Freud's great friend in his solitary and fruitful youth. Since he lived in Berlin, it was by letter that Freud had expounded his ideas, discussed Fliess's ideas and sought his advice.

The year 1937 began with Freud's emotional reaction on learning of the sale of the letters and documents in the possession of Frau Fliess. After Fliess's death, his widow had asked for the return of his letters, but Freud had been unable to find them. Had he burned them or hidden them? In his opinion, Ida Fliess was a bad woman, responsible for the break between her husband and himself, and the correspondence had an intimate note that he was loath to see made public. He offered to repay Marie half of the sum she had paid. She refused. On January 7, she wrote again: "The letters and manuscripts were offered to me on condition that I not resell them at any price to the Freud family, directly or indirectly, for fear of the destruction of this material which is so important for the history of psychoanalysis. That will not keep me from discussing it with you, but you will not be surprised since you know my ideas and feelings: I have a curious aversion to the idea of the destruction of your letters and manuscripts.

"You yourself, dear Father, perhaps do not feel all your greatness. You belong to the history of human thought like Plato, let us say, or Goethe. What a loss it would have been, for us, for posterity, if the conversations with Eckermann had been destroyed, or the dialogues of Plato, these latter out of pity for Socrates, in order to keep posterity from learning that Socrates practiced pederasty with Phaedrus and Alcibiades?

"There can be nothing like that in your letters! Nothing, when one knows you, that could diminish you! and you yourself, dear Father, have written in your beautiful works against the idealization at all cost of great men."

In another paragraph of the same letter, Marie speaks of "this new and unique science, your creation, more important than the theory of ideas of Plato himself." She had had a second visit from Stahl, who brought her the scientific essays of the young Freud. The rest, the letters, were still in Germany and he would bring them to her in a few weeks. She was ready to place the material in a state library, Geneva for instance, "on the express condition that no one should consult it until 80 or 100 years after your death . . ." Furthermore, if it was Freud's wish, she would not read the letters herself. But she had glanced at a few and they were not compromising.

Marie placed this correspondence in a safety deposit box in her name at the Rothschild bank in Vienna. After the events of March 1938, she took them out and carried them away under the eyes of the Gestapo. In 1941, during the occupation of France, she deposited them at the Danish legation in Paris, which was not particularly safe since Denmark was occupied by Germany. The correspondence was to run a further risk, from German mines in the Channel, when it was sent to London in 1945. Finally, the letters were partially published in 1950 in German, and in 1954 in English, in *The Origins of Psychoanalysis*. The German edition had been prepared by Marie Bonaparte, the selection being made by Anna Freud and Ernst Kris; the latter also contributed the introduction and notes. Now the complete correspondence is soon to be published, and sure to provide a major help for understanding how Freud developed his theories by discussing those of the friend who impressed him so greatly.

In February 1937, Géza Róheim returned from his long expedition with enough evidence, he thought, to show—counter to the theses of Malinowski—that the Oedipus complex existed in the matrilinear societies of Melanesia.

On February 8, Málaga fell to Franco's forces, a victory for

Hitler and Nazism. In Vienna there was every reason for anxiety, and intellectuals and artists were leaving the country. Freud was not yet thinking of doing so. The death of Lou Andreas-Salomé, who had been his disciple, a friend and his link with Nietzsche, was a blow to him. He worked with increasing difficulty because of the state of his health, which was worsening despite the efforts of those around him to find a remedy for his suffering and a cure for his disease. Marie visited him at the beginning of March, on her way to Greece, where she arrived on the 15th. She had a very violent discussion with Peter, "his head still turned by that woman," whom he was planning to marry on January 1, 1938. Marie regretted that Loewenstein had kept her from speaking to Peter in the beginning. Freud advised indifference. He also told her that an analyst ought to separate analysis and life.

In Athens, Marie awaited the arrival of her friends Troisier and Annette Berman. The latter had been her patient and had become her secretary. They all went on a cruise through the Greek islands. On April 10, with George, Peter and Eugénie, she left for Crete to spend a week there. As she had hoped the visit was a triumph for George. At last he was received with public acclaim on the island which had seen his downfall. Marie would have preferred not to upset him by telling him about Peter and Irène, but Freud thought it was high time he was informed. The matter, however, was still to be the subject of several letters before Marie could bring herself to speak. The conversation took place on their return to Paris, and George then blamed it all on her. This made her angry at both George and X.

At the beginning of August, Marie arrived, depressed, at Le Lys de Mer. She imagined that George and Eugénie would mourn her, but George would be consoled by the idea of heaven, and Peter would rejoice in his inheritance. Her depression did not last long, and on August 24 she noted that she had recovered her *joie de vivre* and that her foot, which she had burned, had healed. She swam four times a day. The sea was warm. "The greatest happiness of my life is to have met you, to have been your contemporary," she wrote to Freud on September 6. On the 15th, she returned to Paris, where George refused to follow Freud's advice and speak to Peter. "Hard for a mother to become indifferent to her son, but it is a biological and social necessity." She also complained, "The family is disturbing my work."

Before going to Vienna with Eugénie and Topsy, who seemed to have been cured by the X-ray treatments, she went back to Le Lys de Mer. Eugénie was to stay in Vienna until Christmas for an analysis with Freud, who recognized that she had an understanding of what analysis meant.

The year 1938 began quietly enough. On January 1, Marie was back in Greece in her role of Royal Highness. On that day, she attended a ceremony in the Athens cathedral, and on January 9 the wedding of her nephew Paul, brother of King George II, to Princess Frederika of Brunswick-Lüneburg. On January 21, she had a curious dream, in which Kipling and Freud were dead. This dream, which she described to Freud, brought her a response dated "Elysian Fields, 27 January in Vienna." Freud writes once again with spirit and good humor just after a new operation for his malignancy. He jokes: "The stay in this place (the Elysian Fields) has a good effect on one's outer appearance. Perhaps you will even notice that I am even handsomer. Was I not disfigured by a sebaceous cyst, an atheroma that you never spoke to me about, probably out of politeness? They removed this ornament from me at the time of the last—I mean, of course, next to last—operation."[23]

On February 8, Prince Nicholas died in Greece, and the funeral, with torchlight and procession by the populace, was held on the 12th. George and Marie chose their tomb in the royal cemetery of Tatoï. Hitler delivered his ultimatum to Chancellor Schuschnigg, dooming Austria.

Marie returned to Paris on February 16, and on the 17th she had lunch with Prince Dominique Radziwill, who was to become officially engaged to Eugénie the next day. Marie thanked heaven that George was now more kind to his daughter. Freud sent his congratulations, since the Viennese newspapers had reported the engagement. Then events rushed headlong, and Eugénie's joy was soon forgotten.

On March 11, 1938, the Nazis invaded Austria. Marie immediately went into action. She got in touch with Dorothy Burlingham, the American friend of the Freuds who lived in Vienna with her children and worked with Anna, and with Ernest Jones in London. They both decided to go to Vienna to persuade Freud to leave his country.

During the meeting that was held on March 13, the executive committee of the Vienna Psychoanalytic Society urged everyone to flee the country insofar as possible. Jones, after a brief stay in Vienna, returned to London, where he obtained permission from the British Home Secretary, Sir Samuel Hoare, for Freud, his family, servants and personal doctors, as well as a certain number of followers and their families, to settle and work in Great Britain. Marie Bonaparte arrived in Vienna on March 17. She stayed at the Greek legation and took her meals at the Freuds'.

The situation was alarming. The Verlag had already been searched and Freud's will, which showed the existence of property abroad—considered a crime by the regime—had been found. Martin Freud, director of the Verlag, had been present but had not been able to destroy the dangerous documents. On March 22, Anna Freud was summoned to Gestapo headquarters and detained there for the whole day. Freud, who ordinarily did not show his emotions, was very agitated and smoked incessantly. He now made up his mind to leave, but insisted on taking his library and collections. An exit permit was not easy to obtain, especially with all this luggage. The Nazis were converting their "favors" into cash. They had established an exit "tax" (*Reichsfluchtsteuer*) of twenty percent of the value of all property of emigrants. It was a real swindle since they had most often already confiscated their property and seized their bank accounts. Freud, whose coffers had thus been depleted, was unable to pay the tax, which amounted to $4,824. Marie advanced the sum, which he insisted on repaying her the following summer. She devoted this money to the reproduction in London of the *Gesammelte Werke* destroyed by the Nazis.

Marie remained in Vienna until April 10. She spent most of her time with Anna sorting out Freud's correspondence and manuscripts. She even searched his wastepaper basket, and saved documents that Freud would have liked to destroy before his dreaded exile. During this first stay in Vienna, she also gathered numerous recollections of the Freud family, their migrations from the Rhineland to Lithuania, then to Galicia, where Freud's father was born, and later to Freiberg in Moravia, where Freud himself was born. She noted the list of her teacher's brothers and sisters and his screen memories about the death of his brother Julius at the age of eight months when he was a year and a half. On April 8, he told her his Paris memories about Charcot and Richetti.

Marie not only took care of the Freuds, she was ready to help all the endangered people she heard of through her friends. One of them, Dr. Richard Berczeller, a physician, is still living in New York City and remembers "her impressive personality." She was "a handsome woman, extremely warm, a convincing aristocrat." Freud had arranged an appointment in his office. After having listened to Dr. Berczeller's story she immediately called the French ambassador and asked for a residence permit for the young physician, his wife and their six-year-old son. Dr. Berczeller was involved in politics and had already been jailed for a few months. He was sure that the Nazis were going to imprison him again, this time forever; he hoped to find asylum in Paris, where, later, Marie kept in touch with him, though he had not dared to visit her on his arrival, embarrassed as he was by his poverty.

On April 11, Marie left for Saint-Cloud. Her appointment book was full: on the 13th she had lunch with Malinowski. On April 15, she saw Alexis Léger, then the secretary at the Foreign Office, whom she knew through Briand. On the 17th, she returned to Vienna. On the 19th, she went to Cracow to attend the wedding of the sister of her future son-in-law, Dominique Radziwill, while Hitler was entering Vienna.

From April 29 to May 4, Marie was back in Vienna for the final preparations for Freud's departure. She could not stay as long as she would have liked because Eugénie's marriage was to take place on May 30 in Paris, at the church of the Invalides.

On June 5, finally en route to London, Freud stopped over briefly in Paris. Accompanied by the United States Ambassador, William C. Bullitt, Marie went to meet him at the Gare de l'Est. He rested for half a day in the garden of her house on rue Adolphe Yvon, surrounded by his family and Marie's, including Waldemar. The warmth of friendship made them all forget for a day that barbarism was enslaving the spirit.

· 9 ·

PERSECUTION, WAR, EXILE

> "... *nothing being erased in the course of life,*
> *each of us is comparable to a document on which,*
> *in abbreviated form, of course, the whole history*
> *and prehistory of humanity is inscribed.*"
>
> MARIE BONAPARTE,
> *Psychanalyse et Anthropologie, p. 174*

DURING THE FREUD FAMILY'S TWELVE-HOUR STAY AT RUE
Adolphe Yvon, the sun shone over Paris. Prince Waldemar
and Croisy joined them in the garden. Both had come for
the marriage of Princess Eugénie and Prince Dominique Radziwill.
They soon departed, one for England, the other for Denmark, and
with them happiness and celebration vanished.

Marie was haunted by what she had seen in Vienna. She knew
that what she had known and loved had been forever swept away
by the storm of barbarism that was beginning to buffet Europe.
She worried about Freud. His health was deteriorating and the
trip had been strenuous for a man of eighty-two. Dr. Schur had
developed appendicitis and had been unable to accompany his
patient. He and his family left Vienna on June 10, as soon as
possible after the operation. The Schurs stayed for a few days with
Marie Bonaparte on their way to London. Marie was terribly
upset that the children, aged five and two and a half, had been
subjected to the atmosphere of terror and madness in their native
city. During the years that followed, she used her influence and
financial power to rescue close to two hundred Jews persecuted by
Hitler. Dr. Berczeller, who with her help had been able to establish residence in Paris, was one of her go-betweens. Through him,
she channeled funds to Jewish organizations, for the purpose of
saving scientists and physicians from Austria and Germany.
Loewenstein would write later: "Her modesty always opposed the
disclosure of her generosity."[1]

In various ways, she tried to alert public opinion to the realities
of Nazi politics, writing in French newspapers and journals about

Freud's expulsion from his homeland;[2] inviting ministers in the French government to Saint-Cloud, since they might be useful in securing residence permits or transit visas; having Dr. Berczeller lecture at rue Adolphe Yvon on the European political situation. Among her guests were Joseph Paul-Boncour, minister of foreign affairs, Albert Sarrault, minister of the interior, and Jean Zay, minister of education, who was later imprisoned and executed by Pétain's militia. None of them was ready to believe that Western Europe would soon be overrun and ruled by the superior forces of Nazi Germany.

Marie was particularly concerned about Freud's four aged sisters, who had been unable to leave Austria with the rest of the Freud family. By vouching for their support she obtained permission for them to settle in France, but the Austrian National Socialist Government refused them the necessary exit visas; they all perished in extermination camps. But she made it possible for Freud's son Oliver and his family to emigrate to France. She and Loewenstein also succeeded in getting their Austrian friends, Heinz and Dora Hartmann, to Paris, from where they eventually emigrated to New York.

At the end of June, Marie spent three days in London. The Freuds were her real, her chosen family whose worries she shared. In his biography of Freud, Jones recounts how, through the personal intervention of her nephew, the king of Greece, Marie was able to transfer Freud's gold investments to London.[3] Marie took it for granted that the monarch would help the founder of psychoanalysis.

That year, the International Congress of Psychoanalysis was held in Paris, from July 29 to August 3. At this occasion she presented a paper on *L'Inconscient et le temps* (The Unconscious and Time). Freud found her first draft "more poetic and philosophical than analytic." "I do not accept the absolute subjectivity of time," she replied in self-defense.[4] But, as usual, she followed her master's advice and reworked her paper. Now he wrote: "You have given a better explanation of the notions of time and space than I would have done. To tell the truth, as far as time is concerned, I have not kept you completely up to date on my ideas. Nor anyone else either."[5] The paper was published.[6]

After the Congress and again in late October, she visited London. The fall was spent at Le Lys de Mer with Eugénie and her husband. Eugénie seemed content. She translated *Topsy* into

English. (Freud and his daughter, to distract themselves from the political situation and Freud's illness during their last months in Vienna, had done a German version of this little book about Marie's chow-chow which was cured of cancer. Their translation was published in Amsterdam in 1939.)

In September 1938, when peace was in the balance until the Munich Pact assured "peace in our time," Marie was staying with George in their Blain château, "to protect fifteen people (servants and farmers) and our property," as she wrote to Freud.[7] During this time, Freud was operated on again; it was the most painful surgery since 1923. It took him weeks to recover, and he did not wish to see his friend, "our princess," while overcome by pain.

Waldemar's eightieth birthday was celebrated at the end of October. Marie sent him a telegram but did not accompany George to Bernstorff. Instead she went to London and stayed for the first time at Maresfield Gardens, in the house where the Freuds had finally settled with their furniture, books and Freud's collection of antiquities. Everything had arrived in good condition, largely due to Marie's help, as energetic as it was generous.

Marie was satisfied at least with the material conditions of her adored teacher's life, but did not forget the sufferings and impending dangers of those still in Nazi hands. In November, she proposed to William C. Bullitt, the United States Ambassador in Paris, that the United States buy Lower California from Mexico and establish a Jewish state there under its protection. If Lower California were out of the question, why not Guiana or the former German colonies in Africa? She told Bullitt that Freud shared this idea. In his reply, the ambassador expressed his doubts but assured her that President Roosevelt was doing his utmost to help the Jewish refugees. Undaunted, on December 12, she wrote President Roosevelt himself to explain her plan. In the meantime Freud had written that he did not take what he called her "colonial plans" seriously.[8]

During this whole dark period, she had five patients in analysis, but she planned to give them up at the end of the year in order to visit Egypt with her daughter.

The trip began in Athens, where Marie and her family had spent Christmas in their house, and were visited by the king. They sailed on December 31. The first stop was Haifa, where mother and daughter toured the city and its surroundings, including some *kibbutzim*. Marie again saw Eitingon, who had been a professor at the University of Jerusalem since 1933. After Marie and Eugénie had been to Alexandria they settled in the then famous Mena House at the foot of the pyramids. From this base they visited Memphis and Thebes, and the eminent French Egyptologist, Abbé Drioton, took them through the Cairo Museum. George cabled them at Mena House that Waldemar had pneumonia and Marie immediately proposed to join George at his uncle's bedside in Copenhagen. George hoped that the new pneumonia antitoxin would be effective and told her not to come, but three days later Waldemar's condition became critical and George asked her to come. Waldemar died on January 14, just as Marie was arriving. She did not see him. George insisted on remaining alone beside the corpse of his friend.

This death threw Marie into great inner turmoil. She wrote to Freud daily, relating in detail, as was her habit, all the events and her emotional reactions to them. George was exhausted—in four days he had had only eleven hours of sleep. She resented his keeping her at a distance in the Gule Palae, Waldemar's winter residence, where she felt herself a complete stranger. Was it because of her atheism? She should have arrived earlier; she should have been more friendly to Waldemar. The funeral was held on January 18. Waldemar was buried in the royal cemetery, and afterward there was a dinner at his nephew's, King Christian X. Marie wanted to be closer to George. She accused herself frantically. She proposed that her husband be buried in Copenhagen with Waldemar, instead of at Tatoï with her. But George replied that only the soul counted, and he was sure that his would be reunited with Waldemar's in heaven. George was the executor of his uncle's will, and Marie offered to help him buy furniture and houses that had belonged to Waldemar. Nevertheless she was still jealous. It was at this time that she wrote the slender notebook entitled *Le vieux compagnon* (The Old Companion) in which she retraced from the beginning the story of this unique love between uncle and nephew. She felt excluded from George's grief and mourning, just as she had felt excluded from the two men's life. Their passionate attachment provoked irrepressible anger in Marie, who felt more deprived than she would have in the case of adultery. Marie's persistent frigidity made her more vulnerable than others. For thirty years she had felt the indignity inflicted on her condition as a woman and she, so proud of her "virile" mind, suffered from not being able to rival the Old Companion.

Though she stressed her intention not to leave George again for many months, she returned to Paris at the end of January, where the day after her arrival she welcomed her nephew Paul and Princess Frederika, the future sovereigns of Greece. It was a relief to resume her work routine and her various obligations.

After a quick trip to Geneva, she spent two weeks in London to put her papers and manuscripts in safekeeping at the Rothschild bank and above all to be near Freud, whose cancer was spreading. She discussed the medical problems with Dr. Schur, but also consulted the best specialists in London and Paris. She called Professor Lacassagne, Rigaud's successor at the Curie Institute, the radium institute, to London for advice on X-ray treatments. She also saw Queen Mary, the queen mother, whom she hoped to interest in the cause of the refugees. And she found time for an excursion to the country with Anna Freud. George was still in Denmark. Marie went back and forth between Paris and London several times with Professor Lacassagne. She had little time for X. during this period, but she kept him informed about Freud by telephone and letters.

Eugénie was pregnant and confined to bed. Marie went to Normandy and bought her the Val Saint-Martin estate in Beaumont-le-Roger. The international situation was deteriorating. Hitler occupied Czechoslovakia on March 15. On the 28th, Madrid fell to General Franco. It was the end of the Spanish Civil War and the beginning of the long dictatorship. On April 7, Mussolini occupied Albania.

Politics also held sway within the Paris Psychoanalytic Society, from which Marie had been absent for several months. Laforgue had been voted out of the presidency and a rift was slowly developing. His faction, which included his and Pichon's analysands, opposed Bonaparte-Loewenstein and their followers. In this discordant atmosphere, Jacques-Marie Lacan was admitted to full membership in the Society. He had not finished his training analysis with Loewenstein—indeed he never did although he promised to. But it was necessary to support his candidacy in order to secure the election of Heinz Hartmann, already famous for his book, *The Ego and the Problem of Adaptation*; Hartmann was opposed by Pichon because he was a foreigner. Through his wife's family's connections, Lacan had been well launched in Parisian avant-garde literary and artistic circles, and soon he was a force within the society. But by 1939, Pichon, the linguist, had changed his

Prince and Princess George of Greece with their children, Eugénie and Peter

Princess George of Greece and Denmark at the court of King George I of the Hellenes

Prince and Princess George of Greece with their children

Top: *Princess Marie on the hospital ship* Albania, *during the Balkan wars*

Middle: *Princess Marie and her son, Prince Peter of Greece, in Cretan costume, 1912*

Bottom: *Princess Marie, 1919. Photograph dedicated to "Croisy," her children's governess*

Princess Marie with her daughter, Princess Eugénie

Marie Bonaparte, at the beginning of her career as a psychoanalyst

Right: *Aristide Briand*

Below: *Aristide Briand at the helm of a friend's yacht*

Opposite top: *Sigmund Freud with his chow Tofi, 1937*

Opposite bottom: *Marie Bonaparte with members of the Danish royal family, Copenhagen, 1932*

Marie Bonaparte in her later years

Sigmund Freud on his way to London, June 5, 1938, in the garden of rue Adolphe Yvon: Marie Bonaparte, Freud, Mrs. Freud, Ernest Freud, Dr. Josephine Stross

Marie Bonaparte taking Freud's picture in his new study at Maresfield Gardens, London

Prince George of Greece during his 1954 trip to Crete. PHOTO MARIE BONAPARTE

Prince and Princess George of Greece in Venice, 1954

Prince and Princess George of Greece, 1954

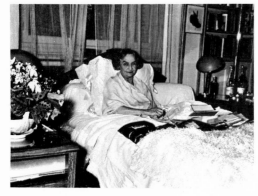

Marie Bonaparte as she often received callers at her home

Marie Bonaparte on the terrace of Saint-Cloud in 1961, one year before her death

mind and he wrote that language for Lacan was "an armor made out of the jargon of a sect and personal preciosity," and that Lacan's style was "hermetically sealed and inexact."[9]

At the end of April 1939, a meeting of British and French analysts was held in Paris. Anna Freud did not attend because of the state of her father's health. George had only just come back from Denmark. On the occasion of Freud's birthday, May 6, Marie spent three days in London. Her diary records her melancholy mood. She knew that her "Great Master" could not survive for long; she was dispirited also by her son's departure; he had left for Madras a month earlier. He had told her often of his wish to fight the Germans and Italians, but he was also thinking of marriage. In early June, Marie was once more in London. Despite the glorious weather, she felt racked by anxiety. George, alone in Paris, was depressed and slept badly. Eugénie was suffering from headaches. Marie took Freud some films of Le Lys de Mer, a place he would never know, others of her trip to Brazil with Eugénie, and some that had been shot by Peter in Tibet. She was at a loss as to how to distract the sick man, for whatever she said or did, there was always a tragic echo.

At the beginning of June, she went to her house by the sea to regain her strength, but she kept in touch with London by telephone. At Le Lys de Mer, she wrote outdoors under the pines. She was pondering a work on the ambivalence of justice, because to her great surprise Annette Berman and Eugénie accused her of being unjust. Once more she worked on herself, endeavoring to understand how and why she could be, or seem to be, unjust. She thought of taking up the theme of the primitive mother who claims to prefer each of her children. At this point in her life, she found "that there were as many kinds of justice as there were people who demanded it; and since one could not satisfy all the contradictory justices, it was impossible to live and be a poet." She turned away from world affairs, to the world within, and to nature, went swimming four times a day, and listened to the nightingales singing. And she mourned Tatoun, the eldest of the chow-chows, who died far away in Annette Berman's office in Paris. Twice, with a month's interval, she went to London. The second trip was with George, from July 30 to August 6. This was her last visit to Freud. They both knew that they were saying adieu. His physical suffering would only end with his life. It would be cruel to want to prolong it.

Events moved rapidly: on the day of Marie's return to Paris, her cousin Lucien de Villeneuve, the youngest of Aunt Jeanne's sons, died. Like the other Villeneuves, he was buried in Valensole, not far from Saint-Tropez. After the funeral, Marie went home to Le Lys de Mer.

Europe inched toward war. The Nazis occupied the Danzig corridor. "We can no longer, at least so I think, go to Munich," Marie wrote to her daughter on August 20. On the 22nd, the Nazi-Soviet pact was signed. Until then, Marie, like everyone else, had tried to lead a normal life. At Le Lys de Mer, she invited colleagues—Flournoy, Morgenstern—to lunch; she took drives in the car; she went to Les Saintes-Maries-de-la-Mer. On August 26, she was in Beaumont-le-Roger to be with Eugénie, who gave birth to a daughter two days later.

Typically, Marie the grandmother immediately started a small red leather diary, *Le Livre de Tatiana* (Tatiana's Book): "On August 28, 1939, at 10:45 P.M., birth of Tatiana-Marie-Renata-Eugénie-Elisabeth-Margueritte, Princess Radziwill, in Rouen, Saint-Hilaire clinic, delivered by Professor Martin at seven months, after twelve hours of labor and Eugénie's trip with me by ambulance from Val Saint-Martin to the clinic." Marie also noted the baby's size and weight. On August 30, Prince George came from Paris to see his granddaughter.

On September 1, Hitler invaded Poland, and two days later England and France declared war. In Marie Bonaparte's notebooks, the first news of the war alternated with events concerning the baby. On September 5, she noted the first air raid alert in Paris and that Tatiana's umbilical cord dropped off. Marie was back in Paris, as was George from Blain, where he had been detained because the British general stationed in the area wanted to requisition the château for a gasoline depot. Finally refugees from Paris were settled there. Marie and George learned from the newspapers that their son had married Irène Outchinikova in Madras. George was desperate. He ordered Marie to inform Peter that he was forbidden to enter their homes in Paris and Athens. Peter had to forfeit all his Greek and Danish prerogatives. He had been cowardly in presenting them with a *fait accompli*. But Marie decided not to deprive Peter of financial support. She let him know this immediately.

Freud died at 3 A.M. on September 23, and she heard of it the next morning. "I will never forget the emotional tones of the BBC announcer when, even before reading the war news, he announced that Sigmund Freud was no more."[10] On the day when her son-in-law Radziwill was leaving for Coëtquiden in Brittany to join the Polish Legion formed by those who had been able to flee the Nazis, Marie left for London to attend the funeral of her master and friend. The cremation took place on September 26 at Golders Green. Stefan Zweig and Ernest Jones gave the eulogies. In accordance with Freud's wishes, his ashes were placed in one of the Greek vases Marie had given him.

Three days after the funeral, Marie returned from London alone. She published an article in the weekly *Marianne*,[11] expressing her grief, her admiration for the greatness of Freud's thought, and her horror of Nazism. She was carried away by her natural lyricism but neither inspiration nor strength of conviction was lacking. She was now in full possession of her intellectual capacities, ready to fight to preserve the spiritual heritage of her teacher.

She had other obligations too. Soon after her return, she was at Val Saint-Martin, writing the *Journal de Tatiana*. On October 2, the baby sucked her thumb for the first time. Marie observed the little girl with her obsessional tendency for precision and detail. She measured everything: the baby's ears, nostrils and genitals.

On November 13, Peter arrived alone in Saint-Cloud. Together they went to see the baby, and then he stayed with his mother for a few days. His father was at rue Adolphe Yvon and would not see him. At the beginning of December, accompanied by her cousin Hedwige, daughter of the Duchesse de Doudeauville, Marie went to Thionville to deliver the ambulances that she was donating to the army. Aside from this unavoidable errand, she remained in Paris, where she had much to do. She had now six patients in analysis—two men and four women. At the end of the year she was in Athens with George. Before leaving Paris, she had decorated a Christmas tree for Tatiana. She wrote an essay entitled "The Legend of the Unfathomable Waters," which related these superstitions to human fascination with return to the womb and death in the amniotic fluid.[12]

Prince Christopher, George's youngest brother, was soon to die of a lung abscess. The family gathered around him. There were Aunts Elena and Alice, as well as the Comte de Paris, whose sister was Christopher's wife. Princess Frederika was four months pregnant, "a nice little woman when you get to know her," Marie wrote to Eugénie.[13] Malinowski had left England. Always faithful, he telephoned from Yale, to tell Marie that he had written Peter that the Department of Anthropology was ready to give him an honorary position as research associate, which would allow the prince-ethnologist to use the university library.

Marie did not forget this transatlantic phone call, for her friend died without their ever meeting again. At this time, Peter and his wife were living at the Hotel Subasio in Assisi, Italy. In India, he had worked with one of Malinowski's pupils, to his satisfaction. But Peter was not interested in exiling himself to the United States. He expected to be called for military service in Greece, although he had no wish to be separated from Irène. Marie saw this union as a poorly resolved Oedipal conflict. "His marriage was against me." He was still reproaching her for having neglected him for other men, and taking his revenge. "Loewenstein only freed him from the superego of Croisy. A mistake, he found another one in Irène."

Loewenstein, Peter's analyst and her former lover, was naturalized as a Frenchman in 1930. He had been mobilized as an auxiliary doctor, but kept in touch with Marie. His second wife was a Hungarian Countess Pallavicini—Amo—whom he entrusted to Marie, along with his three children, in a letter written from Pontarlier on May 28. He had just been demobilized because of age but was re-enlisting for the duration of the war. Marie was in Bénodet, in Britanny, near the Loewenstein family, and gave Amo 20,000 francs.

On April 9, Hitler invaded Denmark and Norway. On May 10, the Germans entered Luxembourg, Belgium and the Netherlands. Marie heard it from Frieda, her Swiss chambermaid, while she was writing in the garden at Saint-Cloud. On the 14th the battle of Sedan took place, and on the 15th, Holland capitulated, followed by Belgium. Italy entered the war on Hitler's side and then, from May 28 to June 4, there was the battle of Dunkirk. Marie visited Eugénie and little Tatiana in Beaumont; the Radziwills were getting ready to leave for Bordeaux, where Marie was to meet them. They were to miss each other in Bordeaux, and the Radziwills found it safer and simpler to go to Le Lys de Mer.

On June 14, the Germans entered Paris. Marie was still in Bénodet and she regretted not being present to watch "this horrible defeat, the greatest catastrophe France had endured since the Hundred Years' War—probably even since Caesar's conquest of Gaul." She thought this wish to observe Hitler's armies occupying Paris was "perhaps the child's regret at not having watched the violent possession of the 'Motherland' by the victorious 'Father.' "[14] On the 16th, Pétain became prime minister, and on the 22nd a Franco-German armistice was signed. On June 18, General de Gaulle launched his famous broadcast appeal from London: "France has lost a battle—she has not lost the war."

On June 20, Marie watched the German troops as they passed through Bénodet. France's armistice with Italy was signed on the 25th. On July 3, the British attacked the French fleet at Mers-el-Kebir, since Admiral Gensoul had refused either to sail to British ports or to scuttle the fleet. Marie had no further reason to remain in Brittany; she had to go back to Paris to see what could be done. She went through Beaumont and discovered that Val Saint-Martin had been ransacked during the "exodus." The doors were staved in, the closets emptied, and the linen stolen. She found clothes strewn about and trampled on, and her finest books scattered and torn.

At Saint-Cloud, she had another surprise. The Germans had burglarized the house. Her cabinets had been smashed, the safe opened with an acetylene torch and only the Empire furniture was intact. All the same, she moved into the devastated house, where, the following day, she had lunch with X., who had stayed in Paris, faithful to his duty as a physician. From him she learned all the details of the German occupation of the city. She soon decided to take everyone to Saint-Tropez and arrived there on August 2. Loewenstein, Amo and the children visited her. There was even a little party for Tatiana's first birthday.

Marie returned to Paris on October 10. On the way she stopped in Arles to see Annette Berman. She found her in tears, living in a miserable room with a wood-burning stove. Marie invited her to Saint-Tropez in December and gave her work. She had begun her essay *Myths of War*. Eugénie had remained at Le Lys de Mer with her demobilized husband. On October 28, Marie wrote her that she and George were applying at the German embassy for visas to travel to Athens. But on that same day, Italy attacked Greece.

In December, Marie was still in Paris. On the 19th, the Nazis returned the remains of l'Aiglon (Napoleon's son) as a gesture to mollify the French, still attached to the memory of the Emperor. Marie saw X. more often, and they even spent a day together in the country. Their relationship had attained a certain serenity. They were now an old couple of lover-friends, happy each time they were together; they enjoyed these precious moments, foreseeing that they would soon be separated, probably forever. In late December, Marie went to Vichy to obtain exit visas for George and herself. Aunt Minnie, George's sister, the widow of Grand Duke George, who had been shot by a Bolshevik firing squad, had died in Athens. The Radziwills wanted to go to Egypt. Finally, they went around Africa and reached Lourenço Marques. From Mozambique they went to South Africa and settled in Durban.

Marie was more depressed than she had been for years, devastated at her country's defeat and torn by the thought of leaving France, but she wanted to be closer to Peter, who was serving in the Greek army. On January 7, 1941, she wrote to him from Vichy that she was ill; once again she had cystitis, flu, sinusitis, otitis. Two weeks later she obtained the visas and returned immediately to Paris to prepare for the departure. She had barely recovered.

Except for her patients, some of whom had left because they were Jews, Marie had no other professional activity. The *Revue* had ceased publication in May 1939, and the Institut de Psychanalyse had closed its doors a few weeks before the arrival of the Nazis. The members of the Society had scattered. Some sought exile, like Loewenstein, who was waiting to leave for the United States. The Swiss had returned to their country. There were only four analysts left in Paris. The others were trying to live inconspicuously in the provinces. Marie Bonaparte had no wish to live under the Nazi occupation—she knew too well what to expect. But exile was even harder for her than she had imagined.

Arriving in Athens in February 1941, she was to remain there only until April 22, when once again she fled before the German onslaught. After spending a few days in Crete, she left for Alexandria with the Greek royal family, two weeks before the German parachute attack on the island. Peter remained behind with the king, for whom he was a liaison officer with the British armies in the Middle East. He soon went to Cairo and Jerusalem, but by then his parents were in South Africa, where they arrived on July 8, 1941, with the rest of the royal family. Eugénie, her husband and little Tatiana were waiting for them in Durban. Marie and George began by traveling through this part of Africa which was new to them and would be their refuge until the end of the war. They saw Kruger Park in Transvaal and Victoria Falls. Both Marie and George were impressed with the wild natural beauty, but

Marie was eager to settle down in Cape Town, where she hoped to resume her career.

Their first house was in Westbrooke. Marie did not like it. They moved into it in a torrential downpour and she noted, "hostile nature." She longed for Europe and most of the time waited in vain for letters from France; the mail from London was not much better. Peter received frequent letters full of complaint, which was not her style. Marie wrote that she wanted to visit him and Irène in Cairo but did not dare to leave George. Her husband was now seventy-two, and still mourning Waldemar; he was aging. Truly alone with him for the first time, Marie could neither leave him nor be satisfied with his company.

At the end of October 1941, things got even worse; the house burned down. The fire started in the kitchen quarters and George and Marie threw valuables out of the windows to the servants below. The family was offered temporary quarters with Jan Smuts, the South African statesman, in his own house in Groote Schuur.

Marie more than ever felt an uprooted exile, and tried to combat her sense of loss and bewilderment with work. During her brief stay in Cairo she had visited the Coptic hospital with Professor Mahfous and had seen two women patients whose clitoris had been excised. Marie had been interested in this practice, which has persisted from the time of the Pharaohs. Freud had discussed it with her and thought that excision of the external clitoris did not interfere with erotic and orgastic possibilities in women because "men in every climate are eager to have voluptuous joinings with their partners." Marie argued to the contrary in *Notes on Excision*,[15] stressing that the bloody and frightening mutilation was but one more step added to societal repression of female sexual enjoyment. She saw this as being aimed at the "virile, phallic" strivings of women. She also continued writing *Myths of War* and started *The Essential Ambivalence of Eros*;[16] these three essays she wrote in English. She resumed her study of Greek, and from mid-November on, she had her first patient.

The presence of her granddaughter distracted her from her morose thoughts and brought her love. Each time she walked the little girl past the burned house, Tatiana blew through her mouth to extinguish the fire, as Marie was pleased to observe, but she also wrote to her Troisier friends: "I long to see the Big Dipper again and hate the Southern Cross."

The double suicide of Stefan Zweig and his wife, early in 1942 in Brazil, affected her deeply. She attributed it to "uprooting and melancholy." During this period she read Nietzsche with her usual passion. By January 1942, she had begun to work twice a week at the library and in the hospital. She attended courses in psychiatry and was invited to address the students. A month later, on March 31, she gave her first lecture on Freud and was asked to teach once a week. She took Professor Fishoek's course in anthropology to be able to participate more closely in Peter's interests. Her life, as in Europe, was divided. Since they shared the same fate as refugees, she became closer to her royal in-laws, especially Princess Frederika, who in May gave birth to a daughter named Irene. She took short trips with George, who was bored, and stayed with him in Caledon to use the spa. In September, he suffered a retinal hemorrhage followed by a variety of illnesses during which she nursed him. Eugénie, who was pregnant again, entered the hospital at the beginning of October, a cesarean had to be performed, and on November 4 Georges-André-Dominique-Jérôme-Pierre-Léon, Prince Radziwill, was born. On November 9, Marie wrote to Anna: "My grandson is born," regretting that she could not give this news to Freud. Eugénie had spent more than six months in bed before the birth. The first time she saw Georges-André, it was Tatiana who wheeled the bassinet into her mother's bedroom.

Marie observed her granddaughter's behavior, drew conclusions about the origin of the superego and wrote long letters to Anna Freud. Similar to the letters she had written her analyst, she discussed everything concerning herself and those around her. The bond between the two women strengthened over the years, and Anna Freud, although younger, retained the role of constant confidante and guide that had been her father's after the end of the analysis. Anna was the first to read the text of "Saint Christopher, Patron Saint of the Motor-car Drivers,"[17] written first in English, then in German, in 1942.

Marie had resumed her professional activities. She organized meetings of psychiatrists and analysts, tried to put refugees in contact with hospitals and universities, exerted herself on their behalf and often had to make the best of a bad job. To Loewenstein she wrote: "Our colleague W. S. is in Johannesburg." Though she did not share his analytic ideas and had no wish to talk to him, she organized a speaking engagement for him before the psychiatrists of Cape Town, where she "tactfully" disagreed with his opinions. Another analyst in Johannesburg, named Peerls, was a pupil of Reich's and was putting his teacher's new biological ideas into practice.

The few lectures given by Marie at the university and elsewhere attracted a considerable audience, but she continued to feel isolated intellectually. The man whom she most enjoyed conversing with was a neurologist from Cape Town, who understood analysis although unwilling to be analyzed himself—which she thought a pity, since in her opinion he would have made a very good analyst. Among her patients Marie had an eighteen-year-old girl, a refugee from Hamburg, who wanted to make analysis her career. The others were in therapeutic analysis: two women doctors and an agoraphobic girl who under Marie's guidance was able to come half the long distance from her home by herself. Marie was also interested in African ethnography and corresponded with Kenyatta, now general secretary of the Kikuyu Central Association.

Outside her professional contacts and her family, she had almost no distractions. She managed to become friendly with Sir Herbert Stanley, the cultivated former governor of Southern Rhodesia, who had been "part of the seedbed of young men surrounding Cecil Rhodes," as she reports, and who lent her Aldous Huxley's *Grey Eminence*. She also met an Anglican bishop, Parker, who invited her to accompany him on a visit to the native chiefs of his Transvaal diocese. She spent a week in his company in Pretoria, though it appears that they spent more time swimming than interviewing the natives.

With Bishop Parker, she met Wolhuter, an ex-ranger famous for a fight he had had with a lion. In talking with him, she elicited his dreams and published them with a psychoanalytic commentary in *A Lion Hunter's Dreams*.[18] It was a trip on which she saw native Africans only at a distance. Her position as a Royal Highness in exile kept her apart from most people. She never stopped repeating how lost she felt. Summing up her state of mind, she wrote to Peter at the end of 1942: "Life is hell. . . ." She had given up all private, intimate life. The passage from maturity to old age was painful for a woman with her powerful erotic drives and such a strong need to be loved, and she sadly missed X.

Hitler had occupied southern France, and Marie grew increasingly worried about Annette Berman, who refused to leave France and her friends, although Marie had obtained a South African visa for her. She sought the same visa for Eitingon. Dissatisfied with her lectures, bored by her work at the military hospital, with

George constantly disgruntled, she dreaded the thought of dying in exile. Once again it was only nature that consoled her. There were flowers, birds, small gray squirrels.

In spite of the irregularity of the mails, Marie made every effort to stay in touch with her friends. She had a gift for friendship, and included Dr. Berczeller among her correspondents. With him she shared her despair at the dullness of her South African life and her concern for Annette Berman. Worrying about others made the major problems more bearable.

In France, the Gestapo was visiting homes and arresting Jews and members of the Resistance. Marie was apprehensive that Oliver Freud and his family might be "denaturalized" and handed over to the Germans. The whole world had been horrified by revelations about the camps in Poland. And there was death unrelated to war: the Duchesse de Doudeauville died. Marie mourned her cousin Lise. Different though they were, they shared many memories. Marie wrote often to Peter, who continued to travel, from Malta to Gibraltar, from Lagos to Léopoldville. In April, he was back in Cairo with his wife, but in July had to leave again for Jerusalem.

Marie was not traveling but she moved. In mid-May, 1942, she changed to a house in the lovely suburb of Chatsworth.

A year earlier, the empty house on rue Adolphe Yvon had been visited by the Germans and on August 15, 1942, it was occupied by them. On November 8 the Allies landed in North Africa. Then came the scuttling of the French fleet at Toulon, and on December 29, at the Cape Town municipal hall, Marie and George attended a "monster rally" to protest Hitler's policy of genocide.

The German capitulation at Stalingrad on February 2, 1943, produced the first tangible hope of victory. George had predicted that the Russians would be decisive in crushing the Germans. There was more good news to cheer Marie: Oliver Freud was safe at last in Barcelona. She finished her essay on *The Ambivalence of Eros*; she rediscovered Rilke and was enthusiastic about *Sonnets to Orpheus* and the *Duino Elegies*, "specially the third and the fourth. . . . When did Rilke know analysis?" she asked Anna Freud in a letter of August 5, 1943. The lack of culture of the people she met appalled her. Giving lifts to soldiers on the roads, she was collecting material for her book about *Myths of War*, but all in all daily life was a burden. And she still suffered from colibacilli cystitis.

On March 15, she wrote to Loewenstein in New York: "It's raining and drizzling, the silhouette of Table Mountain, close as it is, disappears behind a curtain of mist and tiny drops of water, and I feel as melancholy as this foreign sky. . . . My attachment to my native country kept me unduly in France, and then my love for my son. . . . I am here as a princess of Greece, a member of the royal family like any other, and not after all as myself. . . . Just imagine, in leaving for Greece, I did so with the unconscious and even conscious plan of getting myself killed: I would drive an ambulance at the front, I would sail on a hospital ship that would be bombarded or sunk, I would perhaps go by plane to gather up the wounded on the battlefield. . . ." She was still prone to see herself as a romantic heroine, and part of her life was still "wild fantasy." But at the end of August, still depressed, she observed to the same friend: "I thought that with age one acquired serenity. It's not so. When all your life you've had a tormented soul, you probably keep it to the edge of the grave. If only I had taken the boat to America when the Germans marched on Paris. We would all be together." She suffered from being separated from Peter, whom she had to tell that Prince George did not wish to see him. His feelings about Irène had not changed. Furthermore, he was "more and more crippled by pain; he has lost weight; he is tired."

In October, the house-hunting started again. They had hoped to remain in Chatsworth until the end of their stay, but once more had to move. "It is horrible to be a refugee. You are a nuisance for everyone, and everyone lets you feel it. And how strongly," she wrote to Peter on October 30, 1943.

Though the end of the Nazi nightmare could now be foreseen, the year 1944 still began in the debilitating atmosphere of exile. Marie looked at houses but was thinking constantly of the moment when it would be possible to return to France. But would she be able to stay there? "There is good reason why the Russians are in the process of winning the European war, and the wealthier classes have done so many selfish things that the people will not forgive them."[19] The world would not be the same, everything was about to change. Marie was not alone in thinking so. At the age of sixty-two, she was weary. She began to take insulin for her diabetes; her heartbeat was too fast; she caught whooping cough for the second time, and gave it to Tatiana and Georges-André, now called "Porgie."

Her grandchildren were her favorite companions. She spent a

good deal of time with them while their mother was tending the
critically wounded at the military hospital. Marie entertained the
children and this cheered her. She was, however, worried about
Peter, who was in Italy with the Maori troops advancing on Rome.
Mother and son wrote to each other often, once again openly and
affectionately. In March, the family moved to Hellas—another
suburb, another house to adjust to. Fortunately there were three
jacarandas and two pink oleanders.

After the Teheran conference at the end of the previous year, a
second front in Europe was expected. To distract her thoughts
from the slow Allied advance in Italy, Marie decided to learn
Russian. She was as fascinated by Russia as Rilke had been.

On May 16, Anna Freud wrote her a long letter to bring her up
to date on the dissensions within the British Society. Eitingon was
dead, and Jones in Anna's view had gone over to Melanie Klein,
who had long rejected Freudian orthodoxy. Glover had resigned,
and Anna, who was a member of the training committee, no longer
attended its meetings. She was counting on Marie. "You are
needed," she wrote. She was at a loss how to reestablish a committee of five to seven "pure" analysts. She also proposed that Marie
and Arnold Zweig write her father's biography.

Nothing came of this suggestion because Arnold Zweig declined
the offer. Nevertheless Marie once again felt back in her world.
She had an inkling that similar problems would confront her
within the Paris Society, but felt ready to tackle them. A letter
such as Anna's stimulated her.

On June 6, the Allies landed in Normandy. Marie was wholly
absorbed by the news about events in France. By the end of July
she hoped to set up a relief fund for the liberated French. She
believed that socialism could unite Europe and did not fear the
presence of "Cossacks" on the German frontier. Her confidence
was restored. She amused herself by taking her grandchildren and
their cousins, the children of Princess Frederika, to the zoo. She
made new plans for work. She had just about completed *Myths of
War* and hoped to finish writing the memoirs of her childhood
before the end of the war. Time, which had seemed to drag during
the last years, suddenly seemed to quicken. On August 15, the
Americans and the First Army of General de Lattre de Tassigny
landed in Provence; Saint-Tropez was taken the following day; on
August 18, Versailles was in Allied hands; on the 22nd the Americans were in Saint-Cloud; and on August 25, the German garrison

in Paris surrendered. Marie listened to American broadcasts and followed what was happening hour by hour. But the whole household was sick; they had flu and bronchitis. She and the children recovered quickly, but George's state of health worried her. He had chronic tonsillitis. She wanted to take him as soon as possible to London for treatment. On October 9, she learned by telephone that her manuscripts, notes and letters, as well as the Fliess papers, were safe. On October 13, Athens and Riga were liberated.

By the end of the month, Marie and George had left Cape Town. They sailed on the *Empress of Scotland,* leaving Eugénie and their grandchildren behind. When the ship stopped at Casablanca, they visited the city, and she at last saw the Big Dipper again. On November 10 they arrived in London. Three days later, George's larynx was biopsied and he was scheduled for surgery for an epithelioma on November 27. The operation was successful, but the prince had to spend a month in the hospital.

Prince Andrew, George's favorite brother, died suddenly in Monte Carlo, six days after George's operation. George was now the sole surviving son of King George I. On Christmas Eve, Marie accompanied him to church for his first time out of the hospital.

In London, where they remained until February 15, 1945, Marie wasted no time. She saw a good deal of Anna, who had helped them to choose a surgeon and looked after George in the hospital in Marie's absence. Anna was fond of Prince George and got along with him very well. Marie resumed contact with her British colleagues. She saw John Rodker, who in 1938 had founded the Imago Publishing Company, a small firm after Freud's heart, which replaced the destroyed Verlag and published the *Gesammelte Werke.* Rodker was Marie Bonaparte's publisher, and he was henceforth to publish most of her works, in French as well as in English. Marie also saw her niece Marina, the Duchess of Kent, several times.

In this city devastated by the war and still subject to the howling of sirens, she and George spent a sad Christmas, far from their grandchildren. But in early January 1945, Peter arrived, and for Marie, who had eagerly awaited this reunion, it was a happy occasion. She was able to spend time with him, to converse with him as they used to do. Despite George's reservations, Peter's presence helped her cope with all the distressing news. But London was only a way station, en route to her real life. Marie was convinced that the war would be over by spring. She needed to get to work.

Even as she foresaw a period of political upheaval in Europe after the war, she expected turmoil among the French analysts. She could already picture charges and countercharges of those who had joined the resistance and those who had not. Marie thought it best first to dissolve the Society and then reconstitute it, as Jones had done in London during World War I to ensure his control. She wrote of all that to Loewenstein, adding: "I am not overjoyed at returning to that hornets' nest."[20] All the same she planned to play a decisive role in whatever was to happen.

BACK HOME

*"This reflex of taking refuge in writing whenever
I have been hurt by life has remained with me.
Disappointment or grief, far from preventing me
from working, always drives me irresistibly to seek
solace in literary or scientific creation."*

MARIE BONAPARTE,
Five Copy-Books, vol. II, p. 46

MARIE HAD NO ILLUSIONS THAT THE RETURN TO PARIS COULD
recapture the past. Four years of Nazi occupation had
changed people and circumstances, and X., her lover of so
many years, was slowly dying. She had learned of his illness in
London. Parting from him in 1940 had thrown Marie into despair,
but the years of exile without communication had cooled her passion, though she was still attached to him. Her devotion to her
grandchildren, Tatiana and Porgie, had become the center of her
emotional life. She would soon be sixty-three and had a renewed
urge to collect her manuscripts, revise and publish them as soon as
possible.

She and George returned to Paris by way of Newhaven and
Dieppe, where as a child she had first known the sea. She gave no
thought to the house on the rue de l'Hôtel-de-Ville where she had
lived every summer, but was eager to see her house on the shores
of the Mediterranean and to hear the first nightingale at Saint-
Cloud.

The events of the final weeks of the war marked the return to
old habits. On April 24, the day of Mussolini's execution, Marie
and George took their customary walk in Bagatelle. On the 30th,
Hitler's suicide was announced, and on May 2 Berlin fell to the
Russians while the British were entering Hamburg. Two days
later, Holland and Denmark were liberated. On the 7th the armistice was signed; next day, as the first French deportees were
returning from Germany, came the victory proclamation. Marie
and George joined the celebration on the Champs Elysées, where
she had wished to be for the liberation of Paris. She welcomed the

deportees at the rue de Lyon and the Hôtel Lutetia. In her exile, she had often thought of the harsher fate of the deportees and wished that she could have helped them.

Reunions among the French psychoanalysts were not so happy. One might have thought that Hitler's condemnation of psycho-analysis would have prevented problems about "collaboration" among members of the Society, but, there as elsewhere, Marie noticed that the occupation had given rise to suspicions and ac-cusations against those who were not openly allied with the Resis-tance or in French uniform at the liberation; many colleagues were still scattered on military assignments. Marie was disap-pointed by those whom she saw again. After a meeting at Leuba's home, she wrote to Anna Freud: "I feel as though I've come back to an intellectual desert."[1] John Leuba had spent the whole four years of the Nazi occupation in Paris, working at the hospital Sainte-Anne and also as a volunteer at an emergency station. He was going to be president of the Society from 1946 to 1948. More than ever Marie urged the dissolution of the Society in the fall, but receiving no support she gave up the idea. She wrote to Loewen-stein on July 2: "The Paris Society will pretty much have to get along without me (for reasons of health this winter)." She had had persistent angina and otitis. Moreover her diabetes was diffi-cult to control because of the food shortage. "That is one of the reasons—not counting the financial one—why I have not taken up the Institute again. If others want to take it on, it's all right with me. . . . There are very few of us *real* analysts [her italics] in Paris. I'll mention Odier, if he comes back, Schiff and Nacht, whose training is good. Leuba's character is all right, but for him every-thing is psychic. . . . As for Lacan, he is rather too tinged with paranoia and questionable narcissism, allowing himself too much personal interference.

"As for the *Revue*, I cannot go on supporting it either. Besides, it has never done very well. Rodker might be able to found a review in London by reviving *Imago* in three languages—where we would be able to publish our articles in French. One can ex-pect only difficulties from Jones, who wants nothing but his En-glish review with super-Kleinian articles. You know that in London they've split in two. The official group with Jones and the one of Anna Freud, which do not mingle and are about the same size. When one visits London, one goes to the two of them, as formerly in Rome to visit the Pope and the King. The psychoanalytic societies all over the world are anyway going rather to pieces. I'm deeply disgusted by it and above all want to devote myself to my own work...."

Marie worked at Le Lys de Mer. Thanks to the Turveris, their caretakers, the property had not suffered much. The house, occupied first by the Germans and later by the Americans, was intact. Lila Turveri had taken care to hide furniture, books and valuables nearby. Some of the pine trees had been cut down, but every day, as before, Marie could sit outside in the pine grove to write. "Your father always said: Work on, whatever one's state of health," she reminded Anna.[2] In the south that year the weather was hot and beautiful, and she took advantage of it.

She finished her book, *Myths of War*, which she had begun in 1939. In it she analyzes the fables that are created and spread by word of mouth during wars, often the same on both sides. This interesting and well-documented little book, for which she wrote a preface predicting the legend of Hitler's survival a few weeks after the Führer's suicide, was published the following year.

Her other monographs took longer and she did not always have, even at Le Lys de Mer, the peace she needed for her work. After a whole month's solitude, something she seldom achieved, George returned from Denmark. Then Eugénie and the children arrived from South Africa. Prince Radziwill's arrival coincided with the news of the first atomic attack on Hiroshima. Dominique stayed only a few distressing days, during which he and Eugénie argued about their divorce. Marie's writing was considerably interrupted.

When she returned to Paris in October, she made Saint-Cloud ready for General de Lattre de Tassigny. To keep two houses in such close proximity appeared to her a waste in those days of austerity. General de Lattre had rebelled against Pétain at the time of the total Nazi occupation of France, and had been jailed. He managed to escape to Algeria, and returned in command of the French First Army of Liberation, which landed near Saint-Tropez. He had represented France at the German capitulation. Now he and Mme de Lattre were to be Marie's guests for some months.

Eugénie had gone to London with her children to await her divorce. Marie soon followed them. There, a telegram from George informed her of X.'s death. Marie told Eugénie that she no longer had any feelings for X., that she had withdrawn from him, but she returned to Paris immediately. She joined X.'s children when they placed his body in the coffin, and left a bouquet of autumn flowers she had picked in the garden in Saint-Cloud, where she and the Friend had so often made love. After the funeral, she dined with the widow, whom she endeavored to console. The Friend's death coincided with the third birthday of her adored grandson, Porgie. Marie determined not to show her depression. Once again Anna was her confidante, the only person to whom she dared to express her grief, which surged up despite her earlier indifference. Every day she saw X.'s widow, who felt lost without him. "I feel depressed," Marie wrote to Anna Freud, "except for the urge I have to work to finish preparing for publication (that means survival) the manuscripts of my whole life."

Marie looked forward to seeing her grandchildren. She and George went to spend the Christmas holidays in London. Before her departure, in mid-December, she had organized an administrative meeting of the Society at her house on rue Adolphe Yvon. In London, she divided her time between her analyst friends and the family. She dined with Anna and with Rodker; she went to Buckingham Palace for tea, and visited Queen Mary. She saw Anna as often as was possible without interfering with her friend's work. As usual, she took for granted this divided life between the friends she had chosen and who shared her interests, and her royal in-laws, so utterly different, but who had become familiar and dear over the years.

On December 31, 1945, a childhood dream came true. She sailed on an ocean liner for America and took her family with her. She and George first went to Quebec and Montreal, while Eugénie, Tatiana and Porgie stayed on the ship to New York, where Marie and George arrived by train the evening of January 16, 1946. For Marie, this entire stay in the new world was tinged with depression. She was still mourning for X., whose death had touched her more deeply than any since her father had died in 1924. Her mourning for Freud had been interrupted by war and Tatiana's birth. Now she visited a country that her father had forbidden her and which Freud had ridiculed. Her usual *joie de vivre* is distinctly lacking in her diary entries, which are written almost without personal comment and emotional detail.

The arrival in New York did nothing to improve Marie's frame of mind. Her first luncheon, on January 17, was with Ruth Mack-Brunswick, now blind in one eye, like Princess Pierre. Freud and Marie had corresponded at considerable length about the Brunswicks during the thirties, when Ruth had begun to misuse drugs and Mark made his first attempts to disengage himself by brief escapes, sometimes to Paris to see Marie. Freud, still trying to analyze them both, had become caught in a conflicting situation, distressing for both Marie and Freud.

During the war, little news of Ruth had reached South Africa and Marie was unprepared for the state of deterioration brought about in her friend by intensified morphine addiction. This was all the more distressing to her since she still retained her childhood horror of opiates; nonetheless she had tea with Ruth's stepmother and then dinner with Ruth on the 19th. On the 23rd, Ruth, confined to bed, arranged a small dinner party of analysts for Marie. The next day she fell in her bathroom, fractured her skull, and died. This time Marie withdrew without mourning, but the tragic death cast a further pall over her American visit. She did not attend the funeral.

Her days had not been taken up with Ruth alone. She insisted on taking the children herself to the Museum of Natural History and to show them Manhattan. As usual, she and George went their separate ways, he for long discussions with bishops and visits to the dentist, Marie to look up old friends: Loewenstein, now separated from Amo Pallavicini; the family of Oliver Freud; Saussure, Brill and Géza Róheim. At the Saussures' she had dinner with Jean Paul Sartre, who was going to lecture the next day on the freedom of art.

Dr. Berczeller immediately went to the Plaza, where she was staying, to greet his friend and patron. He was delighted to see very little change in her. After six years of separation, she was still an impressive, attractive woman. She asked him about his work and his family. He was practicing medicine in New York City and had no link with the psychoanalytic milieu. Not knowing how distraught she was, he took her looks at surface value. She told him what he expected to hear: she enjoyed being in America, and seemed genuinely glad to see him again, in her usual warm, straightforward manner. Since she did not talk about herself or about her psychoanalyst friends, he never knew that she had lost her enthusiasm and curiosity about life and was still mourning the war's dead and her own.

While visiting her New York friends she was busily arranging to send food packages to those in Europe and urged her friends to do likewise, stressing the still severe food shortage in France. There were visits to New York society as well: on the 21st of February Marie and George were Mrs. Vanderbilt's guests at the Metropolitan Opera for a performance of *Tannhäuser* and on the 23rd they called on Mrs. John D. Rockefeller, Jr., visits she records even more laconically than those to her friends.

On the 25th, she and George went to Palm Beach, where they were entertained by Mrs. van Rensselaer and Mrs. Guest, whose "fabulous swimming pool" she noted, before visiting other parts of Florida. Next, Marie traveled up the East Coast by herself. She went to Richmond, Williamsburg and Washington, where she had lunch with William Bullitt and dined with St.-John Perse, whom she still called Léger. She returned to New York by way of Baltimore, visiting the grave of Edgar Allan Poe. On March 21, she and George sailed for Europe on the *Queen Mary*. Eugénie and the children had left two weeks earlier.

George and Marie stopped in London, where they lunched with the king. Marie dined with her publisher, arrived in Paris on April 7, and had lunch with Mme de Lattre in Saint-Cloud. She began going to concerts again. After hearing Klemperer conduct, she invited him for lunch. Music and musicians would remain her major distraction. And she needed distraction; she had to face a problem utterly new to her—her fortune, which she had thought inexhaustible, was much reduced. Her bankers had warned her and she informed her son: "It's not that I don't want to give you anything, it's that soon I'll no longer be able to. The richest mother can only give what she has. . . . At this rate, we won't have a penny of capital in France in about four years."[3] Actually she was not on the road to bankruptcy, but one of the main sources of her power was slipping away. She would have to curb her generosity.

After the "dark years" of Nazi occupation, it took time for the French to adjust to liberty. Food and fuel were still rationed and in short supply. With four years of curfews, sudden searches and deportations behind them, people tended still to stay close to home and to suspect their neighbors. The predominant mood was one of bitterness, giving rise to rumors and slander. Marie observed the scene and informed Loewenstein of the effect of this atmosphere on the Society: Parcheminey had officially accused Laforgue of collaboration with the Nazis, alleging that the Alsatian analyst had attempted to resume the presidency of the Society: "They didn't have anything precise on him, and no witness appeared—except Leuba, representing the Evolution Psychiatrique group. Under these conditions, they could do nothing against him in our group, this is also the opinion of Anna Freud, to whom I explained the case. I've seen the accused himself. He talked of bringing a libel suit but has dropped the idea. I think that Borel calmed him down considerably. All these group stories disgust me and I'm in a hurry to go to work in peace in Saint-Tropez and not see any more colleagues."[4]

That summer she was not to work as much as she would have wanted, since George and the children were with her at Le Lys de Mer. But she saw her colleagues frequently, both before her departure and after her return.

For the time being, the Society had settled down, but there were still signs of discord. Marie resumed her practice. Dr. Mâle, a well-known psychiatrist and the son of the eminent art historian, Emile Mâle, started his training analysis with her. She had five candidates in analysis and belonged to the Training Committee of the Society.

Correspondence had begun in August with Dr. Ernst Kris and Anna Freud over the publication of the Freud-Fliess material. Marie informed Kris of the circumstances of her purchase of the papers, and Anna worked through the night sorting out her father's letters. (Marie noted that Mme Freud did not show much interest in his letters to Fliess.) A brief visit to London followed, mainly in order to see Anna, but also Rodker and Croisy. From there, Marie went on to give her lecture in Amsterdam. Her crowded schedule allowed her just enough leisure to enjoy Tatiana's first piano lesson and Porgie's first taste of oysters. Anna came to Paris at the end of November to give a lecture at UNESCO and another at the house of Baroness Edouard de Rothschild. Her two days' stay in Saint-Cloud was a boon to Marie, who felt her usual need for intimate communication with a trusted friend.

The year 1947 was busy for Her Royal Highness and for Marie Bonaparte, the analyst. She was in poor health. She had her tonsils out and had whooping cough for the third time. In the spring she went to Corsica with George, Eugénie and the children. The trip began badly, the crossing was very rough, and Porgie was ill with an ear inflammation. Soon after they arrived on the island, King George II died suddenly of a heart attack. He had been recalled to Athens in September 1946 by plebiscite, but his return had not put an end to the civil war, started as soon as German troops had evacuated the territory. A month before the king's death, President Truman had declared that the United States would support the king in fighting the communists. Marie had mixed feelings about the king's policies, but "Georgie's" death grieved her and the fact that neither she nor George was able to attend his funeral in Athens troubled her conscience. On their return to the "continent," they left immediately for Copenhagen, where King Christian X had just died.

But not all was mourning in the family that year. In November, Prince Philip, the nephew who had spent a good part of his childhood in Marie's house in Saint-Cloud, was to marry Princess Elizabeth of England, the future queen. George and Marie were honored guests and Eugénie took her children to the wedding to show them the splendid ceremonies.

In May the International Association held its congress in Amsterdam, and Marie attended in company with Anna Freud and Annette Berman. On the way back, she stopped in Laeken to see Queen Elisabeth of Belgium, who had become a close friend. The "dazzling" park with its flowers and nightingales enchanted her.

The nightingales were still singing when she arrived in Saint-Tropez, but Marie was forbidden to swim because of cystitis. She corrected the English proofs of *Myths of War*, which had finally been published, and started on the essays for *Les Glanes des jours*. She also set about correcting the proofs of all her articles and essays on psychoanalysis and collecting them in volume form. Three volumes of the *Five Copy-Books* remained to be published. She herself drew up the balance sheet in a letter to Loewenstein.[5] She was anxious to finish. "The road still to be traveled is getting visibly shorter." John Rodker came to work with her at Le Lys de Mer. He was translating her biography of Poe for British and American publication.

As Marie had thought many years earlier, she and George were closer in their old days, spending more time together. George had grudgingly accepted the importance of her profession. He had come to appreciate Freud and was affectionate to Anna, who had been so devoted to him in London when he had larynx surgery. Husband and wife no longer had personal lives; they had both lost their loves. So they remained with the ordinary concerns and limitations of ordinary couples—the joy and the trouble that their children and grandchildren were providing, all the habits built up during all those years of married life.

In 1948 she began a new routine, spending each winter in Greece. She liked the climate, which was warmer and more sunny than that of Paris, and she found plenty to do. She joined rounds at the psychiatric hospital, kept up with capable psychiatrists and analysts, organized meetings, addressed the group in Greek, and provided treatment for lepers.

Their nephew Pavlos, a companion in exile, had succeeded his brother and become King Paul I. He had typhoid fever when Marie and George reopened their Athens house on Avenue Franklin Roosevelt for the first time after the war, and Queen Frederika was in Epirus. The civil war still raged. Four policemen followed Prince George wherever he went, to ensure his safety. Marie, however, moved about freely without an escort. On January 10, the couple attended the marriage of their cousin Nane (Princess Anne of Bourbon-Parma, daughter of Princess Margrethe and Waldemar's granddaughter) to King Michael of Rumania. Between Athens and Tatoï, Prince George was leading the family life he loved.

Their fortieth wedding anniversary led Marie to wonder how she had been able to live so long with a man so different from herself, and to love him as much as she did. One evening she questioned him about his religious thoughts. George believed in the transmigration of souls—a medium had assured him that he and Waldemar had been friends some 1200 years earlier—but he thought that Waldemar had not been reincarnated, that he was in heaven, with George's mother, Queen Olga. When Marie asked him which was more important to him, the immortality of the soul or the existence of God, he replied, "But it's the same thing," and added that faith was a question of will. She then reproached him for forgetting grace and added that she was sorry that belief was impossible for her. "Scientific people are like that," he remarked, without seeming moved or distressed. He acknowledged that he loved life and considered suicide the greatest of crimes. There Marie was in agreement with him. It was a crime against life and she detested it.[6]

Marie was happy to return to Paris at the beginning of April, and as always there were walks to Bagatelle with George and to the Trocadéro aquarium with the children. After some commuting between Paris, London and Brussels, she settled down at Le Lys de Mer in July. Rodker again came to work with her. The children were also visiting. Porgie overwhelmed his grandmother with gifts, pressing on her all his little toys. "He wants to express a boundless gratitude but never has enough means to show it." In September, when George came back from Holland, where he had attended the coronation of Queen Juliana, Marie decided to visit the king and queen of Rumania in Villefranche-sur-Mer, and to stop on the way in Vence to question Angèle Leandri, whom she had not seen for fifty years. She had never been able to forget the blackmailer, and wanted at last to get at the truth. Angèle was now seventy-nine, living modestly in a *pension* in the little town. Leandri had died in 1931 of cirrhosis of the liver. Angèle insisted that he had been a religious man and had loved Prince Roland Bonaparte. They had come all the way from Corsica for his funeral. Marie returned to ask more questions. She wanted to know to what extent Angèle was aware that Antoine had entrapped and blackmailed her, to what extent the wife had been an accomplice. The old woman maintained that Antoine and she had been dismissed for interceding for Marie with Prince Roland and Princess Pierre. She seemed innocent and Marie was unable to crack her story.

Back in Saint-Cloud, less than a month later, Marie slipped on a carpet in Tatiana's bedroom and broke her wrist, which did not keep her from continuing with her patients the very next day and from correcting proofs with her left hand.

The proofs she was working on were for articles to appear in the *Revue*,[7] which were to be collected in a book in French in 1951, and in English in 1953, under the title *Female Sexuality*. Marie had cause to feel satisfied and she did. She had debated and discussed her own sexuality and that of other women with Freud for years and she felt her understanding exceeded his. She was now making original contributions to psychoanalytic theory. *Female Sexuality* is probably her most famous work and certainly the most controversial at the time it was published. Marie proved to be far ahead of her time and raised questions that are still with us. She noted that the sexual "masculinization" of women, of which the clitoral fixation would be the "physiological sign," went hand in hand with social masculinization, and she foresaw a lessening in the differences between the sexes.[8] She had assimilated the results of anthropological research and had reflected on the meaning of her own experience. She also treated, with common sense and good humor, another subject that touched her closely: that of incest between a brother and sister. Incest that was never consummated, because of the age of the participants, and which was never discovered. "The brother had, in this case, rendered his little sister a signal service: he had taught her duly to perform her mourning for the impossible Oedipal love; he had shown her how to be able, when necessary, to have recourse to salutary, indispensable infidelity."[9] These lines also help one to understand the manner in which she had earlier treated, openly and healthily, the attraction that had drawn Peter toward her, and her brief temptation. She remained an orthodox Freudian, but her experience as a therapist and her personal experience combined with her lucid imagination had enabled her to write pages that ought not to be neglected by women today. *Female Sexuality* was reissued as a paperback in France in 1977.

During the autumn of the broken wrist, henceforth freed from the happy torments of love, she sought entertainment. She went to a party given by Aldous Huxley and his wife, who were living on Quai Blériot along the Seine; she attended the wedding of Bethsabée de Rothschild, and had tea with the Duchesse de la Rochefoucauld. She entertained herself. She gave a Greek cocktail party, a dinner for the writer and political commentator François Mauriac, and another for Danny Kaye, introduced to her by Peter, who was on a two-year visit to the United States to give lectures on his experiences as an anthropologist in India and Tibet.

Eugénie was thinking of remarrying. In March 1949, in Saint-Cloud, she introduced Prince Raymond von Thurn und Taxis to her mother, who had just come back from Greece with her grandchildren. The prince had inherited Duino Castle, on the Adriatic, where Rilke had written his *Elegies*. If for no other reason, Marie would have looked on him favorably. She found him "cultivated, nice, but Catholic," as she wrote to Anna.[10] She sensed immediately that here was a serious danger of conflict. Eugénie, who was not religious, would have to obtain an annulment of her first marriage in Rome. She was ready to do so, just as she was ready to depart for Athens to announce her future marriage to her father. Her mother preceded her by a few days, with the children. The need for an annulment brought back all Marie's old resentment against the Church. Her atheism and anticlericalism were revitalized. She was never indifferent to questions of God or Church.

Eugénie's marriage plans became general knowledge and Marie spent a difficult month of May. She was "assailed" on all sides by the family. Fortunately, at the beginning of June, a meeting of

French-speaking psychoanalysts in Paris brought her back to her true interest. She gave a reception for the congress at rue Adolphe Yvon and arranged the admission of Kouretas and two other Greeks to the Society as supporting members.

On June 21 she left for Denmark, where, on the 24th, George's eightieth birthday was to be celebrated at Lille Bernstorff with a dinner for forty guests. The next day was Margrethe's fiftieth birthday. Marie's sixty-seventh birthday, on July 2, 1949, was also celebrated at Bernstorff, with twenty-five dinner guests. Then Marie returned to Paris and departed immediately for Saint-Tropez. There she prepared her paper for the Zürich Congress of the International Association. Her talk was entitled "Psyche in Nature, or the Limits of Psychogenesis."[11]

When the congress was over, she went to Saint-Tropez to meet Loewenstein, who had returned to Europe from America for the first time since the war. Annette Berman and Borel were there also; in addition to her colleagues, friends were always coming and going. On the surface, everything was back to normal, but she felt remote from people and events around her.

During this year, Marie did not succeed in dividing her time equally between her work and her family: she and George returned to Greece in November. She had to see to the preparations for Eugénie's wedding, which was to take place on the 28th in the chapel of the royal castle. Prince von Thurn und Taxis had agreed not to await the pope's approval, and the marriage was performed by the "tottering" metropolitan in accordance with the Orthodox rite. Tatiana and her cousin Sophie held the tapers. Marie wrote to Annette Berman that Eugénie was superb.[12] But a few days later, at the parting from Tatiana and Porgie in Piraeus, Eugénie had an attack of despair. She was leaving for Istanbul, the first stop on her honeymoon trip. The children were to spend two months in Athens with their grandparents.

Marie devoted an hour a day to translating George's memoirs. Four days after Eugénie's departure, she learned that Croisy had had a stroke and was paralyzed. She still felt attached to the woman who had lived so long in the intimacy of their household and had shown herself to be so loyal. Croisy died a few weeks later.

The civil war in Greece had ended in the fall, but at the end of the year Marie wondered what "the second half of the century would bring to the world," and mourned for the 28,000 Greek children who had perished in the terrible conflict.

Marie did not return to France until April 1950. She had reviewed her finances and decided to sell the Blain château and the house on rue Adolphe Yvon, keeping only Saint-Cloud, where she would build another house so that George might feel at home among rooms built to resemble those in his Paris residence. These modifications in the framework of her life hardly affected her, but they did George, to Marie's chagrin.

The reopening of the Institute of Psychoanalysis was for her a more important concern. The number of young psychiatrists attracted to psychoanalysis was growing. Younger colleagues with their training behind them were rapidly promoted to training analysts. The group was now large and there was no place to meet, and no library. The Sainte-Anne hospital put at their disposal a hall, shared with another psychiatric group, but this was not a convenient arrangement. In 1949, the Paris Society appealed to its friends, especially those in the U.S.A., for funds to reestablish the Institute. Former members such as Loewenstein and those who had been helped by Marie, such as René Spitz and Heinz Hartmann, and others responded generously. Marie arranged for the transfer of money from America. The new Institute would not only house students for courses but would also have a policlinic. Marie was pleased that at last patients who could not afford high analytic fees would be treated at health insurance rates. Psychoanalysis would finally be "democratized."[13]

Before plans for the Institute had reached this stage, she threw herself into another struggle, one that aroused her indignation and affected her personally. In June, Margaret Williams, an American practicing child analysis in Paris, who enjoyed the respect of her colleagues, was sued by the medical association, the Ordre des Médecins, for practicing medicine illegally. Established medicine maintained that only physicians could practice analysis. The French law in question was very like the Austrian "quackery" statute that had prompted Freud's defense of lay analysis.

In the previous year, 1949, the Training Committee of the Society had officially stated that non-physicians, including psychologists, were qualified for psychoanalytic training. Lacan had drafted this report with the help of Nacht. The Society accepted lay analysts just as Freud had. But the council of the Ordre des Médecins refused, even after the war, to accept them. Some psychiatrists who were not analysts sided with Mme Williams, but the majority opposed her. Eventually, Nacht too joined the opposition. Marie was shocked and furious. She called him "ambitious and greedy" although otherwise endowed with "solid working qualities." Cénac, who in her opinion "had only improved with age," wanted to save the preventive analysis of children, a concept now regarded with some skepticism by most analysts. It was based on early analytic ideas which alleged that dealing with certain conflicts while the patient was a child obviated later problems. Experience has shown that early treatment alleviates these problems, but does not do away with the need for later adult treatment.

"If the French physicians, after having scorned and vilified it, now claim analysis for their own, it is because they have realized how profitable it is," Cénac declared. Marie, though backed by Freud's opinion on the question, had always regretted that she was not a doctor. She had not forgotten Professor Henri Claude's comments on Mme Sokolnicka. Now she was solidly behind Mme Williams and secured a lawyer to defend her. After having tried several male "stars" she chose a woman, Maître Yvonne Netter, who had a perfect grasp of the issues at stake.

As always, Marie went to Saint-Tropez for the summer. There she wrote "Some Bio-physical Aspects of Sado-masochism," the text of her talk to the Seventeenth International Congress of Psychoanalysis, which was to be held the following year in Amsterdam.[14] It was published in 1952, in the volume *Chronos, Eros, Thanatos*.

Marie was still upset about Peter, who asked for additional funds when the Chinese communists invaded Tibet. His wife was ill in Kalimpong. Marie wrote Anna Freud that she could not accept Peter's cruelty toward his old father and that she blamed Irène for this if nothing else.[15] She had vainly attempted to reconcile George and Peter. In her letters to her son she lovingly remembered the past; when she told him that she was reading *The Jungle Book* to Porgie, she recalled the time "when I read it to you, holding you on my lap."[16]

That summer there were fires in the Maures mountains above Saint-Tropez. "[They are] terrible but grandiose, these flaming hills, which at night seem like volcanoes and smolder during the day so as to darken the sun."[17] The children had just come back from the Alps, where their grandmother had sent them for a month. She brought them closer to nature: one evening, walking along the beach, they counted twenty-seven shooting stars together. She taught them the names of the planets. But the end of the holiday at Le Lys de Mer brought separation; the children would remain in the South, attending school in Grasse and living in Malbosc with their mother and stepfather.

Marie and George left for Athens at the beginning of December, earlier than usual, because Philip, now Duke of Edinburgh, and Princess Elizabeth were there on a visit. On December 7, Marie wrote Anna: "Grand dinner at court for Elizabeth and Philip, decorations, tiaras, horror!" The young couple lunched and dined with Marie and George several times. On December 14, there was a Backhaus concert, and next day Marie resumed work on her memoirs. Christmas was approaching, and Eugénie, Raymond and the children arrived to spend the holidays with the grandparents. The day after their arrival, Marie fractured her hip. After the accident, on December 19, she had paroxysmal tachycardia—an abnormally rapid speeding of the heart beat—from six to ten in the evening. She decided to go, accompanied by George, to Massachusetts General Hospital in Boston to have her hipbone operated on by Smith-Petersen. "Anyhow, the whole business is horrible and I am less and less eager for the resurrection of the flesh," she wrote.

Marie chose to see the cause of her accident—there were to be many more—as being psychological. To Anna Freud she wrote her "analysis"[18]: she had turned her repressed hostility toward George against herself.

The operation took place on January 4, 1951. Marie was impatient with the month's wait for the cast to be removed, and it was not until February 15 that she began her first exercises. She asked Eugénie to send her some books: the Littré dictionary, a French grammar, Perrault's fairy tales illustrated by Gustave Doré, and all the little volumes of natural history ("flowers, birds, fish") she could find, as well as her great uncle Charles Bonaparte's book on American birds. Although forced to stay in bed, she did not want to lose contact with nature. The analysts Grete Bibring and Helene Deutsch, whom Marie had known in Vienna and who were practicing in Boston, visited her, and her faithful friend Loewenstein came from New York.

Ten days after the operation, Marie hired a secretary, to whom she dictated her voluminous correspondence. She kept up with the rumblings of discord in the Paris Society. "Lagache has written me that Nacht behaved basely in our elections. He found a way to have Lacan elected vice-president in place of Lagache. Next we'll have this madman as president. It's disgusting. And Nacht has announced his intention of staying on another two years as president"—this is the postscript of her letter of January 23, 1951, to Loewenstein. She was not to leave the hospital until March 10. After a brief stay in New York, where she saw Schur again and the psychoanalysts gave a dinner for her at the Plaza, she sailed with George on the *Queen Mary*. Eugénie, Raymond, Annette Berman, Geneviève Troisier and her two daughters came to meet them at Cherbourg.

Marie was back in her orbit: Mme Williams's trial was coming up. Anna came to stay at Saint-Cloud from May 4 to 6. Together they celebrated Freud's birthday in the garden. Anna like her father urged Marie to write about herself. Marie decided to deposit the manuscript of the last volumes of her memoirs in the Freud Archives in the Library of Congress in Washington. She liked the idea of writing for readers who would have access to uncensored letters of Freud's in the year 2030.

The two friends met again in August at the congress in Amsterdam, where Marie went by car with Annette Berman. Still on crutches, Marie read her paper refuting Freud's death instinct: "I say Destruction and not Death, since for me the instincts of destruction, of aggression, are not identical . . . [with] that silent decline toward death."[19] She was chairman of the symposium on "Mutual Influences in the Development of Ego and Id." Lacan was a participant and as usual exasperated her. Her violent antipathy for him was, as is usual, reciprocated; they were never to be on good terms. At this congress, other antagonisms stirred as well: Nacht attacked Heinz Hartmann, who was elected president of the International Association. Marie, by nature, enjoyed the political side of these meetings, and joined in the battles.

After the congress, she returned to Le Lys de Mer. She was still there at the beginning of November, when she received the news of Mme Freud's death at the age of ninety. She left immediately to attend the cremation, which took place November 5. She stayed on in London for a few days, then returned to Paris, where the trial of Mme Williams began on December 3. Marie testified for the defendant, as did a number of French physicians. A week later came the arguments of the lawyers for the contending parties. On the evening of that day, Marie and George took the Orient Express with Eugénie and Raymond. They made a twenty-four-hour stop at Duino Castle, then left for Athens, where, on December 17, Marie learned that the court had ordered Jacques Millerand, son of the former president of the Republic and the most understanding of the three judges, to obtain additional information in the Williams case.

In 1952, Marie left Greece on January 7, earlier than usual because Eugénie was pregnant and she wanted to spend the last weeks before the delivery with her daughter in Paris. She also wished to be back a few days before the elections of the Society, which were to be held on the 13th and worried her. Traveling alone, she wrote in her Journal: "For the last few days in Athens, I have been trying to soften the violence of the writing scattered through George's memories of Crete. Impossible! He has agreed only to withdraw the epithets of Judas and Traitor, etc., from Venizelos. That's already something. To persist this way in hatred is hardly normal and hardly Christian. One cannot hate with such strength except out of 'duty.' In the same way he has cut off his own son.

"At these moments, he irritates me so much that I cannot help speaking of it to Vandoros [Prince George's aide-de-camp], Frédy [Queen Frederika], and Kouretas [her psychiatrist friend].

"And then today, as I was leaving him, the other side of the ambivalence burst out in me. Sorrow at leaving him. He is eighty-two. Is it the last time that we'll be together in Greece? As the train crossed the intersection with the Tatoï road, which we have so often passed together—my heart was wrung.

"And I wrote him the following letter, which I'll send him from Salonika:

" 'Darling Barleysugar, the trip is going very well, and the train is so heated that it is necessary to open the window a little or else suffocate: Plenty of snow in the mountains, but in the plains I even glimpsed an almond tree blooming in the sun!

" 'As we passed it, I greeted the intersection of the train with the Tatoï road, which we have traveled so many times together, and which now you will be traveling all alone. Then I felt sad at having to leave you behind at the call of the baby who knows nothing about it!

" 'I glimpsed Mount Kithairón in the clouds, the Helicon, Parnassus, and I'm getting ready to greet Thermopylae and Olympus. The sun is striking my bed at this moment and is scorching. Don't be lazy and write what you are doing. I kiss you with all my heart. Marie.'

"And this letter is as sincere as my complaints to my friends in recent days. Such are the fluctuations of the heart."[20]

She was reading Ovid and Virgil's *Georgics*. "It took him seven years to write them. I understand him. Too many worries. I have a craving to become a hermit."[21] Reading had been a solace nearly as great as writing throughout her life.

The next day, she remembered her recent visit to the cemetery in Tatoï and wondered which of the two would be the first to lie there. This was no longer the obsession of her childhood and youth; she would soon be seventy, and death came for her friends and relatives with increasing frequency.

On January 16, she went to Notre-Dame and the Invalides to attend the funeral of Marshal de Lattre de Tassigny. Then, less than a month later, King George VI of England died and Princess Elizabeth became queen. Marie was unable to go to the monarch's funeral, but the following year, with George, Eugénie and the children, she was to be present at the coronation of Elizabeth II.

George was not yet back in Paris when his grandson Charles-Alexandre-Georges-Pierre-Lucien-Marie-Raymond Lamoral Prince von Thurn und Taxis was born, an event that took place on Eugénie's birthday, February 10. Marie witnessed the delivery with Solange Troisier, a gynecologist, the younger daughter of her friend Geneviève. Then she rushed from the American Hospital to the Comédie-Française, where Tatiana was at the classical matinée with a friend, and waited for the intermission in a pastry shop. Tatiana, nearly thirteen, was delighted to have a little brother, and Porgie pronounced himself satisfied too.

Porgie, who was to be ten in November, had just entered analysis with Mme Williams. Anna Freud had insisted on this step. Many times she had pointed out to Marie that he was "a difficult child," but Eugénie had opposed having him analyzed, as had Charlotte MacMillan, the children's nanny since Tatiana's birth. Entrusting Porgie to Mme Williams had reassured everybody. Marie was as blind as the mother; she loved the child so much that she had to believe that there was nothing to worry about.

There were also serious financial problems, which she confided to Anna; Blain had been sold, but not yet the house on rue Adolphe Yvon. The Emperor Bao Dai of Annam, sovereign of Vietnam, had shown an interest in it and then changed his mind. Other prospective buyers had done the same, and George refused to live in the house she had built for him in Saint-Cloud. Although he spent only two months a year in Paris, he remained attached to rue Adolphe Yvon because of Waldemar's memory. It had become impossible for Marie to maintain it. Peter and his wife continued to be a heavy financial burden, and everyone around Marie seemed to count on her to take care of everything.

She asked Queen Elisabeth of Belgium to be the godmother of little Prince Charles-Alexandre. Prince Napoleon would be the godfather. As required, Marie sent the queen the list of guests and organized the ceremony and reception. The baptism was a sumptuous affair, five ambassadors attended, and the family was amply represented. Marie took advantage of Queen Elisabeth's visit to escape to Chartres with her for a day, where they lunched in the woods amid the barely perceptible March spring. These two women, sharply different in their backgrounds, grasped whatever moments of happiness life offered: they savored, once more, the beauty of the cathedral suddenly rising above the Beauce plain.

Elisabeth of Belgium had always been interested in the arts. A Wittelsbach, the widow of Albert I, she had inherited the imagination of her "Aunt Sissi," the Empress Elisabeth of Austria. She was a sculptor and lived among musicians. She had founded the Queen Elisabeth competition, alternating between violinists and pianists, which was held each year before an international jury and brought prestige to the participating young musicians. At the end of May, 1952, Marie was Queen Elisabeth's guest in Brussels. On May 30, she had lunch with Stravinsky, after having heard *Oedipus Rex* the night before. "His spirit is as interesting as is his genius," she wrote. "He told me about his musical education with Rimsky-Korsakov. I asked him whether he had ever composed while dreaming. Twice, he said. The first time he forgot the theme on waking. The second time he dreamed the theme of *L'Histoire du soldat* (the trumpet?)." She attended the concerts and the functions, including the reception given by King Baudouin for his grandmother's prizewinners. Back in France, she wrote to her friend on June 1 that she had returned from Stuyvenberg (the queen's residence) with her soul filled with music and found herself amid the dust of packing and moving. She was clearing out rue Adolphe Yvon before it was sold.

In April, Mme Williams had been "triumphantly acquitted." Much ink had been spilled over the trial, and, except for the Communists, the whole press had been on her side. Marie wrote to Loewenstein: "At last the question of *Laienanalyse* [is] officially settled in France. A statute will have to be drafted, let's hope that it won't be too strict. Nacht gave proof of remarkable cowardice, fawning on the Ordre des Médecins."[22] She thought that Nacht was "disappointed" by the acquittal. He had hoped for an official post in return for his support of the establishment.

In the elections she had voted for him, since Nacht, along with Lagache and Mâle, had prepared a project for training psychologists that she approved. She wanted therefore to keep him on as president of the Society for another year so that he would have to defend this worthy plan himself. Unfortunately, no sooner was he reelected president than he maneuvered Jacques Lacan's election as vice-president, something that Marie judged "inadmissible," since "Lacan does analyses on principle in ten minutes, training analyses."[23] She wondered whether Nacht was not maneuvering to keep the presidency for himself the following year, for "nobody really wants Lacan."

An intense political struggle for control of the Paris Society was under way. The issues were the abbreviated sessions Lacan gave his patients *for full fees*, and the rigor of the training of younger analysts. Lacan made it known that his shorter sessions, linked to linguistics and a kind of acting out of fantasy, were technical advances as against the analytic pursuit of remembering and working through, and represented the future of psychoanalysis.

Marie was becoming isolated. Her knowledge and abilities as well as her experience and her direct link to Freud had won her a leading position, but her male colleagues were all medical doctors and their viewpoints differed from hers. For her part she focused too narrowly on the defense of lay analysis, which interfered with a wholehearted allegiance to any of the political factions. On the other hand, many of the new analysts were unfamiliar with the princess's proven commitment to psychoanalysis and the services she had rendered the cause. They also had to get used to Marie's custom of receiving visitors and patients in bed, dressed in filmy peignoirs.

The re-establishment of the Institute was a coup for Nacht, Marie and other classical analysts. The rules by which future analysts would be trained were those of the International Psychoanalytic Association, which were modeled on the earlier regulations adopted by the American Association. Lacan's ideas about analysis and analytic training and the conduct of his personal practice were antithetical to the Institute's established procedures.

In spite of all this strife, that year, her seventieth, was one of the most productive of her career. Several books appeared: *Chronos, Eros, Thanatos*; *Introduction à la théorie des instincts*, which includes *The Prevention of Neurosis by Prophylaxis in Childhood*; *Psychoanalysis and Anthropology*; *Psychoanalysis and Biology*. She also published articles: "Some Psychoanalytic and Anthropological Insights Applied to Sociology";[24] "Masturbation and Death, or A Compulsive Confession of Masturbation,"[25] and the text of a lecture that she gave in Paris in January and in Brussels at the end of May to the B'nai B'rith Society on "Psychoanalysis of Antisemitism."[26] The last two volumes of the *Five Copy-Books* appeared in English.

Anna Freud shared her joy in authorship (which for Marie was concentrated on briefly looking at the new book and touching it). Anna also commiserated with her worries about the Society and the Institute. Marie kept her informed of all the twists and turns of the various struggles.

In June, the Institute finally became a reality. It was located at 187 rue Saint-Jacques. This was a former printing shop, which Marie described in a letter to Loewenstein: "Two long rooms, with a small one for the caretaker. In one of the rooms, meeting hall and library; in the other, three offices for analysis at a price people can afford. Each analyst will have to supply an analysis. It's modest but we must make a start and take a stand against the Ordre des Médecins, which goes on persecuting us with repeated trials. Elsa Breuer has been called into court for illegal practice, since she has only a Hungarian diploma."[27] Marie Bonaparte had been her analyst and testified in her favor. But Elsa Breuer had made the mistake of signing her patients' health insurance forms "Dr. Breuer." Since she was not recognized as a physician in France, she lost her case.

Because of the Institute, the Society raised its dues fifty percent. It had received $2,300 from America. Marie asked Loewenstein if they couldn't expect more. She herself had subscribed 600,000 francs and Guy de Rothschild and his mother together 900,000 francs. Marie donated furniture, paneling and an important collection of books from the house on rue Adolphe Yvon, which was finally to be sold in November. She left for Saint-Tropez in better spirits.

Anna Freud and George arrived one after the other at the end of June, to celebrate Marie's birthday on July 2. As during every summer, Marie received many visitors, and some guests who came to stay. Queen Elisabeth of Belgium came to spend more than three weeks, and Marie posed for her for a bust. During her visit, Peter and Irène arrived from Calcutta, by way of Copenhagen.

Marie screwed up her courage, as she wrote to her son,[28] and told George of her intention to entertain their son and Irène. "For I've loved you too much to deprive myself of your presence. Now, to my great surprise, and to my great relief, Papa understood. He does not object. He says only that it can only be when he is away." Peter and Irène stayed from August 15 to 25. The days they spent at Le Lys de Mer were without incident, probably because of the presence of Queen Elisabeth, whose holiday no one wanted to spoil.

When Marie saw the couple again in Paris in the autumn, she had to pay their bills: the Hotel Raphaël, Balenciaga, "and the rest." Once again she encountered what she called "Peter's ambivalence." He forgot, for example, to invite his father and mother to his lecture and the showing of his film at the Maison de la Chimie. She recognized that it was high time to "cut the financial umbilical cord," and drew up a list of "Irène's positive and negative qualities." "Good looks. Brilliant intelligence. Feverish activity. Intellectual collaboration with Peter. Attachment to Peter." On the debit side were, "Sterility, prodigality, lack of veracity, lack of tact, and dangerous impulsiveness."[29] She noted their departure from Paris on November 19, adding: "At last!"

On that same day, she wrote to Loewenstein that she was disgusted with the Institute, since "these gentlemen are so eager for official recognition that they are ready to sacrifice *all the psychologists* in order to have Professor Delay and Professor Heuyer on their honorary committee. "In the face of this attitude, I withdraw all support from the Institute. I will give them no more books, or furniture, or money. . . . These are contemptible careerists." Once again she was ready to fight.

UNATTAINABLE PEACE

*"Endowed with a joyful pessimism, I will have
traveled through life without yielding."*

MARIE BONAPARTE,
unpublished notes

MARIE, AT THE AGE OF SEVENTY, STILL POSSESSED THE BONA-
parte vigor. While most French analysts were causing her
grief, some joined her American colleagues in preparing a
festschrift, *Drives, Affects, Behavior: Essays in Honor of Marie
Bonaparte*, edited by Loewenstein. When the book appeared, Marie
reviewed it carefully, summarizing each paper. She wrote that
Ernest Jones in his preface ". . . reminds us of the severe social
handicap Marie Bonaparte, Princess George of Greece, had to overcome in embarking on her career. A handicap which he likens to
that of the legendary starving poet in an attic."[1]

Marie's last decade was, like that of most other people, focused
on sorrow occasioned by the illness and death of close family and
friends, but she remained active in her work and preoccupied with
her sexuality. She dreamed that she was in a hotel with an attractive younger man, who was trying to seduce her. While they were
lying together on the floor, they were surprised by a maid and explained that they were looking for a small purple pencil and Marie's
glasses. She concluded that reading and writing were all that were
left to her now. She was not fully resigned to this state of affairs
and during the summer of 1952 she wrote: "Balance sheet. —A
royal passport. No taxes. No customs duties. Royal musical salutes.
The national anthem . . . On the other hand the life of a female
misfit.

"The most essential needs are to eat, drink, piss, shit, and sleep.
Also, in one's youth, to fornicate.

"Regard for truth involves the absence of regard for oneself and
others.

"Not having spared myself, why spare others when my only regard is for truth?"

But these periods of despairing introspection were infrequent, and she had no inclination to retire from life. Her will sustained her now as it had sustained the unhappy, unloved girl she had been. Psychoanalysis had become her true reason for being.

Contrary to what she had announced to Loewenstein in her letter of October 12, 1952, she was far from indifferent to the Institute of Psychoanalysis. Indeed she continued to be a central figure in the crisis that developed around its reopening.

Marie persisted in her defense of lay analysis, doing battle so that it would not be sacrificed to one faction or another in the deepening political struggles. Lacan, in attacking the rules of the new Institute, alleged that they were an "Americanization" of psychoanalysis. Considering himself as the true "classical Freudian," he rebelled against any such rules. But in a reorganization that had been proposed, only graduates of the Institute and followers of its rules could join the Society. On December 2, 1952, matters came to a head in a stormy meeting during which Nacht resigned as director of the Institute, but by the end of the session he had been temporarily reinstated.

On December 24, Marie wrote to Anna Freud, from Athens, that she foresaw a split in the Society, since in her absence Nacht had resigned again, to be replaced, this time, by Lacan. But Lacan was not interested in the directorship of the Institute; he hoped to become president of the Society in January when Nacht's term expired.

Marie at that time was ready to support Nacht. After the Williams trial, she had lost confidence in him, but on her return from Greece, they had it out between them and she was *"changing sides"* (her emphasis), as she explained to Loewenstein on February 5, 1953.[2] She had believed that Nacht was engaged in a vendetta against all psychologists and lay analysts, while he had thought that she held him in contempt. Thanks to the princess's change of heart, Nacht was again named director of the Institute, while Lacan, as he had hoped, became president of the Society, winning over Marie's candidate, Cénac.

No sooner had she made peace with Nacht than she revived the struggle with Lacan. He had fifteen physicians "in training" as analytic candidates whom he saw for ten-minute "hours" two or three times a week. This was not news anymore. Lacan himself had publicly given his reasons for the briefness of those sessions. "Henceforth the rules of the Institute [will prevail]: at least ¾ of an hour and 4 times a week, but he wants those already analyzed by his 'brief procedure' accepted. . . . We must try to preserve a majority despite the candidates hastily turned out by Lacan."

On February 22, 1953, Loewenstein wrote to her:

"What you tell me about Lacan [his former analysand] is distressing. He has always represented a source of conflict for me; on one hand there is his intellectual worth which I value highly, though I disagree violently with him. Nevertheless the misfortune is that much as we agreed that he would continue his analysis after his election [to the Society], he did not do so. One does not cheat on such an important point with impunity (this between us). I certainly hope that his hastily analyzed (that is to say incompletely analyzed) trainees will not be admitted.

"Here [in New York], as in the American Association, there is a rule requiring a training analysis of *at least* [his underlining] 4 times a week, from ¾ of an hour to 55 minutes, even the Chicagoans insist on this. The worst analysts are those in Washington. There is even a prescribed minimum number of analytic hours (350, I think) and hours of supervision (close to 200, which is too much in my opinion) . . ."

Marie was curious about what was happening in America. She appealed again to "American generosity" for funds. "I will see what I can do myself (but I am more and more financially embarrassed)," she wrote on May 16.

At this time, she wanted to organize a meeting of all the European institutes. "It will be interesting to renew, at the new congress, the tradition of a meeting of the Institutes, the European ones at least, as Max Eitingon had arranged in his time." She had already written a draft of a letter, with Nacht's approval, advocating the first meeting at the London International Congress that July. She did this because she foresaw problems with Lacan and wanted to set machinery in motion to deal with them.

"Lacan had promised, in March 1951, to cease his practice of short analyses, but he has not kept his promise. Nacht confronted him at a meeting with the students (in June, 1953). Lacan said that since he had explained his technique some months ago before the Society, he had been released from his promise, and that more-over he had said that he might change his technique but not that he would do so. Each called the other a liar."[3]

Marie was not present at this meeting on which she was report-ing. She was in London with her family for the coronation of Elizabeth II. She was certain that Lacan had chosen this date for the Society's administrative session knowing she would have to be absent. Her ally, Odette Codet, moved to postpone the heated discussion by calling for a vote of confidence in Lacan to be held two weeks later, when Marie would be back.

In May, Marie Bonaparte had been named honorary president of the Training Committee and of the Executive Council of the Institute. These tokens of recognition touched her, though less than did the differences that set her against some of her colleagues. The psychoanalytic turbulence, however, did not overshadow Stalin's sudden death: "Russia has lost the successor to Ivan the Terrible and Peter the Great." A visit to Queen Elisabeth, in Brussels, pro-vided diversion and she wrote to Anna: "I am alone and can re-cover from the feeling I had for so many months of being a balloon tossed about by many human feet."[4] She gave regular classes at the Institute.

While in London for the coronation, she resumed her role of royal highness, attended the banquet at Buckingham Palace, other palace receptions, and a garden party given by the Archbishop of Canterbury. Her pleasure in these events was vicarious: she ob-served her grandchildren's fascination with court ritual. She herself was now far removed from the pleasure her own royal wedding had given her. In the spectacle, she saw only individuals and flowers, which she occasionally plucked from a bunch or a wreath to sniff or observe more closely. Another paragraph of history was being written at the same time, one that preoccupied her much more: Julius and Ethel Rosenberg, convicted of espionage, were to be electrocuted in the United States on June 19. After her re-turn to Paris, she passionately followed the demonstrations in front of the American embassy. As she had kept a vigil at the hour of the execution of Sacco and Vanzetti, she did the same for the Rosenbergs.

Three days earlier, the Society had met for the vote on Lacan. There had been fourteen votes against him, five in his favor, and two blank ballots. ". . . Lacan has resigned. . . .

"In this situation, the Institute and the *Revue* remain to us—

although they will be able to found others with the gang of Lacan's poorly analyzed pupils who will perhaps, I say surely, follow them.

"But the question of belonging to the International Association will be placed before the next congress and they will be present. I have written to Hartmann about it bringing him up to date on everything. Also to Jeanne Lampl and Sarasin. I'm going to telephone Anna Freud."[5] (These last three were fellow vice-presidents of the International Association, of which Heinz Hartmann was president.) In her letter to Heinz Hartmann, Marie Bonaparte described the split.

There was more bad news; Marie learned on July 15 that Mme Williams's acquittal had been reversed on appeal. Medical supervision was required for all lay analysts; Mme Williams was given the lightest possible sentence: she was forbidden to practice analysis, which forced her to leave Paris for London. It seemed a disaster for the lay analysts, as Marie wrote to Anna, reflecting "a satanic, diabolical fear" of analysis.[6] Established medicine had been pusillanimous. She expressed her solidarity with Mme Williams and the others facing medical supervision. Her own case was different, she was at the height of her career. Indeed, thanks to her passion for medicine and to X.'s instruction, she had a good store of medical knowledge. Heinz Hartmann, when later asked if she had been a doctor, answered: "No, but she was more of a doctor than most doctors are . . . among all of us she was the only one who really understood medicine. . . . She took medicine much more seriously than most analysts do."[7] This was recognition from an equal also analyzed by Freud.

At the International Congress in London, Marie and her allies held sway, and Lacan was not permitted to take the floor. Loewenstein was there and found this exclusion of the dissidents from the debate "abnormal and unjust." Marie thought him too indulgent, and they quarreled. Loewenstein was finally enraged at her oblique attacks on him for the actions of his analysands. Later she wrote him: "You may be surprised to learn that at the moment it is all the same to me whether he [Lacan] is recognized or not, I don't care, not to use a stronger expression. I regret only one thing, namely to be no longer in the least interested in all this. I have decided not to go to the meetings of 'our' Society."[8]

In an earlier period she had mentioned being vindictive; she seemed even more so now, in the old age that she resented and which did not mellow her. Embittered, she withdrew again into melancholy and cruel reflection:

"Penances [sic] for a few mistakes:

"1/Loewenstein was wrong. Once again he believed, in a life crowded by so many women, that I, the mother, would fulfill his desires better than any other. But other women came along. . . . He grew up and I *grew older* [her italics]. Then implacable nature . . .

"2/X. was wrong. He thought to keep me by making me suffer. He needed to forgive himself for his infidelity to [his wife] by maddening me, by humiliating me under his scorn, his sarcasm. . . . He tired me. I left him. What he didn't give me, I sought with others. Without finding it.

"3/ I was wrong. With the blindness of instinct, I took desire for love. In myself and in others. Then the satisfaction of instinct gone, I again found myself poor and naked. I sought to cure myself.

"4/ A bigger error, it is Freud who was wrong. He overestimated his power, the power of therapy. The power of childhood events . . . It was in the depths of the maternal flesh . . . that nature made me, by sex, a female misfit—but otherwise, in the brain, almost a man."

She had proven her strength of character over the years, and overcome most of her problems. She and Loewenstein had it out and the friendship continued. But her obsession with her frigidity, complicated by her stubborn persistence in repeated surgery on the clitoris, still inflamed her old age. Although intellectually she accepted Freud's statement that in cases of obsessional neurosis there was always the danger of understanding a great deal but changing little, emotionally she still reproached him. The major difficulty was that she remained a woman of her time and thus attributed her brains and her accomplishments to her "masculinity."

Her affirmations to the contrary, she remained active in the Paris Society. In 1954, the year of Dien Bien Phu and the end of the Indochina war, an international committee, chaired by D. W. Winnicott, investigated Lacan's French Psychoanalytic Society and opposed its admission to the International. This happened in April while Marie was accompanying George to Crete, where he was heartily welcomed, which gave the old man, whose mind was beginning to fail, immense joy. Marie continued her courses at the Institute, which was officially opened on June 1 by a representative of the Ministry of National Education. The minister himself had stayed away.[9] Nacht was depressed by this but Marie thought that the inauguration had "gone off passably well," and she prepared to leave with the astronomers of the Meudon observatory for the Swedish island of Öland, where she hoped to see a total eclipse of the sun. On the way she stopped in Denmark to celebrate George's eighty-fifth birthday, on June 24.

The major family event of the year was the "Cruise of Kings." King Paul I and Queen Frederika of the Hellenes had invited Queen Juliana of the Netherlands, the Grand Duchess Charlotte of Luxembourg, several dethroned sovereigns and many royal highnesses on board their yacht the *Agamemnon* for a cruise from Naples through the Greek islands. George and Marie, Eugénie and Tatiana were included. All the guests were related and were at ease in seven languages. Marie found the "atmosphere anachronistic," a relic of the past. Tatiana enjoyed herself even though her grandmother observed that she had not yet begun to have flirtations.

Marie was absorbed with worry over Porgie, who had remained at Le Lys de Mer. The boy had become more difficult over the years and that summer he began to report a strange feeling of softness in his cheek. When she returned from the cruise, Marie observed that he was not well and did her best to distract him.

The beginning of the year 1955 was overshadowed by another subject for concern: her son.

Peter and Irène's travels in Iran, Afghanistan, India and Tibet, as well as Irène's Russian ancestry, were causing rumors. The "cold war" had generated little sympathy for dilettantes and ready suspicion of differentness. The queen talked of Peter's "disloyalty" in not having returned to Greece, causing George to remark that "Greece without politics and Frederika would be a paradise." After an article in the London *Daily Mail* on January 21, about spies in Kalimpong, the king and queen advised Peter not to come to Greece.

Marie furiously wrote various members of the family only to discover that the Indian and American governments suspected Peter and Irène of being in the Russians' employ. Marie wrote Peter: "I, the mother of Oppenheimer?"[10] Finally the family counseled him to make peace with Queen Frederika, who responded, "If only someone could get him out of the clutches of that ghastly woman."[11] Loewenstein saw Peter in New York, thought him innocent, and advised Marie to stay out of the matter.[12]

Marie had no choice. She had to play the part of the strong woman, providing funds and support for everybody. But at this time, she was so worried about Peter that she began to have alarming and exhausting attacks of tachycardia. Her only consolation was in having persuaded Kouretas, the Greek psychiatrist whom she judged to be so gifted, to enter analysis with her for three months.

Later she went to Madrid to meet Peter, who was working as a technical adviser for Robert Rossen's film *Alexander the Great*. This trip to Spain enabled her to spend Holy Week in Seville, to visit the Prado and the church of San Antonio de la Florida to see the Goya paintings. She took Peter to lunch at the home of Marañon, a psychiatrist with whose work she was familiar. In her return to France, while eating lunch near the border, she was shaken by the news of Einstein's death. Yet these three weeks were a happy interlude in a crowded schedule.

Because of recurrent episodes of fever, she gave up a trip to Ceylon to observe another solar eclipse, and left for Saint-Tropez, from where she visited Nikos Kazantzakis in Antibes. The Greek writer had been condemned by the Greek synod because his writings were not in conformity with Orthodox doctrine. Marie wrote to Queen Elisabeth asking her to enlist Albert Schweitzer's support for Kazantzakis.[13] She did not abandon any of her interests in literature and the arts. She attended the opening of the Saint-Tropez museum with the writer Colette and the painter Dunoyer de Segonzac. Nor did she neglect her obligations as an analyst. On July 23 she went to Geneva for the Nineteenth International Congress, joining Anna Freud at the Hôtel des Bergues. Both were still vice-presidents; the president, Heinz Hartmann, specified in his report that it was the unanimous view of the Committee that "the Lagache group should not be recognized as a member society of the International Psycho-Analytic Association." This was what the two friends wished to hear.

After luncheons and dinners with their colleagues, they left for Saint-Tropez by the route des Alpes, and stopped at Lurs to see Mme Dominici, the wife of an old peasant who had savagely murdered an English family camping in his field. Marie's fascination with murder persisted. They also went to the Forcalquiers observatory, which Marie, in her renewed passion for astronomy, frequently visited.

At the end of August, probably at the insistence of Anna, who had gone back to London, Eugénie and her mother finally told Prince George about Porgie's illness.

The autumn was somber. Eugénie had to undergo an operation on her spine, in London, and her father had a stroke the day after she was hospitalized. She was bedridden for a month and suffered a pulmonary embolism. Meanwhile George had an episode of mental confusion attributed to hypoglycemia. Marie traveled back and forth between London and Paris. She also dreamed that she was wearing Eugénie's brace, expressing her wish to change places with her daughter, gaining youth in exchange for suffering.

In the following spring of 1956, while George was "struggling against chaos" (he had progressive arteriosclerosis of the brain), Marie studied differential calculus with Tatiana's tutor. The girl was going to the *lycée*. Porgie was at Les Roches, a well-known boarding school in Normandy.

The centenary of Freud's birth was celebrated in Paris with the unveiling of plaques at the Salpêtrière and on the face of the small hotel in the Latin Quarter, rue Le Goff, where Freud had lodged as a student. It was Marie who set up the honorary committee to obtain the necessary authorizations.

Marie left for London to attend the inauguration of the clinic founded by Anna Freud and Dorothy Burlingham, and four days later, the unveiling of a plaque by Ernest Jones on Freud's house at 20 Maresfield Gardens. She also was present at a reception given by the British Psycho-Analytical Society. Less than a month later she was at the Elysée Palace and lunched in Versailles with the king and queen of Greece, who were on an official visit. Her life continued to oscillate between the two poles of psychoanalysis and royalty.

In the summer Marie once again took George to Le Lys de Mer. During this stay he had emergency surgery in Saint-Tropez for a strangulated hernia, performed by a surgeon from Marseilles. She stayed with him and took him home, but he was failing. Admiral Vandoros, his aide-de-camp, took care of him. As every year, the house was full of guests. There were Bishop Parker from South Africa, who swam wearing his cross, and with whom, in the water, Marie debated the existence of God; Kouretas, the psychiatrist from Athens; Kazantzakis and his wife. George and Marie prolonged the stay in Saint-Tropez, and in early October she was still swimming in water at a temperature of 63° F.

Autumn brought the Hungarian uprising, soon crushed by Soviet tanks, and the Anglo-French landing at Port Said. In the middle of November, Marie finally took her often postponed trip to India. Irène herself had invited her many times, and Marie now wished to show support for her son and daughter-in-law. Accompanied by Solange Troisier, as personal physician, she flew to Calcutta and then traveled to Kalimpong, where Peter and Irène had their Himalayan residence. "Superb site. Snow-covered mountains in the background and flowers all around." Irène had a magnificent garden. The two women, adversaries in all else, shared love of nature and of gardening; but the altitude was tiring for Marie. She traveled on to "Delhi, Agra, and Bodh Gaya where were held magnificent celebrations in honor of the 2,500th anniversary of Buddha's enlightenment under the sacred tree, whose shoots one can still see at the base of the temple. The throngs of Tibetans (to whom Peter spoke) were interesting. . . . Their mystical frenzy the last evening was impressive, they ran like madmen around the temple with their prayer wheels and threw themselves on their stomachs hundreds of times to worship Buddha. . . . Calcutta is also very curious with the temple of Kali, where they daily sacrifice goats and buffaloes instead of human beings as before."[14] After a visit to Madras she was back in France, to find George with bronchitis. She had brought gifts for everyone and quantities of stones in order to study the geological formation of India in the neighborhood of Tibet.

This trip had brought her the joy of seeing Peter in the setting that he had chosen, devoting himself to his work as an anthropologist. She was still unaware that the year about to begin would be "the saddest in [her] life after 1924," the year of her father's death.

On March 15, 1957, Marie wrote to Loewenstein consoling him for the death of his and Hartmann's friend and collaborator, Ernst Kris, who had suffered from heart disease for some time and who died dictating his recommendations for new analysts for his patients. At the moment of death he seemed only to have anxiety and concern for his analysands. She counted Kris her friend since the Vienna days and he and Anna Freud had also collaborated with her in editing the Freud-Fliess material.* "A courageous man has died. When will it be the turn of one or the other of us to follow him?

"My sister-in-law Elena, the Grand Duchess of Russia, widow of my brother-in-law Nicholas, has also just died of a heart attack. In her case, probably surrounded by priests and ikons. Each one dies as he has lived. Sometimes one might say: conditioned reflexes. . . . [Peter] has given lectures in Athens with great success. The University of Athens is going to make him a doctor honoris causa.

"Things are finally settled with the family. They have seen each other again, they have even invited [Peter] to review the parade with the king on March 25 [Greek national holiday]; in a word, both sides have wiped the slate clean and are now taking a common stand against Communism, Asiatic and otherwise. . . . This news has of course pleased me."

It was to be the only piece of good news that year, a year filled with sorrow and mourning. The deaths of Ernst Kris and Princess Elena of Greece occurred as George's condition rapidly deteriorated, and Marie struggled with her own heart disease. Eugénie had her first episode of tachycardia. But it was Porgie who upset her most. His health deteriorated dramatically. Her inability to help her beloved grandson and his mother was torture to her. She kept active, but she ceased writing in her diary. She scribbled down her schedule, names and events, without comment or elaboration.

The twentieth International Congress of Psychoanalysis, held in Paris, provided Marie a respite. She went to Saint-Cloud alone to attend it and entertain her friends, Anna, Loewenstein, Hartmann and Jones, who was ill. The meeting of the central executive committee was held at her house.

Now seventy-five, Marie Bonaparte read a brief paper to the Congress summing up the accomplishments of more than half a century of psychoanalysis, among them: "liberation of the irrepressible sexual instincts: greater frankness with our children, greater sexual freedom for women. . . . Mankind has . . . become a little less hypocritical, and, perhaps, a little happier." The final aim of all analysis, she said, was adaptation to reality. How might analysis help mankind face death? In her view religious believers denied reality and were "especially afraid of death." Analysis, fol-

---

* See chapter 10, p. 227.

lowing Freud's example, offered a "greater acceptance and therefore courage in the face of death, that inescapable enemy which it
is better to confront than to deny."[15]

Then she returned to Le Lys de Mer and her concern for Porgie.
In the middle of September, George developed hematuria (the
presence of blood cells in the urine) and became confused. Marie
had him taken by ambulance to Saint-Cloud, where he died on
November 25, 1957, at 2:15 A.M., after days and nights filled with
terror of death. Marie did not leave his side, concentrating her
attention on the husband to whom she was bound by nearly half a
century of shared life. Still she noted, in October, the launching
of Sputnik, and on the 29th she wrote that she had learned from *Le
Figaro Littéraire* of the death of her friend Kazantzakis.

Eugénie, Tatiana, Raymond, the aide-de-camp Admiral Vandoros and Edmond the chauffeur joined her at George's bedside as
he lay dying. Peter came and left again. And Marie wrote: "I
wanted to spend the night of his death alone with my husband. . . .
Then I bent over his cold forehead and kissed it. Not his lips,
which he had always refused me."[16] In her own meticulous way
she recounted, "what we put in the coffin: two small enamel Danish and Greek flags, his wedding ring, [his lock of] Waldemar's
hair and the Saint Christopher medal given by [Waldemar], his
crucifix, and Waldemar's photo in his hands. Our group at his
feet."

The funeral was held two days later. Anna Freud and Mme Williams attended, as did the ambassadors of Greece and Denmark.
Marie took charge of the preparations, assisted by Peter and
Prince Raymond von Thurn und Taxis. The first ceremony was at
eleven o'clock in the chapel on their Saint-Cloud estate, then another at five in the afternoon in the Greek church on rue Georges
Bizet in Paris. Porgie made a scene; tearing Annette Berman's card
from the flowers she had sent, he ran to buy his grandfather, "who
belonged to him, 2,200 francs worth of flowers." He reproached his
mother for not having called him when his "Apapa" was dying.
Marie was moved by his tormented, irrational expression of feeling.

Next day, George's last journey to Greece began. Peter and
Prince Raymond accompanied the body to Toulon. Marie flew to
Athens to prepare for the ceremonies there. She took Eugénie,
Tatiana, Porgie, Princess Magrethe de Bourbon-Parma (Walde-
mar's daughter), Prince Michel of Greece, and Frieda, her cham-
bermaid, with her. The Greek sovereigns and their daughter,

Princess Sophie, along with Princess Alice of Greece, met them in the house on Franklin Roosevelt Avenue where George and Marie had spent their winters.

In Toulon the French navy provided full military honors as the coffin boarded the *Nike*. On December 4 Prince George of Greece was buried in the royal cemetery at Tatoï. Marie placed the Danish flag "brought by Meg," the Princess of Bourbon-Parma, on the coffin, and poured over it some soil from Bernstorff. She noted in detail how her last ten days had been spent and concluded: "I've asked the children to have me cremated." On December 5 she wrote to Annette Berman: "Yesterday we left my husband under the snow at Tatoï . . . he who so *dreaded* the cold."

Porgie had been sent to school in Switzerland, and Marie traveled from Athens to Villars-sur-Ollon for the Christmas holidays. She noted the beginning of 1958: "First year in which he is no more." She felt the emptiness but she finished chapter 135 of her memoirs in three days. Then she returned to Paris, for yet another memorial service for George, this one organized by Greek Orthodox bishops.

Marie was busy distributing George's bequests to lepers, to the Bibliothèque Nationale and to the Malmaison museum, to which he had left his collection of three thousand Empire snuffboxes. She went alone to Saint-Tropez, and then to London with Peter. From there she traveled to Belgium to visit the World's Fair in Brussels. Former King Leopold III came to see her. His mother, Queen Elisabeth, was ill. On her return to Saint-Cloud, before leaving for Athens with Edmond and Frieda, her chauffeur and chambermaid, Marie gave a luncheon for her daughter-in-law Irène, her son-in-law Raymond, and the Indian statesman Krishna Menon. They discussed Hinduism. She had not lost her taste for stimulating company and interesting conversation.

Peter followed her to Greece, but Marie went with Eugénie to Crete to unveil a monument to George's memory at Suda Bay, the place where the prince had landed when he assumed his post as high commissioner. There she met twenty aged veterans from 1897. "Sad and touching ceremony."[17] Later, after spending a few days in Saint-Tropez, she and Peter went to Denmark to settle George's estate; during their visit the military guard of which Peter was an officer celebrated its three hundredth anniversary.

"I am left crushed by the immutability of the past," she noted on March 20. She found it necessary to distance herself from Peter, "who thinks that the disappearance of his father leaves the way open for his wife to enter the royal family,"[18] but it was out of the question, and "if Peter brings his wife [to Denmark]—though, privately speaking, I like her—I will abandon him to shift for himself," she wrote in the same letter to Loewenstein, a letter that contained several postscripts, including: "Work alone provides pure joy." More than ever she felt lonely. Those living in her proximity cared for her since she never ceased to act responsibly. Her servants and friends found her unfailingly thoughtful and generous; but she had changed. She noted in her diary that she was sure of her daughter's love and did not deserve it.

Marie resumed her work. The political atmosphere in France was oppressive. The year 1958 saw the shelling of Sakiet-Sidi-Youssef, a village at the Tunisian border of Algeria—which inflamed public opinion against the Algerian war. After the demonstrations of May 13 on the Champs Elysées, General de Gaulle returned to power.

Ever since the time of the Nazis, Marie had been alert to political events, which she took care to note in her journals. Before the Fifth Republic was proclaimed on October 5, she published the first two volumes of her memoirs: *Derrière les vitres closes* and *L'Appel des sèves*, which recounted, in 1,000 pages, her life up to the royal marriage ceremony. Annette Berman was distressed because the second volume was little noticed. Nor had the first produced "much effect. People prefer Françoise Sagan, too bad," Marie wrote on August 16, while she was at Le Lys de Mer. She went on to observe: "My memoirs will at least have given me the illusion, as long as I live, of some little thing perhaps surviving me. It's not much, but it's a great deal. How many people live and die in the most senseless hope of heaven?" She had little of the author's vanity and could acknowledge the failure of her books, although they meant more to her than her scientific papers. Despite this lack of success, she continued writing her memoirs. She was always daring, in the way she lived and in the way she wrote about herself. Dr. Nacht acknowledged it: "Like Freud himself, she does not hesitate to reveal the most intimate part of her being, painful though that may be, in the sole interest of serving science."[19]

She decided that beginning in 1958 she would no longer attend meetings of the Society. Sasha Nacht had asked her to collaborate on a five-volume psychoanalytic treatise that he was in the process of publishing. He wanted her to write some forty pages for Book III on *Les Troubles de la sexualité chez la femme*, and some fifteen pages for Book V on *Les Applications de la psychanalyse à la mythologie*. In 1955, she had already supplied him with *Psychanalyse et sexologie* for Book II.[20] She had no wish to write the rest. She felt disappointed, however, in men, not in ideas. She was still very involved in discussions concerning psychoanalysis itself. In a letter to Loewenstein of October 11, 1958, she reiterated her idea that aggression was not part of the death "instinct" but, on the contrary, was one of the instincts of life. This was in response to Hartmann's, Kris's and Loewenstein's many additions to psychoanalytic theory, especially their introduction of the "aggressive drive." For the International Congress, to be held in Copenhagen in 1959, she prepared a lengthy contribution, *Vitalisme et psychosomatique*.[21] At the symposium, she also read a paper on two cases of suicidal depression which she had treated.

At this Copenhagen Congress, the French Psychoanalytic Society of Lacan and Lagache, of which Dr. Hesnard was now president, again applied for admission to the International Association. Marie as a vice-president of the organization remained resolute in her opposition to the group. They were rejected and a new committee was appointed to study the matter.

George's book, *The Cretan Drama: The Memoirs of H.R.H. Prince George of Greece*, appeared that year. Marie had arranged for its publication (in the United States) in English and in Greek. It was an act of piety on her part; she sent a copy to the king, with a letter carried by Peter. She continued to do what she regarded as her duty. Her only pleasures were a brief stay by herself in Saint-Tropez when the mimosas and almond trees were in bloom, and a trip to Africa with Tatiana and Solange Troisier to observe the total eclipse of the sun at Fort-Lamy. This trip, organized with the help of the secretary of Queen Elisabeth of Belgium, took them to the Congo, which they visited from September 27 to October 13, the date on which they left Stanleyville for Brussels. Marie remained with the queen for a brief sojourn, while Solange Troisier and Tatiana returned directly to Paris. Later that year Marie spent Christmas with Anna, in her house in Walberswick in Suffolk.

Porgie's condition, Eugénie's impending divorce from Prince Raymond von Thurn und Taxis, and the absence of her "old companion" weighed on Marie. She was no longer distracted by the Paris Psychoanalytic Society or the Institute's politics. Still, she was not ready to retire. She was looking for a cause to which she could dedicate her still strong energy, anxious to play an active role as she was used to doing.

The curious fascination that criminals had for her soon re-emerged and drove her to one of her most extravagant undertakings. For Marie, the year 1960 was entirely dominated by the Chessman case.

Caryl Chessman had spent twelve years on Death Row in the California State Prison at San Quentin. By 1960, at the age of thirty-eight, he had published four books and survived eight execution dates, but he had received a ninth death date for May 2, 1960. He had become a symbol of opposition to capital punishment, the abolition of which Edmund Brown, the governor of California, had sought before this case.

From his adolescence, Caryl Chessman had been a hooligan, but he had a particular aptitude for contrition. At sixteen, he had begun to steal cars, been arrested, escaped, and the next day robbed a drugstore. He had a long police record when he was accused of being the "red light bandit" who had used a police car to prey on lovers in parked cars around Los Angeles. The "red light bandit" also attempted the rape of a seventeen-year-old girl, whose later commitment to a mental hospital was attributed to the crime. Chessman insisted on acting as his own lawyer and was convicted of technical kidnapping, a capital offense in California.

Since July 1948, he had lived in a cell 4½ feet wide, 10½ feet long, and 7½ feet high. He had read or perused ten thousand books and written between two and three million words.

Marie obsessively followed the case of "this aggressive psychopath," as she called him in her article "Réflexions d'une psychanalyste," in which she noted that two British delinquents, who had robbed and killed a passerby, had recently been executed and the same day that they were hanged another British delinquent committed a similar crime.

"A fine example of the [preventative nature] of capital punishment," she commented. Already in 1927, in her article "Le Cas de Mme Lefèbvre," she had spoken out against the death penalty.* She was to write to Loewenstein: "The Chessman case shows the disruptive effect of the death penalty in advanced societies. Who talks about convicted people in Switzerland, in the Scandinavian

* See chapter 7, p. 169.

countries or elsewhere where the death penalty does not exist, where there is only life imprisonment, as in Belgium? People quickly forget."[22]

In November 1959, Marie wrote to Franz Alexander, who was then at Mount Sinai Hospital in Los Angeles, for information about the condemned man. Alexander's reply was detached but informative; he put Marie in contact with Isadore Ziferstein, "lover of lost causes and a good analyst," who suggested to the princess that she send a petition to Governor Brown. Eleanor Roosevelt, Aldous Huxley, Carl Binger, Bernard Glueck, Sr., and Carey McWilliams, editor-in-chief of *The Nation*, had already done so. Marie lost no time. On December 15, 1959, she sent Governor Brown a petition for clemency signed by the most illustrious names of French intellectuals, and members of her family. On January 14, 1960, she wrote to the President of the United States: "Public opinion cannot help feeling that a man, whatever he may have or not have done, who has been twelve years awaiting death, has already suffered more than capital punishment itself." And further on: "We know that it is in your power to influence the Governor of California to grant clemency. Twice already such an influence has been exercised by the White House on State Governors: in 1918 President Woodrow Wilson persuaded the Governor of California to grant clemency to Tom Mooney, and in 1958 Secretary of State John Foster Dulles persuaded Governor Folsom of Alabama to commute the death sentence of James Wilson, a Negro."

To express her gratitude to George's doctor, Marie had invited Professor de Gennes and his wife to accompany her and Eugénie, Tatiana and Solange Troisier to the Far East. The itinerary was Ceylon, Siam, Angkor Wat, Hong Kong and Japan. As planned, the travelers left on March 31, 1960, but on their arrival in Japan, Marie, who "could think of nothing but Chessman," decided to fly to the United States with Solange Troisier to try to save him. Professor and Mme de Gennes returned directly to Paris, while Eugénie and her daughter went to India.

Marie stayed in California from April 23 to 28. She had warned Ziferstein that she would not be able to give any lectures and that because of the lightning nature of her visit she would need the evenings to rest. "I am 77½ years old." In San Francisco she managed to stretch the facts a little and obtain permission to interview

Chessman in his cell as a journalist representing the *Revue Française de Psychanalyse*. The newspapers published pictures of the condemned man and the princess, but when she saw Governor Brown in Sacramento, she was unable to budge him.

She arrived in New York on April 29 with hardly any hope left for her protégé. Loewenstein, who had never seen her so agitated, tried to distract her. He arranged a dinner for her and Solange Troisier, and urged her to visit the Library of Congress in Washington.

On May 2, the day of the execution, Dr. K. R. Eissler wrote to Marie: "I can imagine the state of utter despair in which you probably are." It was indeed total despair for Marie. To have failed in saving this criminal, to whom she had extended a hand, was a crushing defeat. Until then, she had seldom failed in anything she had undertaken. On July 4, she wrote to Loewenstein from the American Hospital in Paris: "My long trip around the world was not a success. Not only do I have the K & Jennikoff syndrome (epilepsia particularis continua) [a form of epilepsy, marked by disturbances of the electrical rhythms of the central nervous system] in the left arm, there are tiny continuous spasms that are very fatiguing (it seems that this usually ends by going away by itself), but since June 17 I have had persistent fibrillation [rapid irregular contractions of the heart muscle], probably chronic I'm afraid. All I needed was to take a trip around the world at my age, and especially to go to Sacramento to see Governor Brown, a fine specimen of filthy politician and Pontius Pilate. . . ."

Marie recovered; on February 15, 1961, she was in San Remo to watch "the magnificent sight of a total solar eclipse that culminated at 8:35 A.M. right in the middle of the 118 minutes total duration. The biggest stars or planets were clearly visible. I could identify Jupiter shining in the east. In spite of the pronounced darkness of the atmosphere, birds went on singing all the time in the garden of the Savoia Hotel where I was watching from the third floor facing east—they did not seem scared."

She signed this notation in her journal "Marie Bonaparte, Princess of Greece, daughter of Prince Roland Bonaparte, ex-President of the Astronomical Society." The need to connect with her father had not disappeared, in spite of all the years filled with work and accomplishments of her own, surpassing his, as it had been her ambition since her youth. Now she no longer felt the urge of competition—all she wanted was to be related to him.

That spring she wrote *Les Faux-pas de la justice*, detailing miscarriages of justice she had witnessed during her life: the Dreyfus case; Sacco and Vanzetti, whom she considered "peaceful anarchists"; the third absurd case cited by her was the hanging of the innocent deranged Evans, who had falsely confessed to a crime subsequently proven to have been committed by the sadist Christie. The last case was that of Caryl Chessman.

Marie had done a great deal of research on the history of the death penalty and alternative punishments. Among the works she noted were those of Melitta Schmideberg, Melanie Klein's daughter, and clinical director of the Association for Psychiatric Treatment of Criminal Offenders in New York City. Simultaneous with her work on criminals, she prepared a study of George Sand, and on April 28, she wrote Queen Elisabeth of Belgium that, stimulated by Gagarin's exploit as the first man in space, she intended to resume her Russian lessons—as did the queen, who was nearing her eighty-fifth birthday at the time.

In July, Marie attended the Edinburgh Congress, in the course of which, on the recommendation of the International Association's Committee of Inquiry the status of "study group" was proposed for the French Psychoanalytic Society. This satisfied no one but did foster further clarifications of issues within the French Society. Most of the members broke with Lacan: they considered his procedures with his patients unethical. The French Society ceased to exist; it became the Association Psychanalytique de France. Lacan founded his own "Freudian School," which abandoned virtually all established standards for the training of young analysts, and which he himself dissolved in 1980. He died in September 1981.

Today one may say that the French analytic movement, which experienced and still experiences so much turmoil, had long been led by Marie Bonaparte. The enmity maintained toward her by Lacan and his disciples—most of whom are too young to have known her—demonstrates the extent of the role she played. In an article published in 1975, Jacques Derrida, one of the most eminent philosophers of the younger generation, took up Marie Bonaparte's defense by denouncing Lacan's "borrowings" from her work on Poe in 1933, in his seminar on *The Purloined Letter*.[23]

Marie's other activities and achievements were mentioned in an article by Professor Pierre Lépine: "Princess Marie's interest in the biological sciences never abated. With a passionate interest she followed research on cancer, infectious diseases and vaccines. As a friend of M. [Émile] Roux she continued to demonstrate an active and generous sympathy for the work of the Institut Pasteur. Thanks to her, the Institute was enabled to build a primate laboratory that permitted Calmette to carry through his experiments with chimpanzees from Guinea, testing the antituberculosis immunity provided by B.C.G. (Bacillus Calmette-Guérin). She also funded the laboratory where Professor Troisier worked up to his death. She repeatedly proved her interest in work in progress by grants, but she wanted her gifts to remain anonymous. She frequently visited our Institute and insisted on being informed about the advances made in chemotherapy and immunology."[24]

In returning to her writings after her failure with Caryl Chessman, she chose the right track; she was linking up with her true vocation, that of writer and scientist. She had saved herself by curing others and by building a body of significant work. But she could no longer work with her habitual intensity. She was impatient with herself and could not conceal her agitation from Frieda, her chambermaid, who found it painful to observe.

Marie, as always, was surrounded by piles of papers and mountains of books. For these last works, she took voluminous notes, giving up George Sand for Dostoevsky. "Exciting. But he was a *true* epileptic, which explains much of his violent, but at the same time ambivalent character. [He was] not a hysteroepileptic, as Freud hypothetically suggests. They didn't have electroencephalograms in Dostoevsky's time. I won't write a study on Dostoevsky until I've read all of him, unfortunately not in Russian despite the study of that magnificent language which I'll continue in October."[25] She wrote only a brief article: "L'Épilepsie et le sadomasochisme dans la vie et l'oeuvre de Dostoïevski."[26]

Marie no longer found pleasure and relaxation in the physical act of writing that since childhood she had enjoyed so much. She misplaced her papers, her fountain pen. She was becoming forgetful. Her heart, which too often beat wildly, interfered with her concentration. But she still had sexual dreams.

She spent the winter in Greece. From there, at the end of 1961, she went to Israel at the invitation of the government, "which says it has not forgotten what I was fortunately able to do before the war for the poor Jews persecuted by Hitler. It is touching to see such gratitude. It is uncommon . . ."[27] The efficiency of all the enterprises there thrilled her: "What has been done is enormous and the army is very impressive with all those young men and women in uniforms. We gave a lift to a nineteen-year-old girl who was giving shooting lessons to her female colleagues. And the kibbutzim . . . What an organization! The resurrection of the Hebrew language contributed to the tremendous work." This she wrote as part of the same letter from Israel.

She returned to Athens, where her journal records the fitting of a lace dress. She very seldom mentions clothes, but in Greece she felt lonely; all her usual interests were untended. She remained in Athens longer than planned and, once again, she broke her hip. This time she stayed in Greece and had surgery there. This accident seemed to disturb her less than the previous ones. As soon as possible, she started working again. She was also planning to attend the Stockholm Congress, to be held in 1963. Her contribution was to be a paper on Jo Ann Baker, the American wife of an Air Force sergeant stationed in Athens, who, on discovering her husband's infidelity, had killed her three children. This modern Medea, who knew nothing of her classical forerunner, intrigued her. Then Marie got absorbed in reading Pasteur, about whom she also wanted to write "a small work." "Very interesting to study for once a man, a genius abnormally normal."

She did not return to Saint-Cloud until the end of June. Her fracture healed with "a wise slowness," but her heart continued to act up. Since her last accident, she seemed to adjust more easily to her age and ebbing strength. "A tender love for her family, devotion to friends, deep love of nature and animals went hand in hand with scientific objectivity and an unflagging intellectual curiosity," wrote Loewenstein.[28]

It was mid-August before she could leave the American Hospital for Le Lys de Mer. There she felt calm and resigned, and found swimming an excellent rehabilitation exercise for her hip. She had herself carried to the sea on one of the chaise longues on which she had spent many days writing. Once in the water she regained the freedom of motion denied her on land. "Mother-sea," her beloved Mediterranean, soothed her pain and renewed her energy. She had in mind "a work on Walt Whitman. 'One must work however much one suffers,' as Freud said! And Claude Bernard: 'Work like a beast!' I've written to Eissler for a biography of Walt Whitman. What a tremendous poet. He's not like Faulkner whose boring books I can never get through."

And in a postscript: "I'll be back in Saint-Cloud at the end of September."

Marie wrote this letter to Loewenstein on August 29, 1962. On Friday, September 14, she had her usual palpitations, but she also had a high fever and spat blood. Eugénie took her to the clinic in Saint-Tropez. Marie exacted Professor de Gennes's promise to tell her the truth. The following Tuesday, when her daughter came to see her in the morning, she was reading Diderot's *Jacques le fataliste*, making notes in the margin. Her choice of this work by the famous Encyclopedist was not accidental: it reflects Marie's joyful pessimism.

In this picaresque novel, embedded among scenes of explicit sexuality, are Diderot's advocacy of atheism, his attacks on Roman Catholicism, his materialistic faith in science and his love of nature. Marie liked the most famous quote about the human need to swear eternal faithfulness in a world where change is inevitable. She had never believed in the fidelity of the flesh, but she was still interested in what makes men and women love and fight, help and cheat each other.

Putting aside the book Marie told Eugénie, "I have leukemia. The doctor has just told me, he has the results of the tests. They're going to treat me with hydrocortisone." Then she went back to *Jacques le fataliste*. A moment later, she wondered aloud: "Will I see another summer?" She had a fever of 104°F. She returned to her reading that day and the following ones.

She asked her daughter to bring her the medical dictionary that always lay on her night table. Eugénie pretended she had forgotten it. She knew that her mother had acute leukemia.

True to her view that psychoanalysis promoted adaptation to reality and that reality included death, Marie, reminiscent of Freud, died with acceptance of this final act of living, on Friday, September 21, 1962, the last day of summer. The nuns at the clinic respected her wishes and did not summon a priest. She was cremated in Marseilles and her ashes taken to Tatoï, to be interred in Prince George's tomb.

As she had asked, there were no religious services and no reception. Only the family, the near relations and friends, and those who had served and loved her attended.

Even as a little girl, Marie had admired what her grandmother described as "those excessive Bonaparte women," a character trait she shared and which made her, truly, "the last Bonaparte."

NOTES

Chapter 1

1. Marie Bonaparte, *Derrière les vitres closes*, p. 174
2. P. Fleuriot de Langle, *La Paolina, soeur de Napoléon*, p. 16
3. J. P. Garnier, *L'extraordinaire Destin des Bonaparte*, p. 32
4. J. P. Garnier, *op. cit.*, p. 167
5. Quoted by J. P. Garnier, *op. cit.*, p. 195
6. J. P. Garnier, *op. cit.*, p. 198
7. François Pietri, *Lucien Bonaparte*, p. 15
8. Eugénie de Grèce, *Pierre-Napoléon Bonaparte*, p. 166
9. Marie Bonaparte, *op. cit.*, p. 212

Chapter 2

1. Marie Bonaparte, *L'Appel des sèves*, p. 670
2. *Le Gaulois*, Thursday, August 3, 1882
3. Marie Bonaparte, *Copy-Books*, I, p. 2
4. ———, *ibid.*, I, p. 139
5. ———, *Derrière les vitres closes*, p. 212
6. ———, *Copy-Books*, I, p. 141, footnote
7. ———, *ibid.*, I, p. 143
8. ———, *ibid.*, I, p. 49
9. All the quotations in this and subsequent chapters, except those with numbered references, are taken from the two volumes of Marie Bonaparte's memoirs of her childhood and youth, *Derrière les vitres closes* and *L'Appel des sèves*.
10. Marie Bonaparte, *Monologues devant la vie et la mort*, p. 78
11. Marie Bonaparte, *The Life and Works of Edgar Allan Poe*, p. 585
12. Marie Bonaparte, *Copy-Books*, I, p. 226

13. ——, *ibid.*, I, p. 1
14. ——, *ibid.*, III, pp. 224–25
15. ——, *ibid.*, III, pp. 339–40
16. ——, *ibid.*, III, p. 166
17. ——, *ibid.*, II, p. 96

Chapter 3

1. Sigmund Freud, *Gesammelte Werke*, I, p. 460
2. Ernest Jones, *Sigmund Freud, Life and Work*, I, p. 269
3. In *L'Appel des sèves*, the Englishwoman is disguised as Miss Kitty, but her name was Hetty. This is what I will call her.
4. Marie Bonaparte, "L'Identification d'une fille à sa mère morte," *Psychanalyse et Anthropologie*, p. 103
5. Marie Bonaparte, *The Life and Works of Edgar Allan Poe*, p. 54
6. Marie Bonaparte, unpublished notebook, 1904–1905

Chapter 4

1. Georges Suarez, *Briand*, II, p. 438
2. Marie Bonaparte, Le vieux compagnon, unpublished notes
3. Marie Bonaparte, Tristesse féminine, an unpublished collection of short texts, 1913

Chapter 5

1. Marie Bonaparte, Tristesse féminine, unpublished manuscript, 1913
2. Jacques Chabannes, *Aristide Briand*, p. 78
3. Marie Bonaparte, *Le Bonheur d'être aimée*, I, Premier printemps plus tard, unpublished
4. Marie Bonaparte, *Les Hommes que j'ai aimés*
5. Georges Suarez, *Briand*, III, p. 87
6. *Ibid.*, IV, p. 41
7. Harold Nicolson, *Peacemaking*

Chapter 6

1. Marie Bonaparte, *Monologues devant la vie et la mort*, p. 51
2. *Five Copy-Books*, I, p. 1
3. Marie Bonaparte, Journal d'analyse, January 7, 1926, an unpublished record of her analysis with Freud

4. André Bourguignon, "Correspondance Sigmund Freud–René La-forgue, Mémorial d'une rencontre," in *Mémoires, Nouvelle Revue de Psychanalyse*, No. 15, Spring 1977
5. Hélène Michel-Wolfromm, *Cette chose-là*, p. 282
6. Marie Bonaparte, draft of a letter to an unnamed addressee, April 16, 1925
7. Institut de France, Publications diverses de l'année 1924–4AA34A, Discours de Jules-Louis Breton, membre libre de l'Académie, le mercredi 16 avril 1924 (mss 33)
8. Marie Bonaparte, *Flyda des mers*, p. 77
9. *Ibid.*, p. 87
10. Princess Eugénie of Greece, unpublished article written for *Reader's Digest*, 1963
11. Bourguignon, *op. cit.*, p. 260
12. *Ibid.*
13. Letter from Marie Bonaparte to Laforgue, April 18, 1925
14. Bourguignon, *op. cit.*, pp. 260–61
15. *Ibid.*, p. 267
16. *Ibid.*, p. 268
17. *Ibid.*, p. 269
18. Journal d'analyse, October 28, 1925

Chapter 7

1. Ernest Jones, *Sigmund Freud, Life and Work*, II, p. 407
2. Marie Bonaparte, Journal d'analyse, October 1, 1925
3. André Bourguignon, "Correspondance Sigmund Freud–René La-forgue, Mémorial d'une rencontre," in *Mémoires, Nouvelle Revue de Psychanalyse*, no. 15, Spring 1977, p. 238
4. Journal d'analyse, January 8, 1926
5. Bourguignon, *op. cit.*, p. 275
6. Letter to Laforgue, September 30, 1925
7. Journal d'analyse, October 22, 1925
8. Journal d'analyse, February 18, 1926
9. Letter to Laforgue, October 7, 1925
10. Journal d'analyse, October 7, 1925
11. Marie Bonaparte, Sommaire d'analyse, December 14, 1925
12. Journal d'analyse, November 16, 1925
13. Journal d'analyse, February 24, 1926
14. Journal d'analyse, October 31, 1925
15. Letter to Laforgue, October 23, 1925
16. Letter to Laforgue, December 12, 1925
17. Letter to Laforgue, October 10, 1925
18. Sommaire d'analyse, November 10, 1925

19. Bourguignon, *op. cit.*, p. 273
20. Sommaire d'analyse, October 28, 1925
21. Jones, *op. cit.*, II, p. 432
22. Sommaire d'analyse, January 31, 1926
23. *Copy-Books*, I, p. 52
24. *Ibid.*
25. Bourguignon, *op. cit.*, pp. 276–77
26. *Copy-Books*, I, p. 62
27. Martin Bergmann and Frank R. Hartman, *The Evolution of Psychoanalytic Technique*, p. 74
28. Letter to Laforgue, August 6, 1926
29. Jones, *op. cit.*, III, p. 292
30. Sigmund Freud, *The Question of Lay Analysis*, 1926, Standard Ed., XX, pp. 230, 233, 248, 249
31. Jones, *op. cit.*, III, p. 292
32. Sigmund Freud, *Postscript to a Discussion on Lay Analysis*, 1927, Standard Ed., XX, p. 258
33. Notes dated December 1966 concerning "the prehistory of the Paris Psychoanalytic Society," sent by the Librarian of the Institut de Psychoanalyse to Princess Eugénie of Greece on March 19, 1970
34. Marie Bonaparte, *Psychanalyse et Anthropologie*, p. 30
35. Jones, *op. cit.*, III, p. 141
36. Journal d'analyse, Winter 1928–1929
37. Marie Bonaparte, Unpublished notes
38. Marie Bonaparte, *Life and Works of Edgar Allan Poe*, p. 110

Chapter 8

1. Ernest Jones, *Sigmund Freud, Life and Work*, II, p. 196
2. *James Jackson Putnam and Psychoanalysis*, bibliographical notes
3. Jones, *op. cit.*, III, p. 79
4. *Revue Française de Psychanalyse*, II, 3, 1928, pp. 541–65
5. ———, III, 3, 1929, pp. 478–81
6. Letter from Freud to Marie Bonaparte, May 2, 1929
7. Jacques Chabannes, *Aristide Briand*, p. 275
8. Max Schur, *Freud, Living and Dying*, p. 505; Jones, *op. cit.*, III, p. 157
9. Letter from Freud to Marie Bonaparte, November 7, 1931, and Marie Bonaparte, *Poe*, note on Kürten, pp. 688–89
10. Letter from Freud to Marie Bonaparte, December 15, 1931
11. Jones, *op. cit.*, III, p. 454
12. *Ibid.*, p. 170
13. *Ibid.*, p. 175

14. *Ibid.*, pp. 181–82
15. Letter from Freud to Marie Bonaparte, February 15, 1935
16. H. D., *Tribute to Freud*, pp. 61–62
17. Letter from Marie Bonaparte to Freud, October 12, 1935
18. *Ibid.*
19. Jacques Lacan, *Écrits*, p. 907
20. Marie Bonaparte, *Psychanalyse et Biologie*, p. 32 and Notes diverses
21. Letter from Marie Bonaparte to Freud, December 18, 1936
22. *Ibid.*, December 28, 1936
23. Schur, *op. cit.*, p. 583

Chapter 9

1. R. Loewenstein, "In Memoriam," in *Journal of the American Psychoanalytic Association*, vol. XI, No. 4, p. 863
2. Articles in *Le Petit Parisien*, June 14, 1938; *Marianne*, June 15, 1938; *L'Ordre*, June 19, 1938; all reprinted in *Psychanalyse et Biologie*, pp. 63, 67, 70
3. Ernest Jones, *Sigmund Freud, Life and Work*, III, p. 227
4. Letter from Marie Bonaparte to Freud, August 25, 1938
5. Letter from Freud to Marie Bonaparte, November 12, 1938
6. *Revue Française de Psychanalyse*, XI, pp. 1–39, later in *Chronos, Eros, Thanatos*, 1952
7. Letter from Marie Bonaparte to Freud, September 30, 1938
8. Letter from Freud to Marie Bonaparte, November 23, 1938
9. *Revue Française de Psychanalyse*, XI, 1, 1939, pp. 107–35
10. Lecture at L'Alliance Israélite universelle, on May 13, 1953, entitled "Du Rôle de quelques penseurs juifs dans l'évolution humaine"
11. *Marianne*, October 4, 1939; reprinted in *Psychanalyse et Biologie*, p. 73
12. *The American Imago*, IV, 1, 1946, and in *Yearbook of Psychoanalysis*, III, 1947; later in French in *Psychanalyse et Biologie*, p. 89
13. Letter from Marie Bonaparte to Princess Eugénie of Greece, January 2, 1940
14. Essai sur le regret obsédant, unpublished, 1941
15. *Psychoanalysis and the Social Sciences*, II, 1948, in French in *R.F.P.*, XII, 2, 1938, then in *Psychanalyse et Biologie*, p. 107
16. *Revue Française de Psychanalyse*, XII, 2, 1948
17. *American Imago*, IV, 49–77, *R.F.P.*, XII, 4, 1948, and *Psychanalyse et Biologie*, p. 124
18. *Psychoanalytic Quarterly*, XVI, 1947: "Les Rêves d'un chasseur de lions," in *Psychanalyse et Biologie*, p. 99

19. Letter from Marie Bonaparte to Loewenstein, January 13, 1944
20. Letter from Marie Bonaparte to Loewenstein, January 6, 1945

Chapter 10

1. Letter to Anna Freud, April 28, 1945
2. Letter to Anna Freud, June 25, 1945
3. Letter to Prince Peter of Greece, April 16, 1946
4. Letter to Loewenstein, April 21, 1946
5. Letter to Loewenstein, September 1, 1947
6. "Idées religieuses de Georges," Athens, February 9, 1948, Notes diverses
7. *Revue Française de Psychanalyse*, XIII, 1, 2, 3, 1949
8. Marie Bonaparte, *De la Sexualité de la femme*, p. 142
9. *Ibid.*, p. 115
10. Letter to Anna Freud, March 10, 1949
11. *Revue Française de Psychanalyse*, XIV, 2, 1950, and *Psychanalyse et Biologie*, p. 159
12. Letter to Annette Berman, December 15, 1949
13. Letter to Loewenstein, November 19, 1950
14. *Revue Française de Psychanalyse*, XV, 4, 1951
15. Letter to Anna Freud, June 21, 1950
16. Letter to Prince Peter of Greece, August 31, 1950
17. Letter to Loewenstein, August 16, 1950
18. Letter to Anna Freud, January 10, 1951
19. Marie Bonaparte, *Chronos, Eros, Thanatos*, p. 141
20. Marie Bonaparte, Unpublished notes
21. Letter to Anna Freud, January 14, 1952
22. Letter to Loewenstein, April 8, 1952
23. Letter to Loewenstein, January 14, 1952
24. *Revue Française de Psychanalyse*, XVI, pp. 313–418
25. *The Psychoanalytic Study of the Child*, Vol. VII, 1952, pp. 170–72
26. *Evidences*, XXV, pp. 5–10
27. Letter to Loewenstein, June 19, 1952
28. Letter to Prince Peter of Greece, July 24, 1952
29. Notes, October 12, 1952

Chapter 11

1. *Revue Française de Psychanalyse*, XVII, 556–67
2. Letter to Loewenstein, February 5, 1953
3. Letter to Loewenstein, June 17, 1953
4. Letter to Anna Freud, May 2, 1953

5. Letter to Loewenstein, June 17, 1953
6. Letter to Anna Freud, July 16, 1953
7. Heinz Hartmann, *The Psychoanalytic Movement Project*, p. 84, The Oral History, Columbia University
8. Letter to Loewenstein, October 1953
9. Letter to Loewenstein, June 17, 1954
10. Letter to Prince Peter of Greece, February 18, 1955
11. Unpublished notes, July 24, 1955
12. Letter from Loewenstein to Marie Bonaparte, August 2, 1955
13. Letter to Queen Elisabeth of Belgium, June 11, 1955.
14. Letter to Loewenstein, December 31, 1956
15. *The International Journal of Psycho-Analysis*, vol. XXXIX, 1958, part 6, pp. 513–15
16. Unpublished notes
17. Letter to Queen Elisabeth of Belgium, June 4, 1958
18. Letter to Loewenstein, February 15, 1958
19. S. Nacht in *Semaine des Hôpitaux de Paris*, supplement 2046, October 20, 1963
20. S. Nacht, *La Psychanalyse d'aujourd'hui*, vol. II, pp. 723–60
21. *Revue Française de Psychanalyse*, 1959, XXIII, 5, pp. 545–54
22. Letter to Loewenstein, December 31, 1960
23. Jacques Derrida, *Le Facteur de vérité*, *Poétique*, 21, Editions du Seuil, 1975, p. 96
24. Pierre Lépine, in *Annales de l'Institut Pasteur*, March 1963, vol. 104, p. 311
25. Letter to Loewenstein, September 14, 1961
26. *Revue Française de Psychanalyse*, 1962, XXVI, 6, pp. 715–30
27. Letter to Loewenstein, January 8, 1962
28. R. Loewenstein, "In Memoriam," in *Journal of the American Psychoanalytic Association*, XI, 4, p. 862

BIBLIOGRAPHY OF MARIE BONAPARTE'S WRITINGS

KEY TO ABBREVIATIONS

Amer. Im.	*American Imago*
I.J.	*International Journal of Psycho-Analysis*
IMP.	Imago Publishing Co. Ltd., London
IUP.	International Universities Press, Inc., New York
PUF.	Presses Universitaires de France, Paris
Q.	*The Psychoanalytic Quarterly*
RFP.	*Revue Française de Psychanalyse*

1920   *Guerres militaires et guerres sociales*, Paris, Flammarion, 240 pp.

1921   "Le Rayonnement d'une gloire," in *Le Martin*, Paris, May 5

1924   *Le Printemps sur mon jardin*, Paris, Flammarion, 226 pp.

"Considérations sur les causes anatomiques de la frigidité chez la femme," published under the pseudonym of A. E. Narjani in *Bruxelles Médical*, April 27, 11 pp.

1927   "Le Cas de Madame Lefèbvre," *RFP.*, I, 149–98

"Du Symbolisme des trophées de tête," *RFP.*, I, 677–732

1928   "L'Identification d'une fille à sa mère morte," *RFP.*, II, 541–65

1929   "Un Petit Accès de kleptomanie larvée," *RFP.*, III, 478–81

1930   "De la Prophylaxie infantile des névroses," *RFP.*, IV, 86–135; in *Introduction à la théorie des instincts*

"Deuil, nécrophilie et sadisme," *RFP.*, IV, 716–34

"Le Soixante-quinzième Anniversaire de Freud," *RFP.*, IV, 426–27

1932   "Le 'Scarabée d'Or' d'Edgar Poe," *RFP.*, V, 275–93

"De l'Elaboration et de la fonction de l'oeuvre littéraire," *RFP.*, V, 649–83

1933   *Edgar Poe*, Paris, Denoël et Steele, 2 vols., 922 pp.

"Les Deux Frigidités de la femme," *Bulletin de la Société de Sexologie*, I, 4

"Une Suggestion pour éviter de nouvelles catastrophes aériennes," in *Le Matin*, Paris, April 1

"Les Bonnes Intentions de l'administration pour les forêts de Paris," in *Le Matin*, Paris, September 25

"L'Homme et son dentiste," *RFP.*, VI, 84–86

"Des Autoérotismes agressifs par la griffe et par la dent," *RFP.*, VI, 192–216

"De la Mort et des fleurs," *RFP.*, VI, 218–22

"La Structure psychique d'Edgar Poe," in *Hygiène Mentale*, XXVIII, 193–201

1934 "La Pensée magique chez le primitif," *RFP.*, VII, 3–18

"Introduction à la théorie des instincts," *RFP.*, VII, 611–54

1935 "Passivité, masochisme et féminité," *RFP.*, VIII, 208–16

"Passivity, Masochism and Femininity," *I.J.*, XVI, 325–33

"Psychologie de la puberté," *Bulletin de la Société de Sexologie*, II, 2–4, 7 pp.

"The Murders in the Rue Morgue," *Q.*, IV, 259–93; in Marie Bonaparte: *Life and Works of Edgar Allan Poe*

1936 "Vues paléobiologiques et biopsychiques," *RFP.*, IX, 422–30

"La Portée de l'oeuvre de Freud," *RFP.*, IX, 532–58

"Animaux amis," in *Paris Soir*, October 12

1937 *Topsy, Chow-Chow au poil d'or*, Paris, Denoël et Steele, 129 pp.

"L'Idole moderne: La Route ne peut pas exiger le sacrifice des arbres," *Paris Soir*, July 28

1938 "Some Palaeobiological and Biophysical Reflections," *I.J.*, XIX, 214–20

"Freud, l'homme et l'oeuvre," in *Le Petit Parisien*, June 14

"Freud à Paris," in *Marianne*, July 15

"Sigmund Freud, l'instinct et la raison," in *L'Ordre*, July 19

1939 *La Mer et le rivage*, Paris, published for the author, 108 pp.

Cinq Cahiers, I, published for the author, 347 pp.

"Apology of Biography" (first published in English), *I.J.*, XX, 231–40

"L' Inconscient et le temps," *RFP.*, XI, 61–105

"La Mort de Freud," in *Marianne*, October 4

1940 *Topsy, the Story of a Golden-haired Chow*, English translation by Princess Eugénie of Greece, Pushkin Press, 79 pp.

1941 "The Myth of the Corpse in the Car," *Amer. Im.*, II, 105–26; in Marie Bonaparte: *Myths of War*

1945 "Notes on the Analytical Discovery of a Primal Scene," in *The Psychoanalytic Study of the Child*, I, 119–25, IUP.

1946 *Mythes de guerre*, IMP. and PUF., 180 pp.

Défense du complexe d'Oedipe: Conférence faite le 16 Mai à l'Institut des Sciences et Techniques, 6 pp.

1947 *Myths of War*, London, IMP., 161 pp.

"The Legend of the Unfathomable Waters," in *The Yearbook of Psycho-Analysis*, IUP., III, 281–90

"A Lion Hunter's Dreams," *Q.*, XVI, 1–10

"Saint Christopher, Patron Saint of the Motor-car Drivers," *Amer. Im.*, IV, 49–77; in *Max Eitingon: In Memoriam*, Jerusalem, Israel Psychoanalytic Society, 1951

1948 *Cinq Cahiers*, II, IMP., 481 pp.

"De l'Essentielle Ambivalence d'Eros," *RFP.*, XII, 167–212

"Notes sur l'Excision," *RFP.*, XII, 213–31; also in *Psychanalyse et biologie*

"De l'Angoisse devant la sexualité," *RFP.*, XII, 475–80

"Notes on Excision," in *Psychoanalysis and the Social Sciences*, IUP., II, 67–83

1949 "De la Sexualité de la femme," *RFP.*, XIII, 1–52, 161–227, 322–41; published in book form in 1951

The Life and Works of Edgar Allan Poe, London, IMP., 749 pp.

1950 "La Légende des eaux sans fond," *RFP.*, XIV, 164–73

"Psyché dans la nature ou des limites de la psychogenèse," *RFP.*, XIV, 174–81

"Les Rêves d'un chasseur de lions," *RFP.*, XIV, 505–12

Les glauques Aventures de Flyda des mers, IMP., 106 pp.

Les Glanes des jours, IMP., 106 pp.

Flyda of the Seas, IMP., 88 pp.

Five Copy-Books, IMP., I, 284 pp.

1951 *Monologues devant la vie et la mort*, IMP., 114 pp.

Cinq Cahiers, IMP., III and IV, 402 and 409 pp.

De la Sexualité de la femme, Paris, PUF., 148 pp.

Des Causes psychologiques de l'antisémitisme, *RFP.*, XV, 479–91

"Some Psychoanalytic and Anthropological Insights Applied to Sociology," in *Psychoanalysis and Culture*, IUP.

1952 *Chronos, Eros, Thanatos*, IMP., 153 pp.; contents—"L'Inconscient et le temps: De l'Essentielle Ambivalence d'Eros," "Réflexions biopsychiques sur le sado-masochisme"

Introduction à la théorie des instincts et *Prophylaxie infantile des névroses*, PUF., 181 pp.

Psychanalyse et biologie, PUF., 190 pp.

Psychanalyse et anthropologie, PUF., 192 pp.

"Quelques Lueurs projetées par la psychanalyse et l'ethnographie sur la sociologie," *RFP.*, XVI, 313–18

"Psychanalyse de l'antisémitisme," in *Evidences*, XXV, 5–10

"Masturbation and Death, or A Compulsive Confession of Masturbation," in *The Psychoanalytic Study of the Child*, IUP., VII, 170–72

Five Copy-Books, IMP., II, 396 pp.

Five Copy-Books, IMP., III, 416 pp.

1953 *Five Copy-Books*, IMP., IV, 329 pp.

Female Sexuality, English translation by John Rodker, IUP.

A la Mémoire des disparus (Derrière les vitres closes, L'Appel des sèves), published for the author, IMP., 1,004 pp.

La Faute d'Orphée à l'envers, *RFP.*, XXII, 221–28

"Du Rôle de quelques penseurs juifs dans l'évolution humaine," lecture at L'Alliance Israélite universelle

"Drives, Affects, Behavior," IUP., review in *RFP.*, XVII, 556–67

1954 "Allocution prononcée à l'occasion de l'inauguration de l'Institut de Psychanalyse le 1ᵉʳ juin 1954," *RFP.*, XVIII, 175–76

"Petit Essai sur la médecine psychosomatique," *RFP.*, XVIII, 276–80

"The Fault of Orpheus in Reverse," *I.J.*, XXXV, 109–12

1956 "Deux Penseurs devant l'abîme," *RFP.*, XX

"Eros, Saul de Tarse et Freud," *RFP.*, XXI, 23–34

"Psychanalyse et sexologie," in S. Nacht: *La Psychanalyse d'aujourd'hui*, II, 723–60

1957 "Kazantzakis, Fils de l'île Minoenne," *Les Nouvelles Littéraires*, November 5

1958 *Edgar Poe—Sa Vie, son oeuvre: Etude analytique*, foreword by Sigmund Freud, Paris, PUF. I—Etude Psychanalytique, 264 pp.; II—Les Contes: Les Cycles de la Mère, 392 pp.; III—Les Contes: Les Cycles du Père and Poe et l'âme humaine, 314 pp.

"Ernest Jones, Nécrologie (1879–1958)," *RFP.*, XXII, 134–36

"La Psychanalyse face aux forces sociales religieuses et naturelles," *RFP.*, XXII, 219–22

1959 "Vitalisme et psychosomatique," *RFP.*, XXIII, 545–54

1962 "L'Epilepsie et le sado-masochisme dans la vie et l'oeuvre de Dostoïevski," *RFP.*, XXV, 715–30

INDEX

279